Scaling Apache Solr

Optimize your searches using high-performance
enterprise search repositories with Apache Solr

Hrishikesh Vijay Karambelkar

PUBLISHING

BIRMINGHAM - MUMBAI

Scaling Apache Solr

Copyright © 2014 Packt Publishing

First published: July 2014

Production reference: 1180714

Published by Packt Publishing Ltd.
Livery Place
35 Livery Street
Birmingham B3 2PB, UK.
ISBN 978-1-78398-174-8

www.packtpub.com

Cover image by Maria Cristina Caggiani (mariacristinacaggiani@virgilio.it)

Credits

About the Author

Hrishikesh Vijay Karambelkar is an enterprise architect with a blend of technical and entrepreneurial experience of more than 13 years. His core expertise involves working with multiple topics that include J2EE, Big Data, Solr, Link Analysis, and Analytics. He enjoys architecting solutions for the next generation of product development for IT organizations. He spends most of his work time now solving challenging problems faced by the software industry.

In the past, he has worked in the domains of graph databases; some of his work has been published in international conferences, such as VLDB, ICDE, and so on. He has recently published a book called *Scaling Big Data with Hadoop and Solr*, *Packt Publishing*. He enjoys spending his leisure time traveling, trekking, and photographing birds in the dense forests of India. He can be reached at http://hrishikesh.karambelkar.co.in/.

I am thankful to Packt Publishing for providing me with the opportunity to share my experiences on this topic. I would also like to thank the reviewers of this book, especially Nick Veenhof from Acquira for shaping it up; the Packt Publishing team, Kartik Vedam and Neil Alexander, for their support during bad times; and my dear wife Dhanashree, who stood by me all the time.

About the Reviewers

Ramzi Alqrainy is one of the most recognized experts within Artificial Intelligence and Information Retrieval fields in the Middle East. He is an active researcher and technology blogger, with a focus on information retrieval.

He is currently managing the search and reporting functions at `OpenSooq.com` where he capitalizes on his solid experience in open source technologies in scaling up the search engine and supportive systems.

His solid experience in Solr, ElasticSearch, Mahout, and Hadoop stack contributed directly to the business growth through the implementations and projects that helped the key people at OpenSooq to slice and dice information easily throughout the dashboards and data visualization solutions.

By developing more than six full-stack search engines, he was able to solve many complicated challenges about agglutination and stemming in the Arabic language.

He holds a Master's degree in Computer Science. He was among the top three in his class and was listed on the honor roll. His website address is `http://ramzialqrainy.com`. His LinkedIn profile is `http://www.linkedin.com/in/ramzialqrainy`. He can be contacted at `ramzi.alqrainy@gmail.com`.

Aamir Hussain is a well-versed software design engineer with more than 5 years of experience. He excels in solving problems that involve Breadth. He has gained expert internal knowledge by developing software that are used by millions of users. He developed complex software systems using Python, Django, Solr, MySQL, mongoDB, HTML, JavaScript, CSS, and many more open source technologies. He is determined to get a top-quality job done by continually learning new technologies.

His other experiences include analyzing and designing requirements, WEB2 and new technologies, content management, service management that includes fixing problems, change control and management, software release, software testing, service design, service strategy, and continual service improvement. His specialties include complex problem solving, web portal architecture, talent acquisition, team building, and team management.

Ruben Teijeiro is an experienced frontend and backend web developer who has worked with several PHP frameworks for more than a decade. He is now using his expertise to focus on Drupal; in fact, he collaborated with them during the development of several projects for some important companies, such as UNICEF and Telefonica in Spain, and Ericsson in Sweden.

As an active member of the Drupal community, you can find him contributing to Drupal core, helping and mentoring other contributors and speaking at Drupal events around the world. He also loves to share all that he has learned through his blog (`http://drewpull.com`).

I would like to thank my parents for their help and support, since I had my first computer when I was eight. I would also like to thank my lovely wife for her patience during all these years of geeking and traveling.

Nick Veenhof is a Belgian inhabitant who has lived in a couple of different countries, but has recently moved back home. He is currently employed at Acquia as a Lead Search Engineer. He also helps in maintaining the Drupal Apache Solr Integration module and also actively maintains and develops new infrastructure tools for deploying Drupal sites on Acquia Cloud with Apache Solr.

He is also advocating open source and especially the open source project, Drupal. This software crossed his path during his young university years and became part of his career when he started to use it for professional purposes in several Drupal-focused development shops.

As a logical step, he is also active in the Drupal community, as you can see in his `drupal.org` profile (`https://www.drupal.org/user/122682`), and tries to help people online with their first steps.

You can easily find out more about him by searching for his name, Nick Veenhof, or his nickname, Nick_vh, on Google.

www.PacktPub.com

Support files, eBooks, discount offers, and more

You might want to visit www.PacktPub.com for support files and downloads related to your book.

Did you know that Packt offers eBook versions of every book published, with PDF and ePub files available? You can upgrade to the eBook version at www.PacktPub.com and as a print book customer, you are entitled to a discount on the eBook copy. Get in touch with us at service@packtpub.com for more details.

At www.PacktPub.com, you can also read a collection of free technical articles, sign up for a range of free newsletters and receive exclusive discounts and offers on Packt books and eBooks.

http://PacktLib.PacktPub.com

Do you need instant solutions to your IT questions? PacktLib is Packt's online digital book library. Here, you can access, read and search across Packt's entire library of books.

Why subscribe?

- Fully searchable across every book published by Packt
- Copy and paste, print and bookmark content
- On demand and accessible via web browser

Free access for Packt account holders

If you have an account with Packt at www.PacktPub.com, you can use this to access PacktLib today and view nine entirely free books. Simply use your login credentials for immediate access.

I dedicate my work to my mentors who inspired my life and made me what I am today: my schoolteacher Mrs. Argade; Prof. S. Sudarshan from IIT Bombay; and Danesh Tarapore, Postdoctoral Researcher at Lisbon, Portugal.

Table of Contents

Preface

With the growth of information assets in enterprises, the need to build a rich, scalable search application has becomes critical. Today, Apache Solr is one of the most widely adapted, scalable, feature-rich, and high-performance open source search application servers.

Scaling Apache Solr is intended to enable its users to transform Apache Solr from a basic search server, to an enterprise-ready, high performance, and scalable search application. This book is a comprehensive reference guide that starts with the basic concepts of Solr; it takes users through the journey of how Solr can be used in enterprise deployments, and it finally dives into building a highly efficient, scalable enterprise search application using various techniques and numerous practical chapters.

What this book covers

Chapter 1, Understanding Apache Solr, introduces readers to Apache Solr as a search server. It discusses problems addressed by Apache Solr, its architecture, features, and, finally, covers different use cases for Solr.

Chapter 2, Getting Started with Apache Solr, focuses on setting up the first Apache Solr instance. It provides a detailed step-by-step guide for installing and configuring Apache Solr. It also covers connecting to Solr through SolrJ libraries.

Chapter 3, Analyzing Data with Apache Solr, covers some of the common enterprise search problems of bringing information from disparate sources and different information flow patterns to Apache Solr with minimal losses. It also covers advanced topics for Apache Solr such as deduplication, and searching through images.

Chapter 4, Designing Enterprise Search, introduces its readers to the various aspects of designing a search for enterprises. It covers topics pertaining to different data processing patterns of enterprises, integration patterns, and a case study of designing a knowledge repository for the software IT industry.

Chapter 5, Integrating Apache Solr, focuses on the integration aspects of Apache Solr with different applications that are commonly used in any enterprise. It also covers different ways in which Apache Solr can be introduced by the enterprise to its users.

Chapter 6, Distributed Search Using Apache Solr, starts with the need for distributed search for an enterprise, and it provides a deep dive to building distributed search using Apache SolrCloud. Finally, the chapter covers common problems and a case study of distributed search using Apache Solr for the software industry.

Chapter 7, Scaling Solr through Sharding, Fault Tolerance, and Integration, discusses various aspects of enabling enterprise Solr search server to scaling by means of sharding and search result clustering. It covers integration aspects of Solr with other tools such as MongoDB, Carrot2, and Storm to achieve the scalable search solution for an enterprise.

Chapter 8, Scaling Solr through High Performance, provides insights of how Apache Solr can be transformed into a high-performance search engine for an enterprise. It starts with monitoring for performance, and how the Solr application server can be tuned for performing better with maximum utilization of the available sources.

Chapter 9, Solr and Cloud Computing, focuses on enabling Solr on cloud-based infrastructure for scalability. It covers different Solr strategies for cloud, their applications, and deep dive into using Solr in different types of cloud environment.

Chapter 10, Scaling Solr Capabilities with Big Data, covers aspects of working with a very high volume of data (Big Data), and how Solr can be used to work with Big Data. It discusses how Apache Hadoop and its ecosystem can be used to build and run efficient Big Data enterprise search solutions.

Appendix, Sample Configuration for Apache Solr, provides a reference configuration for different Solr configuration files with detailed explanations.

What you need for this book

This book discusses different approaches; each approach needs a different set of software. Based on the requirement of building search applications, the respective software can be used. However, to run a minimal Apache Solr instance, you need the following software:

* Latest available JDK
* Latest Apache Solr (4.8 onwards)

Who this book is for

Scaling Apache Solr provides step-by-step guidance for any user who intends to build high performance, scalable, enterprise-ready search application servers. This book will appeal to developers, architects, and designers who wish to understand Apache Solr, design the enterprise-ready application, and optimize it based on the requirements. This book enables users to build a scalable search without prior knowledge of Solr with practical examples and case studies.

Conventions

In this book, you will find a number of styles of text that distinguish between different kinds of information. Here are some examples of these styles, and an explanation of their meaning.

Code words in text, database table names, folder names, filenames, file extensions, pathnames, dummy URLs, user input, and Twitter handles are shown as follows: "You can simply add the following dependency to your pom.xml file to use SolrJ."

A block of code is set as follows:

```
CloudSolrServer server = new CloudSolrServer("localhost:9983");
server.setDefaultCollection("collection1");
SolrQuery solrQuery = new SolrQuery("*.*");
```

Any command-line input or output is written as follows:

```
$tar –xvzf solr-<major-minor version>.tgz$tar –xvzf solr-<major-minor version>.tgz
```

New terms and **important words** are shown in bold. Words that you see on the screen, in menus or dialog boxes for example, appear in the text like this: "The **OK** status explains that Solr is running fine on the server."

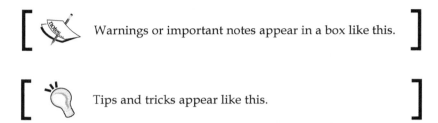

> Warnings or important notes appear in a box like this.

> Tips and tricks appear like this.

Reader feedback

Feedback from our readers is always welcome. Let us know what you think about this book—what you liked or may have disliked. Reader feedback is important for us to develop titles that you really get the most out of.

To send us general feedback, simply send an e-mail to feedback@packtpub.com, and mention the book title via the subject of your message.

If there is a topic that you have expertise in and you are interested in either writing or contributing to a book, see our author guide on www.packtpub.com/authors.

Customer support

Now that you are the proud owner of a Packt book, we have a number of things to help you to get the most from your purchase.

Downloading the example code

You can download the example code files for all Packt books you have purchased from your account at http://www.packtpub.com. If you purchased this book elsewhere, you can visit http://www.packtpub.com/support and register to have the files e-mailed directly to you.

Errata

Although we have taken every care to ensure the accuracy of our content, mistakes do happen. If you find a mistake in one of our books—maybe a mistake in the text or the code—we would be grateful if you would report this to us. By doing so, you can save other readers from frustration and help us improve subsequent versions of this book. If you find any errata, please report them by visiting http://www.packtpub.com/submit-errata, selecting your book, clicking on the **errata submission form** link, and entering the details of your errata. Once your errata are verified, your submission will be accepted and the errata will be uploaded on our website, or added to any list of existing errata, under the Errata section of that title. Any existing errata can be viewed by selecting your title from http://www.packtpub.com/support.

Piracy

Piracy of copyright material on the Internet is an ongoing problem across all media. At Packt, we take the protection of our copyright and licenses very seriously. If you come across any illegal copies of our works, in any form, on the Internet, please provide us with the location address or website name immediately so that we can pursue a remedy.

Please contact us at copyright@packtpub.com with a link to the suspected pirated material.

We appreciate your help in protecting our authors, and our ability to bring you valuable content.

Questions

You can contact us at questions@packtpub.com if you are having a problem with any aspect of the book, and we will do our best to address it.

1
Understanding Apache Solr

The world of information technology revolves around transforming data into information that we can understand. This data is generated every now and then, from various sources, in various forms. To analyze such data, engineers must observe data characteristics, such as the velocity with which the data is generated, volume of data, veracity of data, and data variety. These four dimensions are widely used to recognize whether the data falls into the category of Big Data. In an enterprise, the data may come from its operations network which would involve plant assets, or it may even come from an employee who is updating his information on the employee portal. The sources for such data can be unlimited, and so is the format. To address the need for storage and retrieval of data of a non-relational form, mechanisms such as **NOSQL** (**Not only SQL**) are widely used, and they are gaining popularity.

The mechanism of NOSQL does not provide any standardized way of accessing the data unlike SQL in the case of relational databases. This is because of the unstructured data form that exists within NOSQL storage. Some NOSQL implementations provide SQL-like querying, whereas some provide key-value based storage and data access. It does not really address the problem of data retrieval. Apache Solr uses the key-value-based storage as a means to search through text in a more scalable and efficient way. Apache Solr enables enterprise applications to store and access this data in an effective and efficient manner.

In this chapter, we will be trying to understand Apache Solr and we will go through the following topics:

- Challenges in enterprise search
- Understanding Apache Solr
- Features of Apache Solr
- Apache Solr architecture
- Apache Solr case studies

Challenges in enterprise search

The presence of a good enterprise search solution in any organization is an important aspect of information availability. Absence of such a mechanism can possibly result in poor decision making, duplicated efforts, and lost productivity due to the inability to find the right information at any time. Any search engine typically comprises the following components:

1. Crawlers or data collectors focus mainly on gathering the information on which a search should run.

2. Once the data is collected, it needs to be parsed and indexed. So parsing and indexing is another important component of any enterprise search.

3. The search component is responsible for runtime search on a user-chosen dataset.

4. Additionally, many search engine vendors provide a plethora of components around search engines, such as administration and monitoring, log management, and customizations.

Today public web search engines have become mature. More than 90 percent of online activities begin with search engines (`http://searchengineland.com/top-internet-activities-search-email-once-again-88964`) and more than 100 billion global searches are being made every month (`http://searchenginewatch.com/article/2051895/Global-Search-Market-Tops-Over-100-Billion-Searches-a-Month`). While the focus of web-based search is more on finding out content on the Web, enterprise searches focus on helping employees find out the relevant information stored in their corporate network in any form. Corporate information lacks useful metadata that an enterprise search can use to relate, unlike web searches, which have access to HTML pages that carry a lot of useful metadata for best results. Overall, building an enterprise search engine becomes a big challenge.

Many enterprise web portals provide searches over their own data; however, they do not really solve the problem of unified data access because most of the enterprise data that is outside the purview of these portals largely remains invisible to these search solutions. This data is mainly part of various sources such as external data sources, other departmental data, individual desktops, secured data, proprietary format data, and media files. Let's look at the challenges faced in the industry for enterprise search as shown in the following figure:

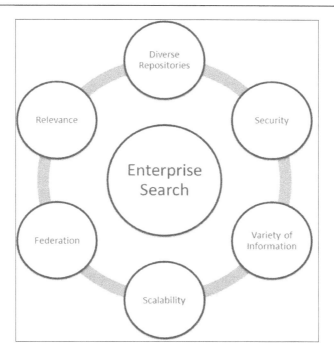

Let's go through each challenge in the following list and try to understand what they mean:

- **Diverse repositories**: The repositories for processing the information vary from a simple web server to a complex content management system. The enterprise search engine must be capable of dealing with diverse repositories.

- **Security**: Security in the enterprise has been one of the primary concerns along with fine-grained access control while dealing with enterprise search. Corporates expect data privacy from enterprise search solutions. This means two users running the same search on enterprise search may get two different sets of results based on the document-level access.

- **Variety of information**: The information in any enterprise is diverse and has different dimensions, such as different types (including PDF, doc, proprietary formats, and so on) of document or different locale (such as English, French, and Hindi). An enterprise search would be required to index this information and provide a search on top of it. This is one of the challenging areas of enterprise searches.

- **Scalability**: The information in any enterprise is always growing and enterprise search has to support its growth without impacting its search speed. This means the enterprise search has to be scalable to address the growth of an enterprise.

- **Relevance**: Relevance is all about how closely the search results match the user expectations. Public web searches can identify relevance from various mechanisms such as links across web pages, whereas enterprise search solutions differ completely in the relevance of entities. The relevance in case of enterprise search involves understanding of current business functions and their contributions in the relevance ranking calculations. For example, a research paper publication would carry more prestige in an academic institution search engine than an on-the-job recruitment search engine.

- **Federation**: Any large organization would have a plethora of applications. Some of them carry technical limitations, such as proprietary formats and inability to share the data for indexing. Many times, enterprise applications such as content management systems provide inbuilt search capabilities on their own data. Enterprise search has to consume these services and it should provide a unified search mechanism for all applications in an enterprise. A federated search plays an important role while searching through various resources.

A federated search enables users to run their search queries on various applications simultaneously in a delegated manner. Participating applications in a federated search perform the search operation using their own mechanism. The results are then combined and ranked together and presented as a single search result (unified search solution) to the user.

Let's take a look at fictitious enterprise search implementation for a software product development company called ITWorks Corporation. The following screenshot depicts how a possible search interface would look:

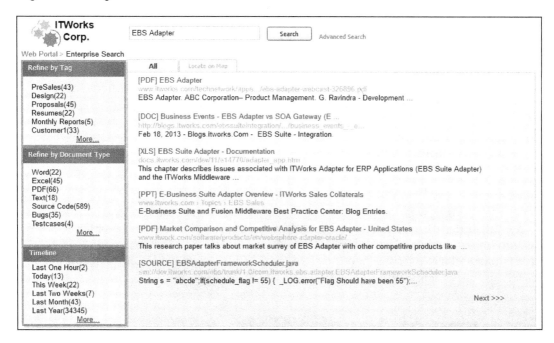

A search should support basic keyword searching, as well as advanced searching across various data sources directly or through a federated search. In this case, the search is crawling through the source code, development documentation, and resources capabilities, all at once. Given such diverse content, a search should provide a unified browsing experience where the result shows up together, hiding the underlying sources. To enable rich browsing, it may provide refinements based on certain facets as shown in the screenshot. It may provide some interesting features such as sorting, spell checking, pagination, and search result highlighting. These features enhance the user experience while searching for information.

Apache Solr – an overview

The need to resolve the problems of enterprise search has triggered interest in many IT companies to come up with an enterprise search solution. This includes companies such as Oracle, Microsoft, and Google who sell their solutions to customers. Doug Cutting created the open source information retrieval library called Apache Lucene during 1997. It became part of `sourceforge.net` (one of the sites hosting open source projects and their development). Lucene was capable of providing powerful full text search, and indexing capabilities on Java. Later in 2001, the Lucene project became a member of the Apache software foundation. The open source community contributed significantly to the development of Apache Lucene, which has led to exponential growth until this point in time. Apache Lucene is widely used in many organizations for information retrieval and search.

Since Apache Solr uses Apache Lucene for indexing and searching, Solr and Lucene index are the same. That means Apache Solr can access indexes generated using Lucene; although, we may just need to modify the Solr schema file to accommodate all the attributes of the Lucene index. Additionally, if Apache Solr is using a different Lucene library, we need to change `<luceneMatchVersion>` in `solrconfig.xml`. This is particularly useful when the client would like to upgrade his custom Lucene search engine to Solr without losing data.

Features of Apache Solr

Apache Solr comes with a rich set of features that can be utilized by enterprises to make the search experience unique and effective. Let's take an overview of some of these key features. We will understand how they can be configured in the next chapter at deeper level.

Solr for end users

A search is effective when the searched information can be seen in different dimensions. For example, if a visitor is interested in buying a camera and he visits online shopping websites and searches for his model. When a user query is executed on the search, a search would rank and return a huge number of results. It would be nice, if he can filter out the results based on the resolution of the camera, or the make of the camera. These are the dimensions that help the user improve querying. Apache Solr offers a unique user experience that enables users to retrieve information faster.

Powerful full text search

Apache Solr provides a powerful full text search capability. Besides normal search, Solr users can run a search for specific fields, for example, `error_id:severe`. Apache Solr supports wildcards in the queries. A search pattern consisting only of one or more asterisks will match all terms of the field in which it is used, for example, `book_title:*`. A question mark can be used where there might be variations for a single character. For example, a search for `?ar` will match with `car`, `bar`, `jar` and a search for `c?t` will match with `cat`, `cot`, `cut`. Overall, Apache supports the following power expressions to enable the user to find information in all possible ways as follows:

- Wildcards
- Phrase queries
- Regular expressions
- Conditional login (and, or, not)
- Range queries (date/integer)

Search through rich information

Apache Solr search can generate indexes out of different file types including many rich documents such as HTML, Word, Excel, Presentations, PDF, RTF, E-mail, ePub formats, the `.zip` files, and many more. It achieves this by integrating different packages such as Lucene, and Apache Tika. These documents when uploaded to Apache Solr get parsed and an index is generated by Solr for search. Additionally, Solr can be extended to work with specific formats by creating customer handlers/adapters for the same. This feature enables Apache Solr to work best for enterprises dealing with different types of data.

Results ranking, pagination, and sorting

When searching for information, Apache Solr returns results page-by-page starting with top K results. Each result row carries a certain score, and the results are sorted based on the score. The result ranking in Solr can be customized as per the application's requirements. This allows the user's flexibility to search more specifically for relevant content. The size of the page can be configured in Apache Solr configuration. Using pagination, Solr can compute and return the results faster than otherwise. Sorting is a feature that enables Solr users to sort the results on certain terms or attributes, for example, a user might consider sorting of results based on increasing price order on an online shopping portal search.

Facets for better browsing experience

Apache Solr facets do not only help users to refine their results using various attributes, but they allow better browsing experience along with the search interface. Apache Solr provides schema-driven, context-specific facets that help users discover more information quickly. Solr facets can be created based on the attributes of the schema that is designed before setting up the instance. Although Apache Solr works on a schema defined for the user, it allows them to have flexibility in the schema by means of dynamic fields, enabling users to work with content of a dynamic nature.

> Based on the schema attributes, Apache Solr generates facet information at the time of indexing instead of doing it on the stored values. That means, if we introduce new attributes in the schema after indexing of our information, Solr will not be able to identify them. This may be solved by re-indexing the information again.

Each of these facet elements contain the filter value, which carries a count of results that match among the searched results. For the newly introduced schema attributes, users need to recreate the indexes that are created before. There are different types of facets supported by Solr. The following screenshot depicts the different types of facets that are discussed:

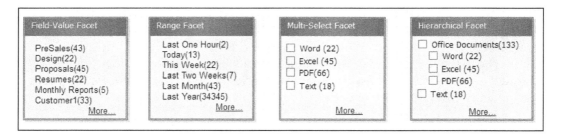

The facets allow you to get aggregated view on your text data. These aggregations can be based on different compositions such as count (number of appearances), time based, and so on. The following table describes the facets and their description supported by Apache Solr:

Facet	Description
Field-value	You can have your schema fields as facet components here. It shows the count of top fields. For example, if a document has tags, a field-value facet on the tag Solr field will show the top N tags, which are found in the matched result as shown in the image.

Facet	Description
Range	Range faceting is mostly used on date/numeric fields, and it supports range queries. You can specify start and end dates, gap in the range and so on. There is a facet called date facet for managing dates, but it has been deprecated since Solr 3.2, and now the date is being handled in range faceting itself. For example, if indexed, a Solr document has a creation date and time; a range facet will provide filtering based on the time range.
Pivot	A pivot gives Solr users the ability to perform simple math on the data. With this facet, they can summarize results, and then get them sorted, take an average, and so on. This gives you hierarchical results (also sometimes called hierarchical faceting).
Multi-select	Using this facet, the results can be refined with multiple selects on attribute values. These facets can be used by the users to apply multiple criteria on the search results.

Advanced search capabilities

Apache Solr provides various advanced search capabilities. Solr comes with a **more like this** feature, which lets you find documents similar to one or more seed documents. The similarity is calculated from one or more fields of your choice. When the user selects similar results, it will take the current search result and try to find a similar result in the complete index of Solr.

When the user passes a query, the search results can show the snippet among the searched keywords highlighted. **Highlighting** in Solr allows fragments of documents that match the user's query to be included with the query response. Highlighting takes place only for the fields that are searched by the user. Solr provides a collection of highlighting utilities, which allow a great deal of control over the field's fragments, the size of fragments, and how they are formatted.

When a search query is passed to Solr, it is matched with the number of results. The order in which the results are displayed on the UI is based on the relevance of each result with the searched keyword(s), by default. **Relevance** is all about proximity of the result set with the searched keyword that is returned by Solr when a query is performed. This proximity can be measured in various ways. The relevance of a response depends upon the context in which the query was performed. A single search application may be used in different contexts by users with different needs and expectations. Apache Solr provides the relevant score calculations based on various factors such as the number of occurrences of searched keyword in the document or the co-ordination factor, which relates to the maximum number of terms matched among the searched keywords. Solr not only gives flexibility to users to choose the scoring, but also allows users to customize the relevant ranking as per the enterprise search expectations.

Apache Solr allows **spell checker** based on the index proximity. There are multiple options available under the label, in one case Solr provides suggestions for the misplaced word when searched, in the other case Solr returns a suggestion to the user with the **Did you mean** prompt The following screenshot shows an example of how these features would look on Apache Solr's client side:

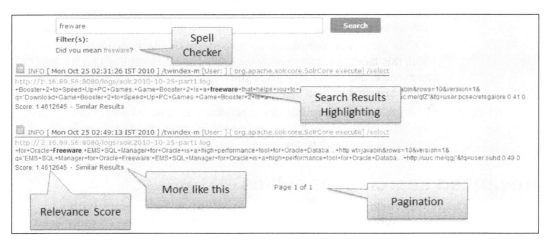

Additionally, Apache Solr has a suggest feature that suggests the query terms or phrases based on incomplete user inputs. With the help of suggestions, users can choose from the list of suggestions as they start typing a few characters. These completions come from the Solr index generated at the time of data indexing from the first top-k matches ranked based on relevance, popularity, or the order of alphabets. Consider the following screenshot:

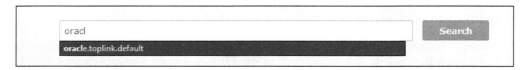

In many enterprises, location-based information along with text data brings value in terms of visual representation. Apache Solr supports geospatial search. A Solr search provides advanced geospatial capabilities in the search by which users can sort the results based on geographical distances (longitude and latitude), or rank the results based on proximity. This capability comes from the Lucene spatial module.

Enterprises are not limited to any languages and often contain a landscape of non-English applications used daily by the employees. Sometimes, the documentation has local languages. In such cases, an enterprise search is required to have the capability to work on various languages instead of limiting itself on one. Apache Solr has built-in language detection and provides language specific text analysis solutions for many languages. Many times, the implementers need to customize the Solr instance to work for us as per their requirements for multi-lingual support.

Administration

Like any other enterprise search operations, Apache Solr facilitates system administrators with various capabilities. This section discusses different features supported at the administration level for Apache Solr.

Apache Solr has built-in administration user interface for administrators and Solr developers. Apache Solr has evolved its administration screen. Version 4.6 contains many advanced features. The administration screen in Solr looks like the following screenshot:

The Admin UI provides a dashboard that provides information about the instance and the system. The logging section provides Apache logging service (log4j) outputs and various log levels such as warning, severe, and error. The core admin UI details out management information about different cores. The thread dump screen shows all threads with CPU time and thread time. The administrators can also see stack trace for threads.

A collection represents complete logical index, whereas a Solr core represents an index with a Solr instance that includes configuration and runtime. Typically, the configuration of Solr core is kept in the /conf directory. Once the user selects the core, they get access to various core-specific functions such as current configuration view, test UI for testing various handlers of Solr, and schema browser. Consider the following features:

- **JMX monitoring**: The **Java Management Extension** (**JMX**) technology provides the tools for managing and monitoring of web-based, distributed system. Since Version 3.1, Apache Solr can expose the statistics of runtime activities as dynamic **Managed Beans** (**MBeans**). The beans can be viewed in any JMX client (for example, JConsole). With every release, MBeans gets added, and administrators can see the collective list of these MBeans using administration interface. (Typically, it can be seen by accessing: http://localhost:8983/solr/admin/mbeans/).

- **Near real time search**: Unlike Google's lazy index update, based on crawler's chance of visiting certain pages, the enterprise search at times requires fast index updates based on the changes. It means, the user wants to search the near real time databases. Apache Solr supports soft commit.

 Whenever users upload documents to the Solr server, they must run a commit operation, to ensure that the uploaded documents are stored in the Solr repository. A soft commit is a Solr 4.0 introduced feature that allows users to commit fast, by passing costly commit procedures and making the data available for near real-time search.

With soft commit, the information is available immediately for searching; however, it requires normal commit to ensure the document is available on a persistent store. Solr administrators can also enable autosoft commit through Apache Solr configuration.

- **Flexible query parsing**: In Apache Solr, query parsers play an important role for parsing the query and allowing the search to apply the outcome on the indexes to identify whether the search keywords match. A parser may enable Solr users to add search keywords customizations such as support for regular expressions or enabling users with complex querying through the search interface. Apache Solr, by default, supports several query parsers, offering the enterprise architects to bring in flexibility in controlling how the queries are getting parsed. We are going to understand them in detail in the upcoming chapters.

- **Caching**: Apache Solr is capable of searching on large datasets. When such searches are performed, the cost of time and performance become important factors for the scalability. Apache Solr does caching at various levels to ensure that the users get optimal performance out of the running instance. The caching can be performed at filter level (mainly used for filtering), field values (mainly used in facets), query results (top-k results are cached in certain order), and document level cache. Each cache implementation follows a different caching strategy, such as least recently used or least frequently used. Administrators can choose one of the available cache mechanisms for their search application.

- **Integration**: Typically, enterprise search user interfaces appear as a part of the end user applications, as they only occupy limited screens. The open source Apache Solr community provides client libraries for integrating Solr with various technologies in the client-server model. Solr supports integration through different languages such as Ruby, PHP, .NET, Java, Scala, Perl, and JavaScript. Besides programming languages, Solr also integrates with applications, such as Drupal, WordPress, and Alfresco CMS.

Apache Solr architecture

In the previous section, we have gone through various key features supported by Apache Solr. In this section, we will look at the architecture of Apache Solr. Apache Solr is a J2EE-based application that internally uses Apache Lucene libraries to generate the indexes as well as to provide a user friendly search. Let's look at the Solr architecture diagram as follows:

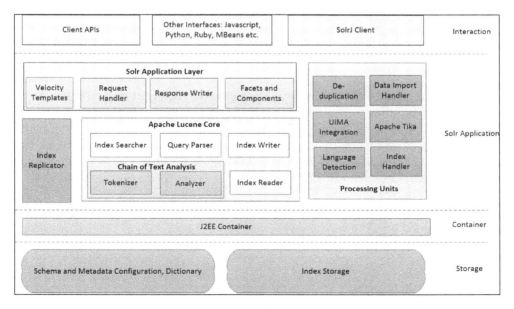

The Apache Solr instance can run as a single core or multicore; it is a client-server model. In case of a multicore, however, the search access pattern can differ. We are going to look into this in the next chapter. Earlier, Apache Solr had a single core, which in turn, limited the consumers to run Solr on one application through a single schema and configuration file. Later, the support for creating multiple cores was added. With this support, one can run one Solr instance for multiple schemas and configurations with unified administrations. For high availability and scalability requirements, Apache Solr can run in a distributed mode. We are going to look at it in *Chapter 6, Distributed Search Using Apache Solr*. There are four logical layers in which the overall Solr functionality can be divided. The storage layer is responsible for management of indexes and configuration metadata. The container is the J2EE container on which the instance will run, and Solr engine is the application package that runs on top of the container, and, finally, the interaction talks about how clients/browser can interact with Apache Solr server. Let's look at each of the components in detail in the upcoming sections.

Storage

The storage of Apache Solr is mainly used for storing metadata and the actual index information. It is typically a file store, locally configured in the configuration of Apache Solr. The default Solr installation package comes with a Jetty servlet and HTTP server, the respective configuration can be found in the `$solr.home/conf` folder of Solr installation. An index contains a sequence of documents. Additionally, external storage devices can be configured in Apache Solr, such as databases or Big Data storage systems. The following are the components:

- A document is a collection of fields
- A field is a named sequence of terms
- A term is a string

The same string in two different fields is considered a different term. The index stores statistics about terms in order to make term-based search more efficient. Lucene's index falls into the family of indexes known as an inverted index. This is because it can list, for a term, the documents that contain it. Apache Solr (underlying Lucene) indexing is a specially designed data structure, stored in the filesystem as a set of index files. The index is designed with a specific format in such a way to maximize query performance.

Inverted index is an index data structure for storing mapping from data to actual words and numbers to its location on the storage disk. The following are the strings:

```
Str[1] = "This is a game of team"
Str[2] ="I do not like a game of cricket"
Str[3] ="People play games everyday"
```

We have the following inverted file index:

```
This {1}
Game {1,2,3}
Of {1,2}
```

Solr application

There are two major functions that Solr supports—indexing and searching. Initially, the data is uploaded to Apache Solr through various means; there are handlers to handle data within specific category (XML, CSV, PDF, database, and so on). Once the data is uploaded, it goes through a stage of cleanup called update processor chain. In this chain, initially, the de-duplication phase can be used to remove duplicates in the data to avoid them from appearing in the index unnecessarily. Each update handler can have its own update processor chain that can do document-level operations prior to indexing, or even redirect indexing to a different server or create multiple documents (or zero) from a single one. The data is then transformed depending upon the type.

Apache Solr can run in a master-slave mode. Index replicator is responsible for distributing indexes across multiple slaves. The master server maintains index update and the slaves are responsible for talking with the master to get them replicated for high availability. Apache Lucene core gets packages as library with the Apache Solr application. It provides core functionality for Solr such as index, query processing, searching data, ranking matched results, and returning them back.

Apache Lucene comes with a variety of query implementations. Query parser is responsible for parsing the queries passed by the end search as a search string. Lucene provides TermQuery, BooleanQuery, PhraseQuery, PrefixQuery, RangeQuery, MultiTermQuery, FilteredQuery, SpanQuery, and so on as query implementations.

Index searcher is a basic component of Solr searched with a default base searcher class. This class is responsible for returning ordered match results of searched keyword ranked as per the computed score. The index reader provides access to indexes stored in the filesystem. It can be used to search for an index. Similar to the index searcher, an index writer allows you to create and maintain indexes in Apache Lucene.

The analyzer is responsible for examining the fields and generating tokens. Tokenizer breaks field data into lexical units or tokens. The filter examines the field of tokens from the tokenizer and either it keeps them and transforms them, or discards them and creates new ones. Tokenizers and filters together form a chain or pipeline of analyzers. There can only be one tokenizer per analyzer. The output of one chain is fed to another. Analyzing the process is used for indexing as well as querying by Solr. They play an important role in speeding up the query as well as index time; they also reduce the amount of data that gets generated out of these operations. You can define your own customer analyzers depending upon your use case. In addition to the analyzer, Apache Solr allows administrators to make the search experience more effective by means of taking out common words such as `is`, `and`, and `are` through the stopwords feature. Solr supports synonyms, thereby not limiting search to purely text match. Through the processing of stemming, all words such as played, playing, play can be transformed into the base form. We are going to look at these features in the coming chapters and the appendix. Similar to stemming, the user can search for multiterms of a single word as well (for example, play, played, playing). When a user fires a search query on Solr, it actually gets passed on to a request handler. By default, Apache Solr provides `DisMaxRequestHandler`. You can visit `http://wiki.apache.org/solr/DisMaxRequestHandler` to find more details about this handler. Based on the request, the request handler calls the query parser. You can see an example of the filter in the following figure:

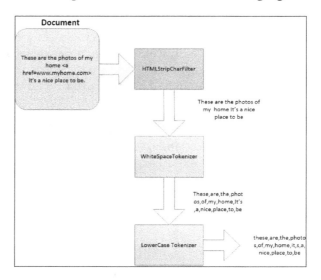

The query parser is responsible for parsing the queries, and converting it to Lucene query objects. There are different types of parsers available (Lucene, DisMax, eDisMax, and so on). Each parser offers different functionalities and it can be used based on the requirements. Once a query is parsed, it hands it over to the index searcher. The job of the index reader is to run the queries on the index store and gather the results to the response writer.

The response writer is responsible for responding back to the client; it formats the query response based on the search outcomes from the Lucene engine. The following figure displays the complete process flow when a search is fired from the client:

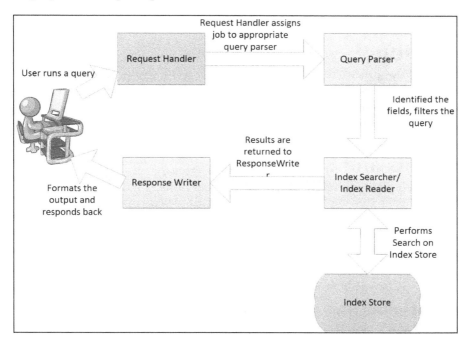

Apache Solr ships with an example schema that runs using Apache velocity. Apache velocity is a fast open source templates engine, which quickly generates HTML-based frontend. Users can customize these templates as per their requirements, although it is not used for production in many cases.

Index handlers are a type of update handler, handling the task of add, update, and delete function on documents for indexing. Apache Solr supports updates through the index handler through JSON, XML, and text format.

Data Import Handler (**DIH**) provides a mechanism for integrating different data sources with Apache Solr for indexing. The data sources could be relational databases or web-based sources (for example, RSS, ATOM feeds, and e-mails).

Although DIH is a part of Solr development, the default installation does not include it in the Solr application; they need to be included in the application explicitly.

Apache Tika, a project in itself extends capabilities of Apache Solr to run on top of different types of files. When a document is assigned to Tika, it automatically determines the type of file, that is, Word, Excel, PDF and extracts the content. Tika also extracts document metadata such as author, title, and creation date, which if provided in schema, go as text field in Apache Solr. This can later be used as facets for the search interface.

Integration

Apache Solr, although a web-based application, can be integrated with different technologies. So, if a company has Drupal-based e-commerce sites, they can integrate the Apache Solr application and provide its rich-faceted search to the user. It can also support advanced searches using the range search.

Client APIs and SolrJ client

The Apache Solr client provides different ways of talking with Apache Solr web application. This enables Solr to easily get integrated with any application. Using client APIs, consumers can run a search, and perform different operations on indexes. The **Solr Java** (**SolrJ**) client is an interface of Apache Solr with Java. The SolrJ client enables any Java application to talk directly with Solr through its extensive library of APIs. Apache SolrJ is a part of the Apache Solr package.

Other interfaces

Apache Solr can be integrated with other various technologies using its API library and standards-based interfacing. JavaScript-based clients can straightaway talk with Solr using JSON-based messaging. Similarly, other technologies can simply connect to the Apache Solr running instance through HTTP, and consume its services either through JSON, XML, or text formats. Since Solr can be interacted through standard ways, clients can always build their own pretty user interface to interact with the Solr server.

Practical use cases for Apache Solr

Publicly there are plenty of public sites who claim the use of Apache Solr as the server. We are listing a few here, along with how Solr is used:

- **Instagram**: Instagram (a Facebook company) is one of the famous sites, and it uses Solr to power its geosearch API

- `WhiteHouse.gov`: The Obama administration's website is inbuilt in Drupal and Solr

- **Netflix**: Solr powers basic movie searching on this extremely busy site

- **Internet archive**: Search this vast repository of music, documents, and video using Solr

- `StubHub.com`: This ticket reseller uses Solr to help visitors search for concerts and sporting events.

- **The Smithsonian Institution**: Search the Smithsonian's collection of over 4 million items

You can find the complete list of Solr usage (although a bit outdated) at `http://wiki.apache.org/solr/PublicServers`. You may also visit to understand interesting case studies about **Contextual Search for Volkswagen and the Automotive Industry**. The scope of this study is beyond Apache Solr, and talks about semantic search (RDF-based) to empower your overall enterprise industry.

Let's look at how Apache Solr can be used as an enterprise search in two different industries. We will look at one case study in detail, and we will understand how Solr can play a role in the other case study in brief.

Now that we have understood Apache Solr architecture and the use cases, let's look at how Apache Solr can be used as an enterprise search in two different industries.

Enterprise search for a job search agency

In this case, we will go through a case study for the job search agency, and how it can benefit using Apache Solr as an enterprise search platform.

Problem statement

In many job portal agencies, the enterprise search helps reduce the overall time employees spend in matching the expectations from customers with the resumes. Typically, for each vacancy, customers provide a job description. Many times, job description is a lengthy affair, and given the limited time each employee gets, he has to bridge the gap between these two. A job search agency has to deal with various applications as follows:

- Internal CMS containing past information, resumes of candidates, and so on
- Access to market analysis to align the business with expectation
- Employer vacancies may come through e-mails or online vacancy portal
- Online job agencies are a major source for supplying new resumes
- An external public site of the agency where many applicants upload their resumes

Since a job agency deals with multiple systems due to their interaction patterns, having unified enterprise search on top of these systems is the objective to speed up the overall business.

Approach

Here, we have taken a fictitious job search agency who would like to improve the candidate identification time using enterprise search. Given the system landscape, Apache Solr can play a major role here in helping them speed up the process. The following screenshot depicts interaction between unified enterprise searches powered by Apache Solr with other systems:

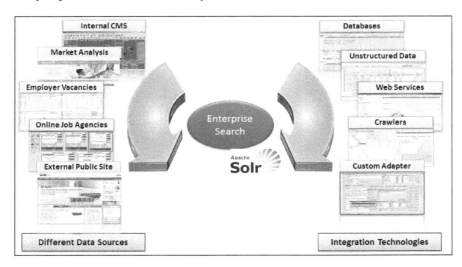

The figure demonstrates how enterprise search powered by Apache Solr can interact with different data sources. The job search agency interacts with various internal as well as third-party applications. This serves as input for Apache Solr-based enterprise search operations. It would require Solr to talk with these systems by means of different technology-based interaction patterns such as web services, database access, crawlers, and customized adapters as shown in the right-hand side. Apache Solr provides support for database; for the rest, the agency has to build an event-based or scheduled agent, which can pull information from these sources and feed them in Solr. Many times, this information is raw, and the adapter should be able to extract field information from this data, for example, technology expertise, role, salary, or domain expertise. This can be done through various ways. One way is by applying a simple regular expression-based pattern on each resume, and then extracting the information. Alternatively, one can also let it run through the dictionary of verticals and try matching it. Tag-based mechanism also can be used for tagging resumes directly from information contained in the text.

Based on the requirements, now Apache Solr must provide rich facets for candidate searches as well as job searches, which would have the following facets:

- Technology-based dimension
- Vertical- or domain-based dimension
- Financials for candidates
- Timeline of candidates' resume (upload date)
- Role-based dimension

Additionally, mapping similar words (J2EE — Java Enterprise Edition — Java2 Enterprise Edition) through Solr really helps ease the job of agency's employees for automatically producing the proximity among these words, which have the same meaning through the Apache Solr synonym feature. We are going to look at how it can be done in the upcoming chapters.

Enterprise search for energy industry

In this case study, we will learn how enterprise search can be used within the energy industry.

Problem statement

In large cities, the energy distribution network is managed by companies, which are responsible for laying underground cables, and setting up power grids at different places, and transformers. Overall, it's a huge chunk of work that any industry will do for a city. Although there are many bigger problems in this industry where Apache Solr can play a major role, we will try to focus on this specific problem.

Many times, the land charts will show how the assets (for example, pipe, cable, and so on) are placed under the roads and the information about lamps are drawn and kept in a safe. This has been paper-based work for long time, and it's now computerized. The field workers who work in the fields for repairs or maintenance often need access to this information, such as assets, pipe locations, and so on.

The demand for this information is to locate a resource geographically. Additionally, the MIS information is part of the documents lying on CMS, and it's difficult to locate this information and link it with geospatial search. This in turn drives the need for the presence of the enterprise search. Additionally, there is also a requirement for identifying the closest field workers to the problematic area to ensure quick resolution.

Approach

For this problem, we are dealing with information coming in totally different forms. The real challenge is to link this information together, and then apply a search that can provide a unified access to information with rich query. We have the following information:

- **Land Charts**: These are PDFs, paper-based documents, and so on, which are fixed information
- **GIS information**: These are coordinates, which are fixed for assets such as transformers, and cables
- **Field engineers' information**: This gives the current location and is continuously flowing
- **Problem/Complaints**: This will be continuous, either through some portal, or directly fed through the web interface

The challenges that we might face with this approach include:

- Loading and linking data in various formats
- Identifying assets on map
- Identifying the proximity between field workers and assets
- Providing better browsing experience on all this information

Apache Solr supports geospatial search. It can bring a rich capacity by linking assets.

Information with geospatial world creates a confluence to enable the users to access this information. It can bring a rich capacity by linking asset information with the geospatial world and creating a confluence to enable the users to access this information at their finger tips.

However, Solr has its own limitations in terms of geospatial capabilities. For example, it supports only point data (latitude, longitude) directly; all the other data types are supported through JTS.

 Java Topology Suite (JTS) is a java-based API toolkit for GIS. JTS provides a foundation for building further spatial applications, such as viewers, spatial query processors, and tools for performing data validation, cleaning, and integration.

For the given problem, GIS and land chart will feed information in the Solr server once. This will include linking all assets with GIS information through the custom adapter. The complaint history as well as the field engineers' data will be continuous, and the old data will be overwritten; this can be a scheduled event or a custom event, based on the new inputs received by the system. To meet the expectations, the following application components will be required (minimum):

- Custom adapter with scheduler/event for field engineers' data and complaint register information providing integration with gateways (for tapping GIS information of field engineers) and portals (for the complaint register)
- Lightweight client to scan the existing system (history, other documentation) and load in Solr
- Client application to provide end user interface for enterprise search with URL integration for maps
- Apache Solr with superset schema definition and configuration with support for spatial data types

The following screenshot provides one of the possible visualizations for this system. This system can be extended to further provide more advanced capabilities such as integration with **Optical Character Recognition (OCR)** software to search across paper-based information, or even to generate dynamic reports based on filters using Solr. Apache Solr also supports output in XML form, which can be applied with any styling and the same can be used to develop nice reporting systems.

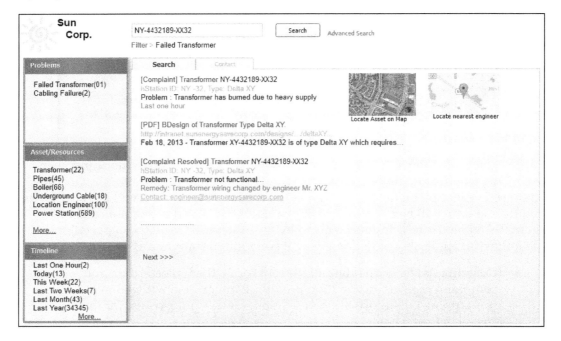

Summary

In this chapter, we have tried to understand problems faced by today's industry with respect to enterprise search. We went through Apache Solr and its features to understand its capabilities, followed by the Apache Solr architecture. At the end of this chapter, we saw a use case about how Apache Solr can be applied in the job search agency as an enterprise search.

In the next chapter, we will install and configure the Solr instance for our usage.

2
Getting Started with Apache Solr

In the previous chapter, we went through the challenges in enterprise search; then, we covered Apache Solr as an enterprise search solution, followed its architecture and features, and finally, we also looked at practical use cases for Solr in different industries. In this chapter, we will focus on starting work with Apache Solr and cover the following points:

- Setting up the Apache Solr server
- Configuring the Solr instance for applications
- Consuming Apache Solr in end user applications

Setting up Apache Solr

Apache Solr is a J2EE-based web application, which runs on Apache Lucene, Tika, and other open source libraries. This section focuses on setting up an Apache Solr instance and running it. Existing users who have Solr instance running can skip this section and move on to the next section.

Apache Solr ships with a demo Jetty server, so one can simply run it through command line. This helps users run the Solr instance quickly. However, you can choose to customize it and deploy it in your own environment. Apache Solr does not ship with any installer; it has to run as part of J2EE.

Prerequisites

Before the installation of Apache Solr, you need to make sure that you have the latest JDK on your machines. You can test this by simply running the `java -version` command on the command line, as shown in the following screenshot:

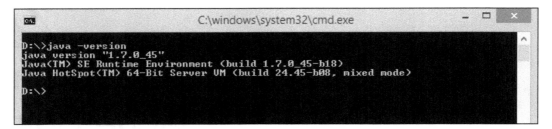

Once you have the correct Java version, you need a servlet container such as Tomcat, Jetty, Resin, Glassfish, or Weblogic installed on your machine.

> With the latest version of Apache Solr (4.0 or higher), the JDK 1.5 is not supported anymore. Versions higher than Apache Solr 4.0 run on JDK 1.6 and higher versions. Instead of going for a preshipped JDK with your default operating system, go for the full version of the JDK by downloading it from `http://www.oracle.com/technetwork/java/javase/downloads/index.html?ssSourceSiteId=otnjp`; this will enable full support for international charset. Apache Solr 4.8 requires at least JDK 7.

Next, you need the Apache Solr distribution itself. You can download the stable installer from `http://lucene.apache.org/solr/` or from its nightly builds running on the same site. To run Solr on Windows, download the zip file from the Apache mirror site. For Linux, Unix, and other such flavors, you can download the `.gzip` or `.tgz` version. In Windows, you can simply unzip your file; in Unix, try the following command to unzip Solr:

```
$tar -xvzf solr-<major-minor version>.tgz
```

> **Downloading the example code**
>
> You can download the example code files for all Packt books you have purchased from your account at `http://www.packtpub.com`. If you purchased this book elsewhere, you can visit `http://www.packtpub.com/support` and register to have the files e-mailed directly to you.

If you are building Solr from source, then you need the Java SE 7 JDK, Apache Ant distribution (1.8.2 or more), and Apache Ivy (2.2.0+). You can compile the source by simply navigating to the Solr directory and running Ant from there. For more information, refer to http://techblogs.razorthink.com/2013/10/how-to-compile-solr-source-code.html.

When you unzip the Solr file, it extracts the following directories:

Directory	Purpose
contrib/	This directory contains all the libraries that are additional to Solr, and they can be included on demand. It provides libraries for data import handler, MapReduce, Apache UIMA, velocity template, and so on.
dist/	This directory provides the distributions of Solr and other useful libraries such as SolrJ, UIMA, MapReduce, and so on.
docs/	This directory contains the documentation for Solr
example/	This directory provides Jetty-based Solr webapps that can be directly used
Licenses/	This directory contains all the licenses of the underlying libraries used by Solr

There are commercial versions of Apache Solr available from a company called LucidWorks (http://www.lucidworks.com). As Solr is a web-based application, it can run on many operating systems such as *nix and Windows. Additionally, you may also need a command-line utility called curl to run your samples. You can also use wget or any other HTTP request-based utility for interaction with Solr.

Some of the older versions of Solr have failed to run properly due to locale differences on host systems. If your system default locale or character set is non-English (that is en/en-US), for safety, you can override your system defaults for Solr by passing -Duser.language=en -Duser.country=US in your Jetty to ensure the smooth running of Solr.

Running Solr on Jetty

Apache Solr ships with the default small Jetty server along with its zip file; you can directly use it for running your Solr instance in a single instance mode. Alternatively, you can use the latest available Jetty server with full features to run Solr on Jetty. You will find the Jetty server in the solr<version>/example directory. Once you unzip the solr.zip file, all you need to do is go to solr<version>/example and run the following command:

```
$ java -jar start.jar
```

The default Jetty instance will run on port 8983, and you can access the Solr instance by visiting `http://localhost:8983/solr/browse`. You will see a default search screen, as shown in the following screenshot:

You can edit the `solr-<VERSION>/example/etc/jetty.xml` file to change the port by changing the system property with the name `jetty.port`. By default, Jetty and Solr will log in to the `logs/solr.log` console. This can be convenient when first getting started, but eventually, you will want to log in just to a file. To configure logging, edit the `log4j.properties` file in `resources`. The `Log4j.properties` file contains the configuration information about the logging done for Apache Solr.

To get Solr on the latest available full Jetty installation, you need to first install the respective JDK version by running the following command with the root user.

```
#apt-get install openjdk-7-jdk
```

You can use `yum install` for Red Hat-based Linux. Download the latest available Jetty from the eclipse site (`http://download.eclipse.org/jetty/stable-9/dist/`) and unpack it in some directory (such as `/pkgs/jetty`) using the following command:

```
$ tar -xvf jetty-distribution-<version>.tar.gz
```

 Jetty 6.0 has a limited support for URL encoded with the Unicode character; the problem has been fixed in Jetty 7.0 and higher versions, so it is always better to go for the latest version of Jetty.

Create a Jetty user and make it the owner of /opt/jetty, using the
following command:

```
$ useradd jetty -U -s /bin/false
$ chown -R jetty:jetty /pkgs/jetty
```

Alternatively, you may also choose to run as a service as the following:

```
$ cp /pkgs/jetty/bin/jetty.sh /etc/init.d/jetty
```

Download Solr from the Apache mirror site (http://lucene.apache.org/solr/
downloads.html), and unpack the example directory in /home/solr:

```
$ wget <apache-mirror site>
$ tar -xvzf apache-solr-<version>.tgz
$ cp apache-solr-<version>/dist/apache-solr-<version>.war /pkgs/jetty/
webapps/solr.war
$ cp -R apache-solr-<version>/example/solr /home
```

Open /etc/default/jetty to add the following settings:

```
JAVA_HOME=/usr/bin/java # Path to Java
NO_START=0 # Start on boot
JETTY_USER=jetty # Run as this user
JETTY_HOST=0.0.0.0 # Listen to all hosts
JETTY_ARGS=jetty.port=8983 # jetty port
JAVA_OPTIONS="-Dsolr.solr.home=/home/solr/example-schemaless/solr
$JAVA_OPTIONS"
```

In the Java options, you can start with Solr without schema. Apache Solr provides
the default /example-schemaless directory that you can use to run by default.
Alternatively, you can also use default collection1, which is part of the Solr release
inside the $SOLR_HOME/example/solr directory.

The schemaless mode is a set for Solr features that, when used
together, allow users to rapidly construct an effective schema
by simply indexing sample data, without having to manually
edit the schema.

With the schemaless mode, you are not required to do any preconfiguration for schema definition, and you can start using Solr in this mode. In this mode, Solr defines two static fields (id and version) and the rest as dynamic fields, for example, *_I as the int field and so on. To enable the schemaless mode, all you need to do is point to this directory instead of example-schemaless. Now, you can start the Jetty service using the following command:

```
$ service jetty start
jetty start/running, process 7299
```

Running Solr on Tomcat

Apache Tomcat is one of the most widely used J2EE containers to run different applications. To start with Apache Tomcat, first download JDK 6 or higher versions as described in the previous section. Now, download tomcat zip (Windows) or tar.gz (*nix flavors) from http://tomcat.apache.org/ (avoid alpha and beta versions) and unzip them in some folder. Start by defining the catalina.home variable as follows:

```
$ export CATALINA_HOME=<path to tomcat folder>
```

Now, enable the Tomcat user login to access the administration UI by adding the following entries in $CATALINA_HOME/conf/tomcat-users.xml as follows:

```
<role rolename="manager"/>
<role rolename="admin"/>
<user username="tomcat" password="tomcat" roles="manager,admin"/>
```

Set the Tomcat port appropriately by modifying the $CATALINA_HOME/conf/server.xml file as follows:

```
<Connector port="8983" protocol="HTTP/1.1"
            connectionTimeout="20000"
            redirectPort="10443" />
```

Download and unzip Solr as described in the previous section. Now, copy the `solr.war` file from the unzipped folder to `$CATALINA_HOME/webapps/solr.war`. Then, you can choose one of the following options for the next step:

- **Java options**: You can set the Java options with the following command so that the container will pick up the Solr collection information from the appropriate location:

  ```
  $ export JAVA_OPTS="$JAVA_OPTS -Dsolr.solr.home=/opt/solr/example"
  ```

  Please look at the previous section to understand more on how to set the `solr.home` location.

- **JNDI Lookup**: Alternatively, you can configure the JNDI lookup for the `java:comp/env/solr/home` resource by pointing it to the Solr home directory. This can be done by creating a context XML file with some name (`context.xml`) in `$CATALINA_HOME/conf/Catalina/localhost/context.xml` and adding the following entries:

  ```
  <?xml version="1.0" encoding="utf-8"?>

  <Context docBase="<solr-home>/example/solr/solr.war" debug="0"
  crossContext="true">

    <Environment name="solr/home" type="java.lang.String"
  value="<solr-home>/example/solr" override="true"/>

  </Context>
  ```

Once this file is created, Apache Tomcat will automatically load it while starting it. Now, start Tomcat by running `$CATALINA_HOME/bin/startup.sh` or `startup.bat`. Once the server is started, you will find `solr.war` getting unpacked in the logs, and automatically, a `$CATALINA_HOME/webapps/solr` directory gets created. Try to access `http://<host>:<port>/solr`.

Apache Solr uses the UTF-8 file encoding which means that a container should be enabled to work with Unicode. In the case of Tomcat, this can be done by simply editing the `startup.bat` or `startup.sh` file with the following code snippet:

```
set "JAVA_OPTS=%JAVA_OPTS% -Dfile.encoding=UTF8"
```

 Since Solr 4.1 Version, Solr now parses request parameters (in URL or sent with POST using content-type application/x-www-form-urlencoded) in its dispatcher code. It no longer relies on special configuration settings that are mandatory for correct Solr behavior.

Apache Solr can be deployed on many open source J2EE containers such as JBoss as well as commercial J2EE containers such as IBM Websphere, Oracle WebLogic, and so on. You need to follow a similar step as explained in the previous section.

Solr administration

In this section, we will understand the Solr administration user interface in brief. Apache Solr provides an excellent user interface for the administrator of the server. A collection in Apache Solr is a collection of Solr documents that represent one complete index. Solr core is an execution unit of Solr that can run on its own configuration and other metadata. Apache Solr collections can be created for each index. Similarly, you can run Solr in multiple core modes. We will be understanding more about these in the following chapters. The following table describes different options available for Apache Solr administrations with the purpose:

Option	Purpose
Dashboard	You see information related to the version of Solr, memory consumption, JVM, and so on
Logging	This shows log outputs with latest logs on top
Logging >Level	This shows the current log configuration for packages, that is, for which package which logs are enabled
Core admin	This shows information about the core and allows its administration
Java properties	This shows the different Java properties set during the run of the Solr instance
Thread dump	This describes the stack trace with information on CPU and user time; it also enables a detailed stack trace
Collection	This demonstrates different parameters of collection and all the activities you can perform, such as running queries and ping status

Access `http://localhost:8983/solr/#/~cores/collection1` to get your Solr instance running. We have gone through the information about administration user interface in *Chapter 1, Understanding Apache Solr*. You can add more cores by navigating to **Core Admin | Add Core** in the administration UI, as shown in the following screenshot:

What's next?

Once you are done with the installation of Apache Solr, you can simply run examples by going to the `examples/exampledocs` directory and running the following command:

```
java -jar post.jar solr.xml monitor.xml
```

The `post.jar` utility is provided by Solr to upload the data to Apache Solr for indexing. When it is run, the `post.jar` file simply uploads all the files that are passed as a parameter to Apache Solr for indexing, and Solr indexes these files and stores them in its repository. Now, try to access your instance by typing `http://localhost:8983/solr/browse`; you should find a sample search interface with some information in it, as shown in the following screenshot:

Common problems and solution

Now, the installation is successful. Let's try to address some of the common problems that you may face during the setup and their solution.

While running Solr, why do I get java.lang.OutOfMemoryError sometimes?

The `OutOfMemory` error is thrown by the **Java Virtual Machine** (**JVM**) that runs Apache Solr, when there is not enough memory available for heap or for PermGen (Permenant Generation Space holds metadata regarding user classes and methods). When you get such an error, you need to restart the container. However, while restarting the container, you must make sure that you increase the memory of JVM. This can be done by adding the following JVM arguments for PermGen:

```
export JVM_ARGS="-Xmx1024m -XX:MaxPermSize=256m"
```

For the Heap Space error, you can specify the following JVM arguments:

```
export JVM_ARGS="-Xms1024m -Xmx1024m"
```

 The size of memory should be specified by the user. We have covered this topic in more detail in *Chapter 8, Scaling Solr through High Performance.*

When I modify the schema.xml file, I do not see any changes immediately

When `schema.xml` is modified, you need to restart the Solr instance to see the effect. You also need to rebuild the indexes, because Solr indexed the data considering the previous schema attributes, and it changed `schema.xml`, which is not incorporated. You can also reload the `schema.xml` changes without restarting the server. Please refer to the reload command as described in `http://wiki.apache.org/solr/CoreAdmin#RELOAD`.

How do I run Solr Jetty in the background mode?

If you create Jetty as a service on Windows/Linux, the server will automatically start at system startup and stop at shutdown. You can manually start the service as a super user with following command:

```
$ service jetty start
```

Stop the service with the following command:

```
$ service jetty stop
```

If you are running it manually, you may try running it using the nohup command:

```
$ nohup java -jar start.jar > output.log 2>&1 &
```

The nohup command will prevent your command from being terminated in the event you log out and will run it in the background. This command will send stdout to output.log and redirect stderr to stdout.

When I create a new core, it fails with the error "Can't find resource 'solrconfig.xml' in classpath"

Apache Solr does not let you create a core unless you have the instance directory and data directory created. So, if you are creating a new core with the instance directory as demo_core and data directory as data, you need to copy the sample configuration folder, conf to $SOLR_HOME/demo_core/conf and the data folder from your sample collection to $SOLR_HOME/demo_core/data.

When copying the Solr configuration files, you should remember to include all the files and the exact directory structure that Solr needs. So, in the directory specified by the solr.solr.home variable, the solr.xml file should be available—the one that describes the cores of your system. Once you have copied it, try creating the new core from the Apache Solr administration user interface.

How to find out whether the Solr server is running or not?

There are multiple ways in which you can find out whether your server is running or not. Typically, many containers provide a manager application to manage all your deployments. In Tomcat, you can access it by calling http://<host>:<port>/manager/html with a login and password, as shown in the following screenshot:

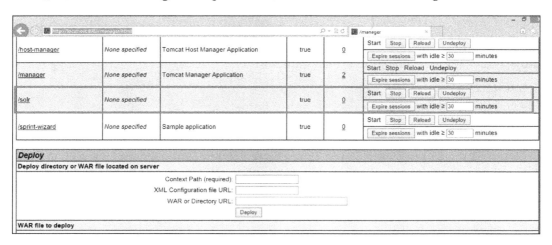

Alternatively, Apache Solr provides you with a ping service that can be accessed from Java clients as well as through the Web by accessing `http://localhost:8983/solr/admin/ping`, as shown in the following screenshot:

```xml
<?xml version="1.0" encoding="UTF-8"?>
<response>
  <lst name="responseHeader">
    <int name="status">0</int>
    <int name="QTime">3</int>
    <lst name="params">
      <str name="df">text</str>
      <str name="echoParams">all</str>
      <str name="rows">10</str>
      <str name="echoParams">all</str>
      <str name="q">solrpingquery</str>
      <str name="distrib">false</str>
    </lst>
  </lst>
  <str name="status">OK</str>
</response>
```

The **OK** status explains that Solr is running fine on the server.

Understanding the Solr structure

Now that your Solr server is set and running, the next step will be to configure your instance for your application. Most of the configuration for Apache Solr can be done through XML configuration files, which go in the `conf/` directory of your Solr core home. Let's go through the configuration for the Solr instance.

When we do the deployments on the container, the `solr.war` file contains the actual web application that can be accessed through the URL. Each container, when started for the first time, unpacks this `.war` file in an internal directory (this is different for each container).

The J2EE container picks up the home directory as specified by Java parameters before starting the instance and looking for `solr.xml`. The `solr.xml` file defines the context that contains information about the core.

A collection in Solr is a combination of one or more indexes spanning one or more cores of Apache Solr. A Solr core or core in Apache Solr is a running instance of the Solr index, along with its configuration.

After understanding `solr.xml`, the loader looks for the directory defined by `solr.solr.home` as a system variable; it gets access to the configuration for further processing. Let's look at the directory structure for Apache Solr.

The Solr home directory structure

The Apache Solr home directory mainly contains the configuration and index-related data. The following are the major directories in a Solr collection:

Directory	Purpose
`conf/`	This directory contains all the configuration files of Apache Solr, and it's mandatory. Among them, `solrconfig.xml` and `schema.xml` are important configuration files.
`data/`	This directory stores the data related to indexes generated by Solr. This is a default location for Solr to store this information. This location can be overridden by modifying `conf/solrconfig.xml`.
`lib/`	This directory is optional. If it exists, Solr will load any Jars found in this directory and use them to resolve any plugins, if they are provided in `solrconfig.xml` (Analyzers, RequestHandlers, and so on) Alternatively, you can use the `<lib>` syntax in `conf/solrconfig.xml` to direct Solr to your plugins.

Solr navigation

By default, there are some of the important URLs configured with Apache Solr that are shown in the following screenshot:

URL	Purpose
`/select`	For processing search queries, the primary RequestHandler provided with Solr is SearchHandler. It delegates to a sequence of SearchComponents.
`/query`	This SearchHandler is similar to the one we use for JSON-based requests.
`/get`	This is the real-time get handler, which guarantees to return the latest stored fields of any document, without the need to commit or open a new searcher. Its current implementation relies on the updateLog feature being enabled in the JSON format.

URL	Purpose
/browse	This URL provides faceted web-based search and primary interface.
/update/ extract	Solr accepts posted XML messages that Add/Replace, Commit, Delete, and Delete by query using the url /update (ExtractingRequestHandler).
/update/csv	This URL is specific for CSV messages and CSVRequestHandler.
/update/json	This URL is specific for messages in the JSON format, JsonUpdateRequestHandler.
/analysis/ field	This URL provides an interface for analyzing fields. It provides the ability to specify multiple field types and field names in the same request and outputs index-time and query-time analysis for each of them. Uses FieldAnalysisRequestHandler internally.
/analysis/ document	This URL provides an interface for analyzing the documents.
/admin	AdminHandler is used for providing administration to Solr. AdminHandler has multiple subhandlers defined. For example, /admin/ping is for health checkup.
/debug/dump	DumpRequestHandler echoes the request content back to the client.
/replication	This URL supports replicating indexes across different Solr servers used by masters and slaves for data sharing. It uses ReplicationHandler.

Configuring the Apache Solr for enterprise

Apache Solr allows extensive configuration to meet the needs of the consumer. Configuring the instance revolves around the following:

- Defining a Solr schema
- Configuring Solr parameters

Let's look at all these steps to understand the configuration of Apache Solr.

Defining a Solr schema

In an enterprise, the data is generated from all the software systems that are participating in the day-to day-operation. This data has different formats, and bringing in this data for Big Data processing requires a storage system that is flexible enough to accommodate data with varying data models. Traditional relational databases allow users to define a strict data structure and SQL-based querying mechanism.

Rather than confining users to define the data structures, NOSQL databases allow an open database with which they can store any kind of data and retrieve it by running queries that are not based on the SQL syntax. By its design, the NOSQL database is best suited for this storage. One of the primary objectives of NOSQL is horizontal scaling, that is, P in the **CAP** theorem at the cost of sacrificing consistency or availability.

The CAP theorem or Brewer's theorem talks about distributed consistency. It states that it is impossible to achieve all of the following in a distributed system:

- **Consistency**: Every client sees the most recently updated data state
- **Availability**: The distributed system functions as expected, even if there are node failures
- **Partition tolerance**: Intermediate network failure among nodes does not impact system functioning

 Roughly, Solr ensures CP in the CAP theorem, and to some extent, it also ensures high availability through no single point of failure as per the new SolrCloud design (refer to `http://wiki.apache.org/solr/NewSolrCloudDesign`) We will look at how it's done in the following chapters.

By design, Solr supports any data to be loaded in a search engine through different handlers, making it agnostic to data format. Solr can be scaled easily on top of commodity hardware; hence, it becomes one of the most efficient eligible NOSQL-based searches available today. The data can be stored in Solr indexes and can be queried through Lucene's search APIs. Solr does perform joins because of its denormalization of data. Overall, the schema file (`schema.xml`) is structured in the following manner:

```
<schema>
  <types>
  <fields>
  <uniqueKey>
  <defaultSearchField>
  <solrQueryParser defaultOperator>
  <copyField>
</schema>
```

Solr fields

Apache Solr's basic unit of information is a document, which is a set of data that describes something. Each document in Solr composes fields for the Solr schema. Apache Solr lets you define the structure of your data to extend support to search across the traditional keywords searching. You can allow Solr to understand the structure of your data (coming from various sources) by defining the fields in the schema definition file. Once defined, these fields will be made available at the time of data import or data upload. The schema is stored in the `schema.xml` file in the `conf/` folder of Apache Solr. Apache Solr ships with a default `schema.xml`, which you have to change to fit your needs.

 If you change `schema.xml` in a Solr instance running on some data, the impact of this change requires a regeneration of Solr index again with the new schema.

In schema configuration, you can define field types, (for example, string, integer, and date) and map them to the respective Java classes.

```
<field name="id" type="integer" indexed="true" stored="true"
required="true"/>
```

This enables users to define the custom type if they wish to. Then, you can define the fields with names and types pointing to one of the defined types. A field in Solr will have the following major attributes:

Name	Description
Default	This sets the default value if it is not read while importing a document.
Indexed	This is true, when it has to be indexed (i.e. can be searched, sorted, facet creation).
Stored	When this is true, a field is stored in the index store, and it will be accessible while displaying results.
compressed	When true, the field will be zipped (using gzip); it is applicable for text-based fields.
multiValued	This is a field that contains multiple values in the same import cycle of the document/row.
omitNorms	When true, it omits the norms associated with fields such as length normalization and index boosting. Similarly, it has omitTermFreqAndPositions (If this is true, it omits term frequency, positions, and payloads from postings for this field. This can be a performance boost for fields that don't require this information. It also reduces the storage space required for the index) and omitPositions.
termVectors	When this is true, it also persists metadata related to the document and returns this when queried.

With Solr 4.2, the team has introduced a new feature called DocValue for fields. DocValues are a way of building the index that is more efficient for some purposes. While Apache Solr relies on inverted index mechanism, the DocValue storage focuses on efficiently indexing the document to index storage mechanism. This approach results in a reduction in memory usage and the overall search speed. DocValue can be enabled on specific fields in Solr in the following fashion:

```
<field name="test_outcome" type="string" indexed="false" stored="false" docValues="true" />
```

If the data is indexed before applying DocValue, it has to be reindexed to utilize the gains of DocValue indexing.

Dynamic Fields in Solr

In addition to static fields, you can also use Solr dynamic fields to get the flexibility in case you do not know the schema affront. Use the `<dynamicField>` declaration to create a field rule. Solr understands which datatype to be used. In the following sample, any field imported and identified as `*_no` (for example, id_no and vehicle_no) will in turn be read as an integer by Solr. In this case, `*` represents wildcard. The following snippet shows how you can create a dynamic field:

```
<dynamicField name="*_no" type="integer" indexed="true" stored="true"/>
```

 Although it is not a mandatory condition, it is recommended for each Solr instance to have a unique identifier field for the data. Similarly, ID name-specified uniqueKey cannot be multivalued.

Copying the fields

You can also index the same data into multiple fields using the `<copyField>` directive. This is typically needed when you want to have multi-indexing for the same data type. For example, if you have data for the refrigerators of a company, followed by the model number (WHIRLPOOL-1000LTR, SAMSUNG-980LTR), you can have these indexed separately by applying your own tokenizers to different fields. You might generate indexes for two different fields: Company Name and Model Number. You can define tokenizers specific to your field types. Here is the sample copyField from schema.xml:

```
<copyField source="cat" dest="text"/>
<copyField source="name" dest="text"/>
<copyField source="manu" dest="text"/>
<copyField source="features" dest="text"/>
```

Field types

You can define your own field types in Apache Solr; they cater to your requirements for data processing. A field type includes four types of information:

- Name
- An implementation class name (implemented on `org.apache.solr.schema. FieldType`)
- If the field type is `TextField`, it will include a description of the field analysis for the field type
- Field attributes

The following XML snippet shows a sample field type:

```
<fieldType name="text_ws" class="solr.TextField"
positionIncrementGap="100">
  <analyzer>
  <tokenizer class="solr.WhitespaceTokenizerFactory"/>
  </analyzer>
</fieldType>
```

The `class` attribute indicates which Java class the given field type is associated with. `PositionIncrementGap` determines the spacing between two words. It's useful for multivalued fields where the space between multiple values of the fields is determined. For example, if the `author` field has John Doe and Jack Williams as values, when `PositionIncrementGap` is zero, a search for Doe Jack will match with these fields. This is because Solr treats this field as John Doe Jack Williams. To separate these multivalued fields, you can specify a high `PositionIncrementGap` value.

The name attribute indicates the name of the field type. Later, when a field is defined, it uses the type attribute to denote the field type associated, as shown in the following text:

```
<field name="name" type="text_ws" indexed="true" stored="true"/>
```

Other important elements in the Solr schema

The following table describes the different elements in schema.xml:

Name	Description	Example
UniqueKey	The uniqueKey element specifies which field is a unique identifier for documents. For example, uniqueKey should be used if you ever update a document in the index.	`<uniqueKey>id</uniqueKey>`
default SearchField	If you are using the Lucene query parser, queries that don't specify a field name will use the defaultSearchField. The use of default search is deprecated from Apache Solr 3.6 or higher versions.	`<defaultSearchField></defaultSearchField>`
similarity	similarity is a Lucene class responsible for scoring the matched results. Solr allows you to override the default similarity behavior through the `<similarity>` declaration. Similarity can be configured at the global level; however, with Solr 4.0, it extends similarity to be configured at the field level.	`<similarity class="solr.DFRSimilarityFactory">` `<str name="basicModel">P</str>` `<str name="afterEffect">L</str>` `<str name="normalization">H2</str>` `<float name="c">7</float>` `</similarity>`

Configuring Solr parameters

Once the schema is configured, the immediate next step is to configure the instance itself to work with your enterprise. The configuration can take place in the following manner:

- Understanding solrconfig.xml
- Understanding solr.xml and Solr cores
- Solr plugins

There are two major configurations that go in the Solr configuration: solrconfig.xml and solr.xml. Let's look at them one by one.

solr.xml and Solr core

The `solr.xml` configuration resides in the `$SOLR_HOME` directory, and it mainly focuses on maintaining configuration for logging, cloud setup, and solr core. The Apache Solr 4.x code line uses `solr.xml` to identify the cores defined by the users. In the newer versions of Solr 5.x (planned), the current `solr.xml` structure (which contains the `<core>` element) will not be supported, and there will be an alternative structure used by Solr.

solrconfig.xml

The `solrconfig.xml` configuration primarily provides you with an access to RequestHandlers, listeners, and request dispatchers. Let's look at the `solrconfig.xml` file and understand all the important declarations you'd be using frequently, from the following table:

Directive	Description
luceneMatchVersion	This tells you which version of Lucene/Solr this configuration file is set to. When upgrading your Solr instances, you need to modify this attribute.
Lib	If you create any plugins for Solr, you need to put a library reference here so that it gets picked up. The libraries are loaded in the same sequence as that of the configuration order. The paths are relative; you can also specify regular expressions, for example, `<lib dir="../../../contrib/velocity/lib" regex=".*\.jar" />`.
dataDir	By default Solr uses the `/data` directory to store indexes. However, this can be overridden by changing the directory for data using this directive.
indexConfig	This directive is of complexType, and it allows you to change the settings of part of the internal indexing configuration of Solr.
Filter	You can specify different filters to be run at the time of index creation.
writeLockTimeout	This directive denotes the maximum time to wait for `write Lock` for IndexWriter.
maxIndexingThreads	This denotes the maximum number of indexed threads that can run in `IndexWriter`. If more threads arrive, they have to wait. The default value is 8.
ramBufferSizeMB	This denotes the maximum RAM you need in buffer during index creation, before the files are flushed to the filesystem.
maxBufferedDocs	This limits the number of documents buffered.

Directive	Description
lockType	When indexes are generated and stored in the file, this mechanism decides which file-locking mechanism should be used to manage concurrent read-writes. There are three types: single (one process at a time), native (native operating system driven), and simple (based on locking using plain files).
unlockOnStartup	When this is true, it will release all the write locks held in the past.
Jmx	Solr can expose the statistics of runtime through MBeans. It can be enabled or disabled through this directive.
updateHandler	UpdateHandler is responsible for managing the updates to Solr. The entire configuration for updateHandler goes as a part of this directive.
updateLog	You can specify the directory and other configurations for transaction logs during index updates.
autoCommit	This enables automatic commit when updates are happening. This could be based on documents or time.
Listener	Using this directive, you can subscribe to update events when IndexWriters are updating the index. The listeners can be run either at the time of "postCommit" or "postOptimize".
Query	This directive is mainly responsible for controlling different parameters at the query time.
requestDispatcher	By setting parameters in this directive, you can control how a request will be processed by SolrDispatchFilter.
requestHandler	RequestHandlers are responsible for handling different types of requests with a specific logic for Apache Solr. These are described in a separate section.
searchComponent	SearchComponents in Solr enable additional logic that can be used by the search handler to provide a better searching experience. These are described in a separate section.
Update Request ProcessorChain	This defines how update requests are processed; you can define your own updateRequestProcessor to perform things such as cleaning up data, optimizing text fields, and so on.
queryResponse Writer	Each request for query is formatted and written back to the user through queryResponseWriter. You can extend your Solr instance to have responses for XML, JSON, PHP, Ruby, Python, CSV, and so on by enabling the respective predefined writers. If you have a custom requirement for a certain type of response, it can easily be extended.

Directive	Description
`queryParser`	The query parser directive tells Apache Solr which Query parser should be used for parsing the query and creating Lucene Query Objects. Apache Solr contains predefined query parsers such as Lucene (the default one), DisMax (based on the weights of fields), and eDismax (similar to DisMax, with some additional features).

The Solr plugin

Apache Solr provides easy extensions to its current architecture through Solr plugins. Using Solr plugins, you can load your own code to perform a variety of tasks within Solr from custom RequestHandlers to process your searches, custom analyzers, and token filters for the text field. Typically, the plugins can be developed in Solr using any IDE by importing `apache-solr*.jar` as the library. The following types of plugins can be created with Apache Solr:

Component	Description
SearchComponents	These plugins operate on a result set of a query. The results that they produce typically appear at the end of the search request.
RequestHandler	RequestHandlers are used to provide a REST endpoint from the Solr instance to get some work done.
Filters	Filters are the chain of agents which analyze the text for various filtering criteria such as lower case and stemming. Now, you can introduce your own filter and package it along with the plugin JAR file

Once the plugin is developed, it has to be defined as part of `solrconfig.xml` by pointing the library to your JAR.

Other configurations

RequestHandlers in Solr are responsible for handling requests. Each request handler can be associated with one relative URL, for example, `/search`, `/select`. A RequestHandler that provides a search capability is called a search handler. There are more than 25 RequestHandlers available with Solr by default, and you can see the complete list here:

```
http://lucene.apache.org/solr/api/org/apache/solr/request/
SolrRequestHandler.html
```

There are search handlers that provide searching capabilities on Solr-based indexes (for example, DisMaxRequestHandler and SearchHandler among others). Similarly, there are update handlers that provide support to upload documents to Solr (for example, DataImportHandler, CSVUpdateRequestHandler, and so on). RealTimeGetHandler provides the latest stored fields of any document. UpdateRequestHandlers are responsible for updating the index. Similarly, CSVRequestHandler and JsonUpdateRequestHandler take the responsibility of updating the indexes with CSV and JSON formats. ExtractingRequestHandler uses Apache Tika to extract the text out of different file formats. Additionally, there are other configuration files that appear in the configuration directory. We are listing them in the following table with the description of each configuration:

Filename	Description
protwords.txt	In this file, you can specify protected words that you do not wish to get stemmed. So, for example, a stemmer might stem the word "catfish" to "cat" or "fish".
currency.txt	This stores the exchange rates between different countries. This is helpful when you have your application accessed by people from different countries.
elevate.txt	With this file, you can influence the search results and make your own results among the top-ranked results. This overrides Lucene's standard ranking scheme, taking into account elevations from this file.
spellings.txt	In this file, you can provide spelling suggestions to the end user.
synonyms.txt	Using this file, you can specify your own synonyms, for example, cost : money and money : dollars.
stopwords.txt	Stopwords are those that will not be indexed and used by Solr in the applications. This is particularly helpful when you really wish to get rid of certain words. For example, in the string, "Jamie and joseph," the word "and" can be marked as a stopword.

Understanding SolrJ

Apache Solr is a web application; it can be used directly by its customers to search. The search interface can be modified and enhanced to work as an end user search tool to search in an enterprise. Solr clients can directly access Solr URL through HTTP to search and read data through various formats such as JSON and XML. Moreover, Apache Solr also allows administration through these HTTP-based services. Queries are executed by generating the URL that Solr will understand.

SolrJ is a tool that can be used by your Java-based application to connect to Apache Solr for indexing. SolrJ provides Java wrappers and adaptors to communicate with Solr and translate its results to Java objects. Using SolrJ is much more convenient than using raw HTTP and JSON. Internally, SolrJ uses Apache HttpClient to send HTTP requests. It provides a user-friendly interface, hiding connection details from the consumer application. Using SolrJ, you can index your documents and perform your queries.

There are two major ways to do this. One way is by using the `EmbeddedSolrServer` interface. If you are using Solr in an embedded application, this is the recommended interface suited to you. It does not use an HTTP-based connection. Here is the sample code:

```
System.setProperty("solr.solr.home", "/home/hrishi/work/scaling-solr/
example/solr");
CoreContainer.Initializer initializer = new CoreContainer.
Initializer();
CoreContainer coreContainer = initializer.initialize();
EmbeddedSolrServer server = new EmbeddedSolrServer(coreContainer, "");
ModifiableSolrParams params = new ModifiableSolrParams();
params.set("q", "Scaling");
QueryResponse response = server.query(params);
System.out.println("response = " + response);
```

The other way is to use the `HTTPSolrServer` interface, which talks with Solr server through the HTTP protocol. This is suited if you have a remote client-server based application. It uses the Apache Commons HTTP client to connect to Solr. Here is the sample code for the same:

```
String url = "http://localhost:8983/solr";
SolrServer server = new HttpSolrServer( url );
ModifiableSolrParams params = new ModifiableSolrParams();
params.set("q", "Scaling");
QueryResponse response = server.query(params);
System.out.println("response = " + response);
```

You can use ConcurrentUpdateSolrServer for bulk uploads, whereas CloudSolrServer communicates with Solr running in a cloud setup. SolrJ is available in the official Maven repository. You can simply add the following dependency to your `pom.xml` file to use SolrJ:

```
<dependency>
        <artifactId>solr-solrj</artifactId>
        <groupId>org.apache.solr</groupId>
        <version>1.4.0</version>
        <type>jar</type>
        <scope>compile</scope>
</dependency>
```

To use the EmbeddedSolrServer, you need to add the `solr-core` dependency too:

```
<dependency>
        <artifactId>solr-core</artifactId>
        <groupId>org.apache.solr</groupId>
        <version>1.4.0</version>
        <type>jar</type>
        <scope>compile</scope>
</dependency>
```

Apache Solr also provides access to its services for different technologies such as JavaScript, Python, and Ruby. The following table describes different interactions with various technologies and Apache Solr:

Technology	Interaction with Solr
JavaScript	Apache Solr can work with JavaScript in the client-server model through XMLHTTP / standard web interface; you can use libraries such as ajax-Solr and SolrJS for interaction.
Ruby	For Ruby, there is a project called sunspot (`http://sunspot.github.io/`) that enables Solr-powered search for Ruby Objects. You can also use DelRuby through APIs and SolrRuby libraries.
PHP	PHP can talk with Solr in many ways. You will find more details on this in *Chapter 7, Scaling Solr through Sharding, Fault Tolerance, and Integration*.
Java	Java can directly talk with Solr through SolrJ APIs, or through standard HTTP calls, as Solr supports HTTP interface.
Python	Python can utilize the Solr-Python client API library to contact Solr for searching.
Perl	CPAN provides Solr libraries (`http://search.cpan.org/~garafola/Solr-0.03/`) to utilize the Solr search. However, you can also use HTTP-based lightweight client to talk with Solr
.NET	There are many implementations available to consume Solr in .Net-based applications such as SolrNET (`https://github.com/mausch/SolrNet`) and Solr Contrib on CodePlex (`http://solrcontrib.codeplex.com/`).

Summary

In this chapter, we have set up the Apache Solr instance and tried to configure it for the J2EE container. We went through various ways to configure the Apache Solr instance in depth, finally ending and consuming the capabilities of Solr. In the next section, we will see how to work with various applications and their dataset and analyze their data using the capabilities of Apache.

3
Analyzing Data with Apache Solr

Many organizations suffer when dealing with huge amounts of data generated in different formats, due to incremental IT enablement of their business processes. Dealing with vast varieties of data becomes a challenge for any enterprise search engine. This data may reside in a database, or would be streamed over HTTP protocol. To address these problems, many companies provided tools to bring in data from various sources into one form. These were **Extract Transfer Load** (ETL) tools mainly used for **business intelligence** (BI) and analytics solutions. Luckily, Apache Solr provides different ways of dealing with different data types, when it comes down to information collection. We have already read about indexing in *Chapter 1, Understanding Apache Solr*. In this chapter, we are going to look at analyzing different types of data and how to deal with them. We will focus on the following topics:

- Configuring handlers
- Apache Tika integration
- Importing data from the database
- Dealing with streaming data
- Customized indexing
- Advanced Text Analytics with Solr

While going through these topics, we will also look at adding content to Solr for indexing, modifying, or deleting it.

Understanding enterprise data

Many enterprise search applications consolidate data from various data sources. Each separate system may also use a different method of data organization and/or format. To use Apache Solr effectively in these systems, all the important data that is to be searched must be fed to the Solr engine, and it goes through a complete process chain (which is explained in brief in *Chapter 1, Understanding Apache Solr*). Interestingly, since this data is fed only to generate indexing, we do not really have to worry about the formatting, and other presentation aspects of this data. However, if the expectation from enterprise search engines is also to provide an excellent browsing experience, each data element should carry structure information. This information is extracted by Apache Solr and is used to provide further dimensional navigation for a better user experience, that is, facets.

> Each unit of data objects is called a document in Solr. Each document contains multiple fields; each field carries its name and content. This content can be empty; however, each document must have a unique ID (just like the primary key in relational databases). The field names are defined in Apache Solr's `schema.xml` file in the `conf` directory.

Most data warehousing projects consolidate data from different source systems. Common data source formats are relational databases and flat files, but may include non-relational database structures. Enterprise search deals with the different types of data explained in the next section.

Categorizing by characteristics

Each document that enterprise search might deal with, has one important aspect—its characteristics. Each data/document carries one of the characteristics listed in the following table:

Name	Description	Example
Structured data	A structured data carries a certain structure or schema or definition of its representation. This kind of well-formed data provides a lot of information to Solr, and it can be easily indexed in Solr.	Relational databases (tables, columns, and relations), XML data with a predefined XSD (schema), and APIs from various enterprise applications, which provide information in a well-formed manner.

Name	Description	Example
Semi-structured data	This data is not completely structured, but you can definitely extract the required information from it. It requires extraction of certain properties and their values. This requires additional work on Apache Solr.	E-mails (with subject and message), XML (without schema), Word documents, and PDFs.
Unstructured data	This data carries no definite structures and it becomes challenging for Apache Solr to extract the necessary information.	Audio files, video files, CLOBs and BLOBs in databases, and so on.

Many times, unstructured data and semi-structured data are combined together while referring them.

Categorizing by access pattern

Another aspect while looking at data access is how the data is getting generated; this means frequency of data generation and its availability to Apache Solr, as shown in the following table.

Name	Description	Example
Streaming data / sequential access	This data deals with real-time information, and this information should be made available in real-time / near real-time to Solr search. This data is mainly associated with time. This is mainly sequential access.	Sensor data, live transmission of video/audio, stock quotes, and server logs.
Random access / direct access	This data is mainly stored in certain storage and allows random access.	Databases, flat files, and csv.

Categorizing by data formats

In enterprise, data formats can differ from application to application. Many times, the data resides in databases and can be queried using SQL, sometimes, data is transmitted using wires over HTTP in JSON and XML format. The documents can be in PDF/Word/Excel format. Apache Solr has to deal with data in different formats including custom formats. Solr has built-in tools that understand many standard formats, but when it comes down to custom format, it does not provide any tools for extracting information from these formats in a structured manner.

Since Solr uses this data to create one time indexes, the good news is that we do not really have to bother about how to feed in a table from a word document to Apache Solr. It's more focused on how one can extract attributes out of them as per `schema.xml`. Interestingly, sometimes this information might even be coming from a different application all together, and that information has to be fed together along with a document. This information has to make logical sense. Let's look at the upcoming example to understand this.

ABC Company has a content management system, which has different types of documents; each document is associated with user IDs (ABC-12345). The content management system does not maintain the usernames. However, one can find usernames from the Corporate LDAP. The tricky part is that when these documents are fed to enterprise search, association with user ID is not going to help anyone here, because employees will never search on user IDs, they instead require a name, maybe a role, and a department to understand which document belongs to which department. This means, for each document, Apache Solr must be fed with the author name, and a department. So, it requires additional metadata from LDAP to be fed to Apache Solr while uploading documents for indexing. Such requirements drive a need for custom adapters/agents, which can integrate information from various sources to create sensible indexes.

Loading data using native handlers

Apache Solr supports add, delete, and update operations on its index store. It ships with inbuilt native handers to work with JSON, XML, and CSV format. These handlers can be called over HTTP by posting a message to them in one of these formats through an update call. Apache Solr also provides an inbuilt posting tool (client application), that can be used to upload data to an Apache Solr server.

Quick and simple data loading – post tool

Apache Solr provides a command-line tool by default for posting your XML information directly to the Apache Solr server. Using this tool, one can upload a document file/folder or it can also be provided through a standard input (STDIN), that is, typed using your keyboard. `$SOLR_HOME/example/exampledocs/post.jar` provides this data upload capability. There are some example files that you can use to upload to Solr Server. You can run it using the following command:

```
$ java <arguments> -jar post.jar <filenames/raw data/URL>
```

Let's look at the following table that lists some of the important arguments used in this tool:

Name	Description	Examples
`-Ddata=<name>`	`<name>` can be web, stdin, files, or args; the default is files. Args mainly provides instructions, such as delete a document; web is a simple crawler that crawls through a URL; stdin is where you can provide your data through the command line itself; and files is where you can point to your files to load. You may also use a regular expression (`*.xml`).	• `java -jar post.jar *.xml` • `Java -Ddata=web -jar post.jar http://www.packtpub.com` • `java -Ddata=args -jar post.jar '<delete><id>42</id></delete>'`
`-Dtype=<mime-type>` and `-Dauto=<yes/no>`	The content type and auto go together. When auto is true, the tool determines the file type from its extension; similarly, when auto is no and the user specifies a content type, the tool will assume the file in that content type.	• `java -Dtype=text/csv -jar post.jar *.csv` • `java -Dauto=yes -jar post.jar test.pdf`

Similarly, there are `recurse=<yes/no>` to enable recursive import of files in local folders and subfolders, `filetype=<pdf/xml/json....>` to define the types of files. You can also perform batch commit by passing `-Dcommit=no`, and finally committing at once for an atomic operation.

Working with JSON, XML, and CSV

Apache Solr provides an inbuilt handler called `UpdateRequestHandler` to work with JSON, XML, and CSV data. In `solrconfig.xml`, this information goes under the `<requestHandler>` XML tag as shown in the following screenshot:

```
<requestHandler name="/update" class="solr.UpdateRequestHandler">

</requestHandler>


<requestHandler name="/update/json" class="solr.JsonUpdateRequestHandler">
    <lst name="defaults">
      <str name="stream.contentType">application/json</str>
    </lst>
</requestHandler>
<requestHandler name="/update/csv" class="solr.CSVRequestHandler">
    <lst name="defaults">
      <str name="stream.contentType">application/csv</str>
    </lst>
</requestHandler>
```

It requires a data to pass its content type. All the handlers allow users to add new data, update the existing data index in Solr, or to delete it. While updating and deleting, indexes are matched with a certain unique ID, or query pattern. This is one of the reasons why each record uploaded in Apache Solr must have one unique identifier. Each of the handlers has the configuration and parameters associated with it, you may refer to the Apache Solr reference guide (`https://cwiki.apache.org/confluence/display/solr/Apache+Solr+Reference+Guide`) to look at the configuration aspects in depth.

> In earlier versions of Solr 3.x and so on, there were separate handlers for CSV and JSON data, that is, `JsonUpdateRequestHandler` for JSON requests, `CSVRequestHandler` for CSV request. These are not required in newer Solr releases, but they exist for backward compatibility, as shown in the preceding screenshot. There is a fixed content type parameter associated with the request handler that is passed to Solr at the time of loading the configuration. Hence, these handlers do not require any content type to be passed unlike `UpdateRequestHandler`.

For JSON and XML request handlers, there is a newly introduced feature called atomic updates. This feature allows you to update on a field level rather than on a document level (in the previous versions). This feature allows users to just send the delta (differences) to Apache Solr instead of sending the complete document.

If the document schema defines a unique key, then the `/update` operation to add a document will by default overwrite (replace) any document in the index with the same unique key. If no unique key has been defined, no replacement will take place. Unless the field is marked with `required=false`, the field will be required to be present in the Solr document. Whenever a handler is called through CURL to add a new data element, Apache Solr returns a response that looks like the following screenshot:

```
C:\>curl "http://localhost:8983/solr/update/csv?stream.file=exampledocs\books.cs
v&stream.contentType=text/csv;charset=utf-8&commit=true"
<?xml version="1.0" encoding="UTF-8"?>
<response>
<lst name="responseHeader"><int name="status">0</int><int name="QTime">301</int>
</lst>
</response>

C:\>_
```

When a document is uploaded in Apache Solr, a commit operation has to take place to finalize the changes. A commit operation makes index changes visible to new search requests.

A hard commit also runs synchronization on the index files to ensure they have been flushed to stable storage and no data loss will result from a power failure. A soft commit is much faster since it only makes index changes visible and does not synchronize index files or write a new index descriptor. If the JVM crashes or there is a loss of power, changes that occurred after the last hard commit will be lost unless you have update logs enabled. When Apache Solr is shut down with command instead of crashing, it fires a hard commit on the documents to ensure that there is no data loss. Search collections that have near-real-time requirements (that want index changes to be quickly visible to searches), will want to soft commit often but hard commit less frequently.

Many handlers support boosting of fields. To increase the scores for certain documents that match a query, regardless of what that query may be, one can use field-based boosting.

Handling JSON data

JavaScript Object Notation (JSON) is one of the most popular lightweight data interchange formats. JSON is built on the following two structures:

- A collection of name/value pairs
- An ordered list of values, for example, array, vector, list, or sequence

JSON offers a smallest footprint of the message to be transmitted across the system; hence, many applications prefer a JSON-based message-passing mechanism for collaboration. The JSON content type is either marked with `application/json` or `text/json`. Let's try this with an example as follows:

1. Use `people.json` from the dataset available in the book, as the initial dataset to load in your Apache Solr system. First, copy the file in the `exampledocs` directory under `$SOLR_HOME/ example`.

2. We need to enhance the existing Solr schema to support additional attributes such as `people.json`, so add the following changes in the `schema.xml` file under the `<schema>` tag:

   ```
   <field name="gender" type="text_general" indexed="true"
   stored="true"/>
   <field name="company" type="text_general" indexed="true"
   stored="true"/>
   ```

   You will not require the name and ID field to be defined in `schema.xml`, as it's seeded.

3. Now, run the following command, this will load the data into Solr. The Solr console will show uploaded information in the log files as follows:

```
curl 'http://localhost:8983/solr/update/json?commit=true' --data-binary @people.json -H 'Content-type:application/json'
```

4. Access `http://localhost:8983/solr/browse`, and you can search for relevant information. Similarly, you can call `http://localhost:8983/solr/get?id=1` if one does not wish to edit the schema, as shown in the next screenshot:

```
localhost:8983/solr/get?id=1

{
  "doc":
  {
    "id":"1",
    "name":"Frieda Lamb",
    "gender":"female",
    "company":"Globoil",
    "_version_":14571353135235727736}}
```

In this manner, Solr includes the essential benefits of schemaless configuration as explained in *Chapter 2, Getting Started with Apache Solr.*

Working with CSV data

Similar to the JSON format, CSV files can be uploaded to the Apache Solr instance directly through `UpdateRequestHandler` using the standard HTTP post. For each CSV file, the first row maps to Solr schema attributes defined in `schema.xml` in configuration directories. This CSV data can be uploaded by running a `curl` command:

```
curl http://localhost:8983/solr/update/csv --data-binary @<csv file>
-H 'content-type:text/plain; charset=utf-8'
```

When the file is available locally, one can avoid going through the longer HTTP route, and instead this file can be uploaded directly to the Solr server by enabling remote streaming. Using remote streaming, a user can provide a direct path to the file location, and the same can be uploaded without going through the HTTP route. To enable remote streaming, one has to set `enableRemoteStreaming` to `true` in the `solrconfig.xml` file:

```
<requestParsers enableRemoteStreaming="true"
                multipartUploadLimitInKB="2048000"
                formdataUploadLimitInKB="2048"
                addHttpRequestToContext="false"/>
```

The `enableRemoteStreaming=true` parameter enables remote streaming. The `multipartUploadLimitInKB` attribute sets an upper limit in kilobytes on the size of a document that may be submitted in a multipart HTTP POST request and the `addHttpRequestToContext` attribute adds the `HttpServletRequest` object to `SolrQueryRequest`. Since it is not used by any of the Solr components, it can be set to `false`. Once remote streaming is enabled, you can directly pass your CSV file to Solr. You may use `book.csv` provided for CSV uploading, as shown in the following snippet:

```
curl "http://localhost:8983/solr/update/csv?stream.file=exampledocs\
books.csv&stream.contentType=text/csv;charset=utf-8&commit=true
```

Working with XML data

XML data is the most widely used data across organizations. It carries various formats. Apache Solr supports the upload of XML data, but in a certain format. This is one of the biggest drawbacks of this handler, which means every XML message/document you wish to push to Apache Solr needs to be transformed. There are many transformation tools available to transform one type of XML into another. One of the most common ways to do it is to simply apply XSLT Transformation.

To add a new document(s), the XML schema recognized by the update handler for adding documents is very straightforward as follows:

- The `<add>` element introduces one or more documents to be added
- The `<doc>` element introduces the fields making up a document
- The `<field>` element presents the content for a specific field

An example of a sample document can be seen in the following snippet:

```
<add>
  <doc>
    <field name="Id">05991</field>
    <field name="name">Harry Potter</field>
    <field name="author">J. K. Rowling</field>
  </doc>
  [<doc> ... </doc>[<doc> ... </doc>]]
</add>
```

To understand how XML data can be transformed and uploaded, let's assume that we have received a book's information from a store in a certain format (please refer to `books.xml` from the book samples). This XML message can simply be transformed using associated XSLT (`visualize.xsl`). By opening `books.xml` in the web browser, the transformation takes place and you see the Solr understandable `books.xml` file.

Similar to add, the delete operation can also be performed with the `<delete>` tag. A single delete message can contain multiple delete operations:

```
<delete>
  <id>1123</id>
  <id>1124</id>
  <query>title:Harry Potter</query>
</delete>
```

Working with rich documents

We have seen how Apache Solr has inbuilt handlers for CSV, JSON, and XML formats in the last section. In any content management system of an organization, a data item may be residing in documents which are in different formats, such as PDF, DOC, PPT, XLS. The biggest challenge with these types is, they are all semi-structured forms. Interestingly, Apache Solr handles many of these formats directly, and it is capable of extracting the information from these types of data sources, thanks to Apache Tika! Apache Solr uses code from the Apache Tika project to provide a framework for incorporating many different file-format parsers such as Apache PDFBox and Apache POI into Solr itself.

 The framework to extract content from different data sources in Apache Solr is also called Solr CEL, solr-cell or more commonly Solr Cell.

Understanding Apache Tika

Apache Tika is a SAX-based parser for extracting the metadata from different types of documents. Apache Tika uses the `org.apache.tika.parser.Parser` interface for extracting metadata and structured text content from various documents using the existing parser libraries. Apache Tika provides a single parse method with the following signature.

```
void parse(InputStream stream, ContentHandler handler, Metadata
metadata)
     throws IOException, SAXException, TikaException;
```

This method takes the stream of the document as input and generates the XHTML SAX event as the outcome. This way, the Tika provides a simple, yet powerful interface to deal with different types of documents. Apache Tika supports the following types of document format:

- Rich Text format (RTF)

- HTML, XHTML
- All types of XML formats
- Microsoft office formats (Excel, Word, PowerPoint, Visio, Outlook)
- Open Office Formats
- Portable Document Format (PDFs)
- Electronic Publication Format (ePub)
- All types of text files
- Different types of compression formats (zip, gzip, bzip, bzip2, tarball, and so on)
- Audio formats (mp3, MIDI, wave formats). The lyrics, title, subject can be extracted from these formats
- Images: Support for only the metadata extraction is provided by Tika; it does not support optical character recognition on scanned documents
- Source Code: Different source code such as Java, Jar, JSPs are supported

Apache Tika will automatically attempt to determine the input document type (Word, pdf) and extract the content appropriately. Alternatively, you can specify MIME type for Tika with `stream.type` parameter. Apache Tika generates XHTML stream, through SAX parser. Apache Solr then reacts to SAX events by creating fields for indexing. Tika produces metadata information such as Title, Subject, and Author for the documents parsed.

Using Solr Cell (ExtractingRequestHandler)

Apache Solr supports Apache Tika for rich documents through Solr plugin. Apache Solr's `ExtractingRequestHandler` uses Tika to allow users to upload binary files to Solr and have Solr extract text from it and then index it optionally.

 Solr allows you to load custom code to perform a variety of tasks within Solr—from custom Request Handlers to process your searches, to custom Analyzers and Token Filters for your text field, even custom Field Types. These are called SolrPlugin.

Let's run a small example to load your HTML page using Tika to Apache Solr. Although we use curl throughout this book for testing, the real production instance has to rely on more robust mechanisms such as SolrJ, custom application, and adapter.

```
curl "http://localhost:8983/solr/update/extract?literal.
id=doc1&commit=true" -F "myfile=@<your page>.html"
```

The `literal.id=doc1` parameter provides the necessary unique ID for the document being indexed. The `commit=true` parameter causes Solr to perform a commit after indexing the document, making it immediately searchable. For optimum performance when loading many documents, don't call the commit command until you are done. This is because a hard commit causes time consuming disk IO. The `-F` flag instructs curl to POST data using `Content-Type multipart/form-data` and supports the uploading of binary files. The `@` symbol instructs curl to upload the attached file. The `myfile=@page1.html` argument needs a valid path, which can be the absolute or relative location of `$SOLR_HOME`. You may look at Apache Solr reference guide for configuration details.

Now, you should be able to execute a query and find that document. You may notice that although you can search the text in the sample document, you may not be able to see that text when the document is retrieved. This is simply because the `content` field generated by Tika is mapped to the Solr field called `text`, which is indexed but not stored. This is done via the default map rule in the `/update/extract` handler in `solrconfig.xml` and can be easily changed or overridden. Similarly, mapping of Tika fields with Solr fields can be provided through `fmap`. For example, `fmap.content=mytext` will move the content generated by Apache Tika to be moved to the **mytext** field. In `solrconfig.xml`, `ExtractingRequestHandler` can be found as shown in the following snippet:

```
<requestHandler name="/update/extract"
                startup="lazy"
    class="solr.extraction.ExtractingRequestHandler" >
............... . .
</requestHandler>
```

Adding metadata to your rich documents

Since Apache Tika takes complete control over what gets parsed using its own parser, we are constrained to limiting ourselves to using Tika with its capabilities. This works well for pure text searches, but when it comes down to adding different dimensions to your search (faceted search), extracting the right fields is most challenging. Tika provides an automated extraction, which in turn limits us to extract fields based on the real-world requirements for enterprise search.

To deal with such cases, it may be required to build a wrapper on top of Tika to extract additional metadata for a given document for indexing. This can be done through SolrJ APIs.

Look at the following example (from sample code `CustomDocsManagerUploader.java`):

```
public void indexFile(String filePath, Map<String,String> metadata)
throws Exception {
        SolrServer solr = new CommonsHttpSolrServer(urlString);
        ContentStreamUpdateRequest up = new
ContentStreamUpdateRequest("/update/extract");
        for (String key : metadata.keySet()) {
            //set the literals
            up.setParam("literal." + key, metadata.get(key));
        }
        up.addFile(new File(filePath));
        up.setAction(AbstractUpdateRequest.ACTION.COMMIT, false,
false);
        solr.request(up);
    }
```

Each document must have a unique identifier. Any custom field that represents uploaded metadata should be passed as literal.`<field-name>`, to make it appear as the schema element. You can also use the simple post tool to post your rich document to Apache Solr through `ExtractingRequestHandler`. For example, refer to the following code:

```
java -Durl=http://localhost:8983/solr/update/extract -Dparams=literal.
id=myId1 -Dtype=text/html -jar post.jar home.html
```

Importing structured data from the database

Many applications in the enterprise world store their important data in relational databases. The databases become one of the important data sources for Apache Solr for searching. Apache Solr provides `DataImportHandler` to deal with this type of data source. With `DataImportHandler`, you can also load only the deltas instead of the complete data set again and again. Many times, this can be set as off-time scheduled job activity to minimize the impact of indexing on day-to-day work. In case of real-time updates, this activity has to be scheduled with a fixed frequency.

Traditionally, `DataImportHandler` supports pull mechanism, but in the newer release of Apache Solr, `DataImportHandler` supports push operation as well. Some of the interesting features of `DataImportHandler` are listed as follows:

- Imports data from RDBMS/XML/RSS/ATOM in Solr using configuration across multiple tables

- Data is denormalized, and it supports full as well as incremental import of data

- `DataImportHandler` is a separate library from Solr Core, and it is a plugin of Apache Solr

- Allows extension of existing APIs with customizations

- Better error handling and rollback

- Event listeners

- Data push to Apache Solr

- Works on JDBC-based data connections. This means virtually any database can be connected through `DataImportHandler`

Configuring the data source

One of the important steps before importing data from the database to Apache Solr is to configure the data source. A data source is pointed to the location where data resides. In this case, it could be a relational database such as Oracle, MySQL, SQL Server, and HTTP URL. The data source configuration is required to define the following:

- Where to fetch the data from (database connection, URL, and so on)

- How to fetch data from a data source (query or other information)

- What to read (tables, SQL, resultset, columns, and so on)

- Mapping it with Solr Schema (database attributes to field mapping)

A data source can be defined in `solrconfig.xml` or it can simply point to another file containing the configuration (in our case `data-config.xml`). Each data source configuration has the `<dataSource>` and `<document>` elements. `<dataSource>` focuses more on establishing contact to data through different protocols such as JNDI, JDBC, and HTTP. Each `<document>` has `<entity>`. Each entity represents one data set. An entity is processed to generate a set of documents, containing multiple fields, which (after optionally being transformed in various ways) are sent to Solr for indexing. For a RDBMS data source, an entity is a view or table, which would be processed by one or more SQL statements to generate a set of rows (documents) with one or more columns (fields). You can create a custom data source by writing a class that extends `org.apache.solr.handler.dataimport.DataSource`.

Apache Solr `DataImportHandler` supports the data source types, listed in the following table, that can be used along with `DataImportHandler`:

Type	Description
ContentStreamDataSource	This mainly focuses on POST data and is useful for HTTP-based stream data.
FieldReaderDataSource	This can be used where a database field contains XML, which you wish to process using the `XpathEntityProcessor`. You would set up a configuration with both JDBC and FieldReader data sources, and two entities. One entity will be placed under the other one to pass SQL output to XPath resolver.
FileDataSource	This can be used to fetch files from the disk.
JdbcDataSource	This is the default data source that works with JDBC.
URLDataSource	This supports HTTP, it can also be used with `file://` as of now.

Entity processors extract data, transform it, and add it to a Solr index. There are different types of entity processors that work with different types of data sources, starting with SQL Entity Processor, XPath-based entity processor, and Apache Tika-based entity processor, file list entity processor, line entity processor and plain text entity processor.

Transformers manipulate the fields in a document returned by an entity. A transformer can create new fields or modify the existing ones. You may refer to *Apache Solr reference guide* to understand various configuration parameters.

Importing data in Solr

Apache Solr supports two types of data imports possible with structured data sources through `DataImportHandler` which are discussed in the following sections.

Full import

The full import mechanism is useful where it is required to read the data source snapshots at any given point of time. The usage of this import varies from case to case. Full import can be used when the underlying data is not changing frequently, and the enterprise search demand is not for a near-real time search.

When the full-import command is executed, Apache Solr notes different timings in a `dataimport.properties` file under `$SOLR_HOME/conf`. From Apache Solr version 4.1 onwards, this file location can be changed by modifying `data-config.xml`:

```
<dataConfig>

...

<propertyWriter dateFormat="yyyy-MM-dd HH:mm:ss"
type="SimplePropertiesWriter" directory="data" filename="dataimport.
properties" locale="en_US"/>

...

</dataConfig>
```

The content of the `$SOLR_HOME/conf/dataimport.properties` file is as shown in the following snippet:

```
#Tue Jan 14 19:14:07 IST 2014
last_index_time=2014-01-14 19\:14\:06
department.last_index_time=2014-01-14 19\:08\:55
id.last_index_time=2014-01-14 19\:14\:06
```

These timestamps are used with the delta-import mechanism that we will take a look at in the next section. While performing full import of data, the Apache Solr search does not block itself. Based on the commit pattern, the new imported data starts appearing in the search results.

A full import operation can be started by hitting the URL `http://<host>:<port>/solr/dataimport?command=full-import`.

Delta import

This import is similar to full import, but it offers to reflect the change of state of your data source in Apache Solr. This import focuses on incremental updates and change detection. This operation will be started in a new thread and the status attribute in the response should be shown as busy now. Depending on the size of your data set, this operation may take some time.

When the delta-import command is executed, it reads the start time stored in `conf/dataimport.properties`. It uses that timestamp to run delta queries, and after completion, updates the timestamp in `conf/dataimport.properties`. The following example shows a sample delta-import data source configuration file:

```
<dataConfig>
    <dataSource ..../>
    <document>
        <entity name="EntityName" pk="ID"
                query="select * from department"
                deltaImportQuery="select * from department where ID='${dih.delta.id}'"
                deltaQuery="select id from department where last_modified &gt; '${dih.last_index_time}'">
            <entity name="department_code" pk="ID"
                    query="select department_code from department where item_id='${EntityName.ID}'">
            </entity>
            <entity name="department_name" pk="ID"
                    query="select department_name from department where item_id='${EntityName.ID}'">
            </entity>
        </entity>
    </document>
</dataConfig>
```

For delta import, a query is separately specified, and the entities are marked inside the entity. The query gives the data needed to populate fields of the Solr document in full-import. The `deltaImportQuery` gives the data needed to populate fields when running a delta import. The `deltaQuery` gives the primary keys of the current entity, which have changed since the last index time. This time is read from the `dataimport.properties` file under `conf`.

> One important point to note while working with delta import is that it does not offer any smart tracking over what is changed in the database from the last run; it is the responsibility of the application to maintain a flag/column (last-modified-on) for each table, and keep it updated as and when there is change. Databases such as Oracle support such columns with default values as SYSDATE to avoid inserting queries that pass additional column name and values.

Delta import operation can be started by hitting the URL `http://<host>:<port>/solr/dataimport?command=delta-import`.

Loading RDBMS tables in Solr

Let's go through the complete flow of how the overall configuration takes place while configuring `DataImportHandler`. The following steps describe how the overall import will take place:

1. Load data from the sample database provided (`deptdb: create_db.sql`). This sample is built upon MySQL database.

2. Since `DataImportHandler` is not part of Apache Solr core release, one has to add its request handler in `solrconfig.xml`:

```
<!-- my handler starts -->
<requestHandler name="/dataimport" class="org.apache.solr.handler.dataimport.DataImportHandler">
<lst name="defaults">
  <str name="config">data-config.xml</str>
</lst>
</requestHandler>
<!-- my handler ends -->
```

3. Create a `data-config.xml` file as follows (please change URL, user, and the password attributes appropriately) and save it to the `conf` directory:

```
<dataConfig>
   <dataSource type="JdbcDataSource"
               driver="com.mysql.jdbc.Driver"
               url="jdbc:mysql://localhost:3306/deptdb"
               user="<user>"
               password="<password>">
   </dataSource>
   <document name="departments">
     <entity name="id"
             query="select id,department_code,department_name from
department">
       <field column="id" name="id"/>
        <field column="department_code" name="department_code"/>
        <field column="department_name" name="department_name"/>
     </entity>
   </document>
</dataConfig>
```

4. Since `DataImportHandler` is not part of the Solr core, you need to package the following two jars in `solr.war` (WEB-INF/lib), or put them in the classpath of your container as follows:
   - `solr-dataimporthandler-extras-<version>.jar`
   - `solr-dataimporthandler-<version>.jar`

5. Similarly, you will also need to package your respective database JDBC driver JAR file in the classpath or `solr.war`.

6. Extend your schema file to incorporate additional attributes from your SQL queries as follows; attribute ID is seeded in `schema.xml`, so you do not need to add that:

```
<field name="department_name" type="text_general" indexed="true"
stored="true"/>
    <field name="department_code" type="text_general"
indexed="true" stored="true"/>
```

7. Access `http://localhost:8983/solr/dataimport?command=full-import` and you will see an XML message in the following manner, which signified a successful import:

```
localhost:8983/solr/dataimport?command=full-import

- <response>
  - <lst name="responseHeader">
      <int name="status">0</int>
      <int name="QTime">16</int>
  </lst>
  - <lst name="initArgs">
    - <lst name="defaults">
        <str name="config">data-config.xml</str>
    </lst>
  </lst>
  <str name="command">full-import</str>
  <str name="status">idle</str>
  <str name="importResponse"/>
  - <lst name="statusMessages">
      <str name="Total Requests made to DataSource">1</str>
      <str name="Total Rows Fetched">1</str>
      <str name="Total Documents Skipped">0</str>
      <str name="Full Dump Started">2014-01-14 19:14:04</str>
    - <str name="">
        Indexing completed. Added/Updated: 1 documents. Deleted 0 documents.
      </str>
      <str name="Committed">2014-01-14 19:14:05</str>
      <str name="Total Documents Processed">1</str>
      <str name="Time taken">0:0:0.531</str>
  </lst>
  - <str name="WARNING">
      This response format is experimental. It is likely to change in the future.
  </str>
</response>
```

It is recommended that users specify batchSize in the `data-config.xml` file when the data in tables is huge, this is required due to `DataImportHandler` picking rows one-by-one, and processing it.

Advanced topics with Solr

We have dealt with various data and their types. Most of the cases in enterprise search can be addressed by the different techniques we have gone through. In this section, we will go through some advanced topics for analyzing your data with Solr. We will also try to explore integration with NLP tools to make the incoming data more sensible and effective.

Deduplication

Deduplication in Apache Solr is all about avoiding duplicate documents from entering in the storage of Apache Solr. Apache Solr prevents these duplicates at the document as well as the field level. This is a new feature of Apache Solr 4.x release. The duplicates in the storage can be avoided by means of hashing techniques. Apache Solr supports native de-duplication techniques through the <Signature> class. As of now, Apache Solr 4.6 supports MD5 (MD5Signature), 64-bit hashing (Lookup3Signature) and fuzzy hashing (comes from Nutch, TextProfileSignature).

To enable deduplication, users need to modify solrconfig.xml with the following changes as a part of UpdateRequestProcessorChain:

```
<updateRequestProcessorChain name="dedupe">
  <processor class="solr.processor.SignatureUpdateProcessorFactory">
      <bool name="enabled">true</bool>
      <str name="signatureField">id</str>
      <bool name="overwriteDupes">false</bool>
      <str name="fields">category, author, name</str>
      <str name="signatureClass">solr.processor.Lookup3Signature</str>
  </processor>
</updateRequestProcessorChain>
```

Similarly, schema.xml can be modified with a new field for signature, and finally the requestHandler should allow all the /update queries to go through the deduplication layer. The code snippet will look like the following:

```
<requestHandler name="/update" >
  <lst name="defaults">
    <str name="update.chain">dedupe</str>
  </lst>
</requestHandler>
```

Extracting information from scanned documents

In a content management system, the documents are scanned and preserved in image or PDF format. Although the information is preserved, it is not usable as the information is not readable to human eyes. In such cases, enterprise search becomes useless, and Apache Solr does not provide any direct support to such images/scanned documents. To make the scanned documents readable, we primarily need Apache Solr integration with **Optical Character Recognition (OCR)** software. The overall architecture for this scenario looks like the following screenshot:

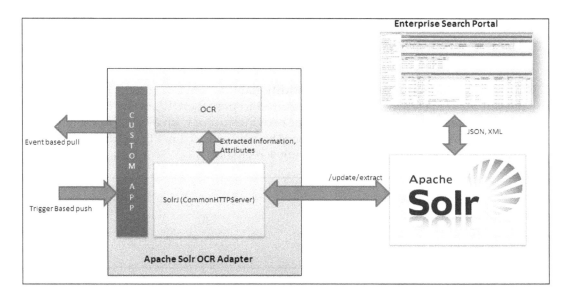

The overall integration with any OCR (in our case it is Tesseract OCR) can be modeled as a custom adapter developed to interact with Apache Solr. A sample code (`ImageInformationExtractor.java`) should be able to address some of the aspects of it. In the sample implementation, the integration is done at the command level, since Tesseract does not provide any API-level access.

Searching through images using LIRE

Apache Solr allows a search over images through **Lucene Image Retrieval** (**LIRE**) Library. (Visit http://demo-itec.uni-klu.ac.at/liredemo/) The LIRE library allows users to enable a search through images, based on the properties of images. The image histogram is used to calculate the relevancy of the image with the searched image.

Today, LIRE supports the following five histogram algorithms:

- Color histogram layout (cl_ha)
- Pyramid histogram of oriented gradients or PHOG (ph_ha)
- Opponent histogram (oh_ha)
- Edge histogram (eh_ha)
- Jc_ha

LIRE configuration requires creation of additional filters in solrconfig.xml (by default it is /lireq), and users are required to pass the URL of the image they would like to search. The output of a filter provides users with a list of documents when searched for an image (http://localhost:8983/solr/lireq?url=<image-absolute-url>), as shown in the following screenshot:

```
{
  "responseHeader":{
    "status":0,
    "QTime":41,
    "params":{
      "url":"http://localhost:8983/solr/imagedb/Photo-14.jpg"}},
  "RawDocsCount":"12",
  "RawDocsSearchTime":"6",
  "ReRankSearchTime":"1",
  "docs":[{
      "id":"perigreen_falcon1.jpg",
      "title":null,
      "d":0.0},
    {
      "id":"perigreen_perching.jpg",
      "title":null,
      "d":55.9769},
    {
      "id":"965.jpg",
      "title":null,
      "d":65.53736}]}
```

The following screenshot demonstrates how effectively, LIRE can possibly match the images using `cl_ha`:

Visit `https://bitbucket.org/dermotte/liresolr` to understand how it can be used to query as well as configure LIRE. There are three primary changes required in the configuration, which are as follows:

- Copying LIRE jars in the classpath of Solr
- Modifying `schema.xml` to incorporate new schema elements to store the weights of each histogram
- Modifying `solrconfig.xml` to introduce a new filter for LIRE

With this book, we have provided the sample configuration files with changes required for LIRE marked accordingly. Data loading can be done using `DataImportHandler`; please refer to `solr-data-config.xml`.

Summary

In this chapter, we have understood various ways of analyzing data while working with Apache Solr. We also looked at different data types that Apache Solr might encounter while working in the role of enterprise search, and how to deal with them. We have looked at some practical examples of how users can load data from different data sources.

Designing Enterprise Search

Finding the right information to make relevant decisions is an important aspect in running a successful and effective business. This is the place where good enterprise design comes into play. Enterprise search is used by different organizations to capitalize on their internal knowledge by providing quick access to all internal information.

Enterprise search not only helps users in discovering new information but also collaborates across organizational and geographical boundaries by creating the necessary conditions. Enterprises suffer from many problems due to poor design of enterprise search for their organizations. These include issues such as:

- Amount of information tweaking required to work with search engines
- Time wasted by employees due to ineffective search, resulting in lower productivity
- Cost of managing such ineffective search servers
- Unavailability of important information (lost value)
- Misleading and irrelevant information, resulting in losses by making wrong decisions

Not finding the right information or finding it too late, duplicated efforts, productivity impacts, and missed opportunities make a huge cost impact to an organization. Many times, this impact is further cascaded throughout the organization. The impact grows as the organization needs are on a real-time/up-to-date search. In this chapter, we will understand the aspects of designing a search solution for enterprise. We will look at the following topics:

- Designing aspects for enterprise search
- Referencing enterprise search architecture
- Designing workflows to process data
- Integrating data sources
- Case study – designing enterprise search for the IT industry

Designing aspects for enterprise search

Every business day, employees need to access information stored in various enterprise applications and databases. Employees want one entrance to all corporate information. They often perceive the company intranet as one fuzzy cloud of information, while in reality it is a set of highly isolated information silos. Enterprise search is meant to address this need by providing access to relevant information, consolidating all the results, and presenting it properly. How does one achieve this? The larger the organization, the more divergent is its information access needs. Implementing enterprise search in organizations must follow a well-established process to build a mature, usable application. The process of implementation of enterprise search requires the following aspects:

- Identifying and establishing the business requirement
- Identifying the right set of technologies
- Proof of Concept using the technologies
- Implementation of enterprise search solution
- Integrating search interfacing with the relevant client
- Testing and rollout
- Monitoring

Identifying requirements

Identification of requirements is one of the key aspects of the enterprise search implementation lifecycle. The first step in designing the enterprise search solution will be to identify the relevant stakeholders who will use this search, and have a discussion with them regarding the expectations. The intent will be to identify what information they are really looking for from the existing systems, and what benefit can they expect out of the solution once it's available for use.

To identify the requirements properly, one may have to find answers to the following questions:

- What information is the customer looking for as part of search implementation?
- What are the key benefits of implementing search engines in organizations?
- Which applications does a customer expect the search engine to find?
- How can data on these applications be accessed?
- Do applications support search using their APIs?
- What is the frequency of data generated by each application?
- What kind of delay can a customer live with in terms of indexing the data from various applications? Is it real-time/near real-time search that has to be performed?
- How and in what form is a customer expecting the search user interface to appear?
- Is the customer looking for multilingual support?
- What kind of security over search is expected by the customer?

Enterprise search provides a presentation/UI layer to all its end users; however, underlying systems design aspects that are equally important, and they impact the overall enterprise search usability and its value. We have gone through some of the aspects in the first chapter. We will look at the rest now. We will consider Apache Solr-based search as a reference model for these design discussions. The following image illustrates different design aspects you should consider before implementing an enterprise search solution:

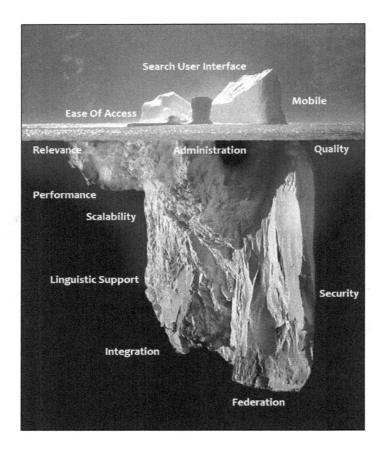

Matching user expectations through relevance

A relevance of results in enterprise search enables users to reach the information they are looking for in the quickest possible way. The results in any search engine are ordered by the relevancy score for the searched term. The topmost search elements carry the highest scores, and it's based on the relative scoring of elements.

Apache Solr uses the **TF-IDF**-based scoring model for the relevance scope of documents. TF stands for Term Frequency, and IDF stands for Inverse Document Frequency. Term frequency signifies the frequency of a searched term appearing in the document. Higher term frequency means the document is more relevant to the searched subject. Inverse document frequency represents the rareness of a searched term in the document repository. If the term is rare, the score of the term is higher. Together, the TF-IDF algorithm enables the search results to provide the order of the document that has maximum occurrences and avoids common words by inclusion of rareness.

Additionally, the Apache Solr scoring also involves coordination factor and field length. The coordination factor identifies the number of query terms present in the document, and based on that, the scoring is determined. The more the query terms in the document, the higher the scores. For example, if a user searches for "black dog", a document that will have both terms together will score relatively higher than the ones with "black" or "dog". Similarly, the length of the field also impacts the scoring of each document. A document that has fields with more words will carry a low score.

You can find more on Apache Solr scoring at the Javadoc of `org.apache.lucene.search.Similarity` class:

```
http://lucene.apache.org/core/3_5_0/api/core/org/apache/lucene/
search/Similarity.html
```

The problem arises when documents with a lot of common words get indexed, and the overall search is influenced by them. For example, one organization has a recruitment wing and they would like the search to work upon resumes. So, they load resumes in the Apache Solr search engine. Every time a user searches for `Java + JDBC`, many of the resumes start appearing right on top of the result. This becomes a problem for a user who is genuinely looking for Java projects in the organization. Apache Solr resolves such problems by boosting the search results.

Boosting is a process that allows Apache Solr administrators to modify the document scores, thereby enabling them to influence the result ordering. Score boosting can be done at indexing time or at query time. Boosting can either be positive boosting or negative boosting.

Index time boosting can be done by simply adding boost attributes to your document/fields. The following XML snippet shows how it can be achieved:

```
<add>
  <doc boost="2.4">
    <field name="doc_id">223</field>
    <field name="department" boost="2.0">Information Technology</
field>
    <field name="person_name">Hrishikesh Karambelkar</field>
  </doc>
</add>
```

The default value of boost is 1.0. In our example, the document (boost value is 2.4) is boosted by influencing the relevancy scores of the searched keyword. Similarly, the field department with boost value 2.0 influences the search results for field-related searches.

Access to searched entities and user interface

Another aspect while designing the search solution is providing ease of access to searched results. The enterprise landscape has a variety of applications that are to be indexed and searched. Typically, documents/contents are huge and the search solution cannot render a complete document in line. So, when a search matches with a number of documents, it renders a snippet of a matched search on the results screen/UI components.

Search engines are not designed to store user data and provide querying capabilities. They do not only provide internal repositories to store data residing at different application-specific storage systems but also involve unnecessary duplication of information.

It's more intuitive to provide a way for users to access the complete document or content through a detailed link. The following screenshot demonstrates a sample log-based search engine that points to a complete logfile:

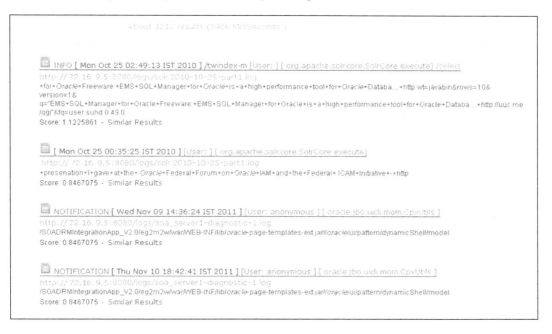

When the information resides in a different application, it has to be linked with search results and a user interface. The biggest problem lies with application privacy and security. These applications do not allow the external world to access information through web-based methodologies. Access to searched entities can be achieved using the following different ways:

- Direct access to resource (through standard protocol files such as HTTP/FTP/URL-based)
- Indirect access:
  - Through pluggable user interfaces (for example, portlets and web toolkits by different vendors)
  - API level information access (this requires the UI to be rebuilt)
  - Web services or other such service-based approach
  - Application-specific adapters

While preparing the design for enterprise search, different applications and their user interface access patterns have to be studied upfront. Depending upon the integration pattern, administrators might need to spend effort in getting access to other applications from Solr UI. This might involve getting into authorization similar to **Single-Sign-On** (**SSO**) or even building user interfaces that can be portable. Sometimes, Apache Solr is also referred to as the NOSQL database because it allows indexing for any kind of data. However, one point to note here is that the primary objective of Apache Solr is to provide enterprise search application capabilities and not to store the documents.

Improving search performance and ensuring instance scalability

The performance of enterprise search is of the utmost importance. The search engine should respond to user queries as soon as possible to keep users from abandonment. With every second's delay in response time, the percentage of user abandonment increases (reference: `http://blog.kissmetrics.com/loading-time/`). There are other factors that impact the page load on the end user's browser interface; these include network latency, Internet speed, page size and references, browser page load time, and so on, besides search response. So, a simplistic page design with the quickest page loading time enables users to save their time.

The optimization of enterprise search can be achieved at both the indexing and querying levels. To maintain the same performance of enterprise search with growing data, one should also review the density of the content that is getting generated along with the current capabilities of search. Search performance can be measured in different ways: it can be the time taken for search results to appear when queried, or it can be the time to index and the indexing frequency. The performance of the search is impacted due to one of the following reasons:

- Growing rate of data inflow to search application
- Increased refresh rates for indexing
- Demands for real-time/near real-time search
- Increased number of queries run per unit time
- Slow response of the underlying application that provides Enterprise Search data
- High runtime response time of federated search
- Type of queries/complexity of query (such as wildcard search)

Given the factors impacting the performance of the search, architects can look for reducing data loading before the indexing phase by removing unnecessary information and reduction in index creation with techniques such as stemming and synonyms. As demand grows, the landscape can be transformed into clusters of search.

Every organization data grows day-by-day. Enterprise search solution should provide a scalable search engine that can grow along with the data. We will look at different patterns of enterprise search solutions in the next section. Apache Solr provides a scalable high-performance search application that can be used for high-performance requirements.

Working with applications through federated search

Applications often provide their own search APIs, and unified search solutions should utilize the capabilities of this application's search APIs to search and merge the results in runtime. The following block diagram demonstrates how the federation works in enterprise search:

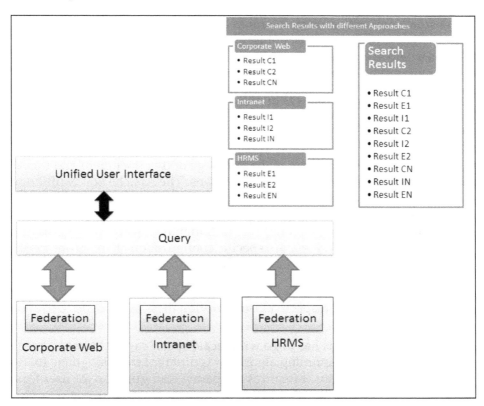

Although federated search works in the same fashion as enterprise search, it works for a limited scope. Enterprise search, when working with federated search engines, can directly integrate at a lower level and start consuming indexes generated by federated searches; this association can be more lightweight when enterprise search engines pass user queries to federated search, which in turn returns the results, which are later merged in unified enterprise search. After federation, a step of deduplication is required to remove data redundancy.

Other differentiators – mobiles, linguistic search, and security

Enterprise search can provide a differentiator by enabling access over user mobiles. This is very useful for customers to browse external content and employees to access internal information. It also saves time and cost because of its availability to respective stakeholders all the time. To address such requirements, one has to build a mobile application that can talk with the enterprise search server dynamically. Today's technology provides various options to architects.

Supporting mobile introduces its own challenges for design. Given that the mobile screens are small, and only a limited content can be displayed, the UI is required to be reworked or transformed for mobile apps. Enterprise search content can be published as a web service and consumed in mobile applications directly. Many times, customer implementation demands for mobile support.

Another design aspect to consider is linguistic support for the enterprise search solution. Customers might have data defined in a non-English locale; in such cases, the expectation is that the other locales used by customers should be supported by the enterprise search implementation. When a document is processed, parsing and tokenization of the module determine the language of that document and break up the stream of input text into distinct units or tokens. The Apache Solr Multilingual feature provides an out of the box solution to language-specific problems. Additionally, Apache Solr Multilingual provides a way to offer language-specific searches for different languages at once on multilingual websites. It supports a non-English locale. However, there are specific configuration changes one needs to do in different configuration files, which are:

- **Protected words/stop words**: This file requires locale-specific changes in the word list of their respective configuration files (`protwords.txt` and `stopwords.txt`).

- **Word stemming**: This has to go with locale-specific word stems. Unfortunately, the stemming algorithm is different from language to language, which means it requires a separate configuration for user locale.

- **Spell checking**: This needs to work with newer locale for spelling corrections.

Security is one of the design aspects to consider. This aspect talks about authorization and authentication. Authentication demands only authenticated users can come for enterprise search access, and authorization demands the enterprise search instance should have fine-grained access control. It helps each user access only what he is allowed to access. Security is more challenging because the data comes from various applications. Now, each application holds authorization information for the data.

In case of Apache Solr, one can use the application server-based authentication methodology. Apache Solr does not support any direct way of working with document-level security. So, an intermediate proxy has to be built around Solr and the client. This proxy can hide the Solr implementation from the outside world, and it can also hold a security wrapper layer to provide document-level fine-grained access control. Apache Solr allows users to run queries across multiple indexes; the proxy can protect these types of queries and ensure they are limited to respective search cores. You can find information on Solr security on the `https://wiki.apache.org/solr/SolrSecurity` wiki page.

Enterprise search data-processing patterns

Enterprise searching has evolved over time from a basic web-crawling document search to a more sophisticated structured/unstructured content search providing a lot of user interactions. As the data grows, there is a paradigm shift, and more focus is shifting towards the effective use of distributed technology to handle such a high volume of data. At the same time, the cost of enterprise storage needs to be controlled. Enterprise-ready search also demands support for high availability and scalability. By design, the enterprise search implementation should be capable of handling large indexes. With more growth, single server capacity of handling index becomes a limitation of the search server. In this case, sharding of index is most important.

 Sharding is a process of breaking one index into multiple logical units called "shards" across multiple records. In case of Solr, the results will be aggregated and returned.

Let's look at different data processing workflows for an enterprise search application.

Standalone search engine server

This configuration uses a single high-end server containing indexes. This type of configuration is mostly suitable for development and in some cases for production, where there is a control over data to be indexed. This is a single-node configuration. We have already seen Apache Solr in a single-node configuration in previous chapters. In this configuration, a server is responsible for managing the indexing enterprise data and search on indexed data. The advantages of such a system are:

- Many enterprise search systems come with a single-node readymade setup. This in turn enables developers to easily configure the instance and manage them.

- During enterprise search implementation, such configuration can be part of the development stage, where the validation of the search solution on a small subset of data can take place. This kind of environment is best for development stages.

- This pattern is well-suited for enterprises with a small/mid segment. With one standalone search server, it is easy to back up/restore due to its simplicity.

The disadvantages of standalone search engine servers are:

- Although the standalone search provides an easily manageable instance, it becomes difficult to scale the single node. As the indexing data grows, it faces limitations in terms of memory and processor capabilities. The cost of maintaining hardware with a higher data requirement becomes a challenge and expensive affair.

- Standalone search servers are not failsafe, and they cannot ensure high availability, unless you move them to a cluster. However, by ensuring a proper backup and recovery strategy, certain levels of data loss can definitely be prevented.

Distributed enterprise search pattern

This pattern is suitable for large-scale indexes, where the index is difficult to store on one system. In a distributed pattern, the index is divided among various shards, and they are stored locally on each node. Whenever a search query is fired by the user, the load balancer effectively balances the load on each node, and the query is redirected to a node that tried to get the results. Some distributed searches such as Apache Solr do not use load balancer, and instead, each participating node handles load balancing on its own by distributing the queries to respective shards. This pattern offers ample flexibility in terms of processing due to multiple nodes participating in the cluster or distributed search setup. The results are collected and merged. The following diagram shows an example of distributed enterprise search with a load balancer:

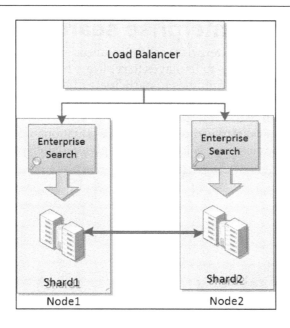

In case of Apache Solr, distributed search is supported but has its own limitations. A lot of features of Apache Solr, such as MoreLikeThis and Joins, are not supported. Note that the feature support for MoreLikeThis is introduced for distributed Solr in Version 4.1. Check the reference website `https://issues.apache.org/jira/browse/SOLR-788`.

The advantages of this system are:

- The distributed search approach provides excellent scalable capabilities to search. With the facility to scale horizontally by adding more hardware, distributed search becomes scalable.
- Compared to the previous approach, the cluster approach does not demand high-end hardware; the overall cost of implementing such a cluster is relatively cheaper.

The disadvantages of this system are:

- As the size of the cluster node grows, it becomes difficult for administrators to manage such a configuration. Many search engine vendors provide an administration console to manage the nodes and its configuration. Sometimes, such configurations also require load balancing software to handle the flow of request, and distribute them in an optimized manner to ensure the maximum utilization of available resources. Such clusters are difficult to manage by administrators.

The replicated enterprise search pattern

In this mode, more than one enterprise search instances exist; among them, the master instance provides shared access to its slaves to replicate the indexes across multiple systems. The master instance continues to participate in index creation, search, and so on. Slaves sync up the storage through various replication techniques such as rsync utility. Using replication of the enterprise search index, one can ensure high availability of instance. This kind of pattern is most suitable for situations where data size is finite and predictable and the customer is looking for high-availability features.

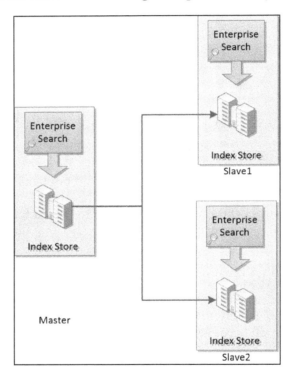

In case of Apache Solr, a system includes a Java-based replication that uses HTTP protocol for communication. This replication is recommended due to its benefits over other external replication techniques.

The advantages of this system are:

- With the replication abilities, enterprise search achieves high availability of the solution for end users. With index sync operation between multiple servers, all the indexes are replicated, and whenever the master instance fails, any slave can become a master.

The disadvantages are:

- Although this configuration provides high availability to end customers, it often requires an intermediate proxy between the search engine master and the consumer. This proxy hides the master details from the end user. In case of failure, the proxy redirects all the requests to another slave.

- Data upload operation is marked as complete only when the master and all the slaves hold indexes for that data. This in turn slows the overall indexing operation during real-time replication. Alternatively, if data sync is not in real time, it runs periodically between the master and slaves. With periodic sync, the possibility of losing the data whenever a failure happens during the time between two data sync operations is high. In case of Apache Solr, it replicates in real time, so the possibility of loss of data is minimal.

Distributed and replicated

This mode combines the best of both worlds and brings in the real value of a distributed system with high availability. In this configuration, the system has multiple masters, and each master holds multiple slaves where the replication has gone through. A load balancer is used to handle the load on multiple nodes equally. The following schematic shows a sample configuration with a distributed and replicated cluster:

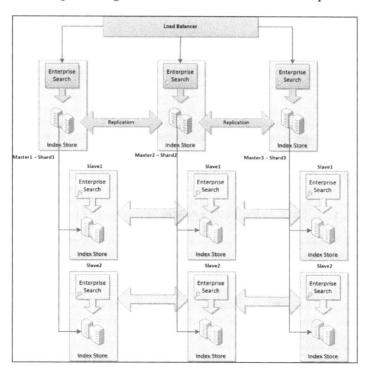

If Apache Solr is deployed on a Hadoop-like framework, it falls into this category. Solr also provides SolrCloud for distributed Solr. We will look at different approaches in the next section.

The advantages of this system are:

- This configuration combines the best of both worlds (that is, distributed and replicated). It enables scalability and high availability for this kind of configuration.

The disadvantages of this system are:

- Since the number of cluster nodes required for the distributed and replicated approach is high compared to other approaches, the cost of managing such a configuration is high
- With multiple nodes participating in the cluster activities with various roles (replicated and distributed), the management of such clusters becomes a bigger challenge for users

Data integrating pattern for search

Enterprise search solutions work on multiple data sources. Integration of these data sources with a search engine is an important aspect of search solution design. The data sources can vary from applications to databases and web crawlers. Like ETL tools of data warehouse, the data loading in search solutions goes through similar cycles. The important part here is how and which data should be loaded in the search engine. In this section, we will look at different approaches while working with the integration of data sources with a search engine. Many times, during the design of a search engine, architects end up using one or more of these data integration patterns for the design. Most application integrations fall under one of the following patterns. Each of them offer unique benefits and drawbacks; the architects have to choose the best-suited pattern based on the landscape.

Data import by enterprise search

This type of data integration is used for most cases. It is applicable for the cases where the system landscape is already established, and those applications provide access to their information through a standard interface or filesystem. Enterprise search is capable of reading data that an application exposes through its interfaces. This interface can be web service based, API based, or any other protocol based. The following schematic shows the interaction between an application/database and enterprise search:

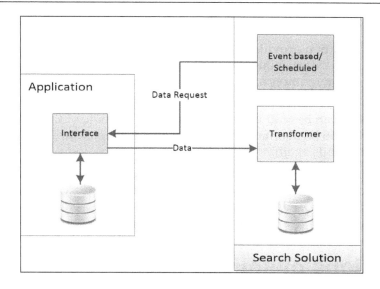

A data request is sent to the application's interface from enterprise search through a trigger. This trigger can be a scheduled event, or it can be an event triggered from applications itself, signifying the change in the state of data. When this data is requested, it is important for enterprise search to remember the last state of this data so that an incremental data request can be sent to interface, and the same can be returned by the application. When data is received by Enterprise Search, it is transformed into a format in which enterprise search can create a new index for the given data and persist it in its own repository. This transformation is generally predefined.

In Apache Solr search, a system provides predefined handlers to deal with various such data types. For example, DataImportHandler can connect to a relational database and collect data in either the full import or delta import form. This data is then transformed into indexes and preserved in the Solr repository.

Data import by enterprise search provides the following advantages over other approaches:

- No/minimum impact on the current system landscape due to applications not being impacted by the introduction of enterprise search; all the configuration is done on the enterprise search application and applications do not require a change of code

- Enterprise search becomes a single entity to manage all the integration; such configuration becomes easy to manage by administrators

This approach offers the following challenges during implementation:

- Each application provides different ways of communication. Legacy applications expose non-standard ways of integration, so this kind of integration requires a complex event-based mechanism to work with applications.

- While data can be read through integration, the state of the last data read pointer has to be maintained by a search engine to ensure there are no duplicate reads again.

- Sometimes, it becomes difficult to provide real-time search capabilities on this system. This is applicable when the enterprise search solution-based data integrators import data in between certain intervals (polling-schedule-based approach). Search is always near-real time, in such cases.

Applications pushing data

In this integration pattern, the applications are capable of extending themselves to work as agents to connect to an enterprise search solution. This pattern is applicable when the enterprise system landscape is going through changes, and applications can accommodate the additional logic of pushing data on their own to enterprise search. Since this approach is followed as and when the new information arrives on the application side, this does not require polling- or event-based mechanisms to work with. Enterprise search hosts an interface where this information can be passed by the application agents directly. The following schematic describes this integration pattern:

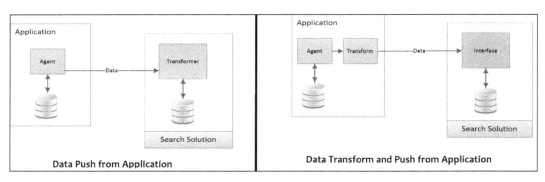

There are two major types of applications pushing data to enterprise search. The first is where applications simply push data in some format, for example, XML, and the data transformation takes place in enterprise search. Enterprise search then converts data into indexes through its own transformation logic. Typically, such supported configurations are published affront by search software and are part of its standard documentation library.

In the second approach, the application owns the responsibility of complete transformation and pushes ready indexes/data to the search interface or directly to the search repository. Apache Solr supports this approach by providing different types of extractors for data. It provides extractors for the CSV, JSON, and XML formats of information. This data integration pattern offers the following benefits:

- Since the data import part is out of enterprise search's objectives, the focus remains on searching and managing the indexes. Enterprise search becomes faster because data transformation is no longer managed by the search engine.
- A search engine does not require complex modules such as event-based data reader or the scheduler, making the overall search much simpler to configure and use.
- Enterprise search can provide real-time search abilities due to data sync happening from the data source itself.

This approach has the following drawbacks:

- The characteristics and search schema are exposed to the outside world, and applications carry the burden of keeping search engines in sync with the changes done with the application data
- It is a huge impact on the system landscape; any system integrated with enterprise search has to use search dependency

Middleware-based integration

The middleware-based integration pattern is a combination of the earlier patterns. This is applicable when enterprise search does not provide any mechanism to pull data of a certain type, and the application too does not provide any mechanism to push data to the search engine. In such cases, architects end up creating their own applications or agents that read information from applications on the trigger of an event. This event can be a scheduled event, or it can be coming from the application itself. The following schematic describes the interaction cycles between the middleware, application, and search application:

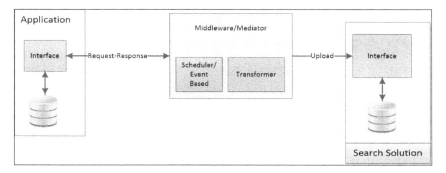

Once a request is sent to the application interface, it returns the required data. This data is then transformed by the intermediate agent or mediator and passed to search an application through another interface call.

Apache Solr provides an interface for applications or middleware to upload the information onto the server. When a request is for a nonconventional data source that does not provide any support for the previous two patterns, for example ERP and CRM applications, this approach can be used.

The middleware-based integration approach has the following benefits:

- Due to the presence of middleware, the current system landscape can function without awareness of the introduction of a new enterprise search engine.
- Similarly, applications and enterprise search do not carry any dependencies as they never interact with one another.
- To achieve middleware-based integration, there are many middleware tools available in the market, ranging from open source to commercial supported products. The cost of development of such middleware can be utilized here.

This approach has the following drawbacks:

- Creation of mediators/middleware introduces more applications to manage for administrators.
- Agents work with the store-forward methodology. By introducing agents, there is the addition of one more stage between the source and target data. This can impact when the data migrated is huge in size. It also increases the point of failures in a complete landscape.

We will look at a case study where all these integration patterns are used in the designing of a search engine in the next section.

Case study – designing an enterprise knowledge repository search for software IT services

We have now gone through various design aspects of building enterprise search. Now, let's see how one can build an enterprise knowledge repository search. We intend to create a unified search experience across all enterprises dealing in software IT services. Since this is a case study, we will limit ourselves in terms of the definition of the problem and design solution. In a real project, you will have more detailing done for each aspect of it. So, let's try and identify the requirements first.

Gathering requirements

Let's understand the requirements regarding search engines. We will now try answering some of the questions that are described in the first section of this chapter one by one, as they help us define a complete problem statement.

> *Problem Statement: What information is the customer looking for as part of the search implementation?*

The customer is looking for the following information:

- Tenders/contracts floated on the web on a specific site
- Rates of all the contractors
- Information from internal pre-sales repositories containing responses
- Information regarding projects successfully completed and delivered from the project repositories
- Information on various resource capabilities available with organizations from the HR portal

Additionally, customers want this information to be accessible at a single place, with access to the original resource.

What are the key benefits of implementing search engines in organizations?

Today, it is difficult for a customer to access this information at one place; the pre-sales bidding team often has to visit different websites or talk with different teams to access this information. With a unified search in place, our organization hopes to speed up the responses of bidding and also help them shortlist the bids that can be effectively handled by this company.

What applications does a customer expect the search engine to index?

A customer intends to integrate the following:

- Internet-based websites for tender access and contractor rates
- Internal knowledge management repository for pre-sales
- Project management repository, that is, ERP
- Custom applications holding employee HR information
- How can data on these applications be accessed?

Each of these applications has different ways of providing data:

- Typically, websites hold information in HTML tags, which has to be extracted, cleansed, and converted into information. This work is beyond the simple crawler. Another interesting option could be to identify if there are any RSS or ATOM feeds posted by the site regularly, in which case RSS can be accessed through RSS readers.

- The internal knowledge management repository provides access to its information through APIs and the WebDAV protocol.

- ERP provides APIs and web services to access its information.

- Custom applications do not provide any way of accessing its data in a straightforward manner. However, they do expose its database to end users.

Designing the solution

We have the clarity over user expectations. In terms of technology, Apache Solr clearly covers all the expectations of the users for this problem. We will be looking at various aspects of designing a complete Solr as enterprise search engine. To start with, we will look at designing the overall schema and how data can be captured and loaded for indexing with Apache Solr.

Designing the schema

It is important to have standardization of data definitions and data structures by using a common conceptual schema across a collection of data sources. There are multiple ways in which a schema can be designed; it mainly depends upon the expectations from the customer. Let's go through one of the designs for a schema. To design a schema, we need to understand the different types of attributes all the information sources bring into Apache Solr. We have four different types of information sources, and each of them bring a set of attributes/records. Each of the recordings will carry a unique identifier. We simply list down attributes that are required by search engines from information sources.

Information source	Attributes
Tender sites	Tender name, client name, technologies, bidding cost, contact person, functional information, deadline, and time of upload.
Pre-sales repository	Responses for RFP, efforts, technologies, estimated cost, client name, tender name, outcome, reason for failure, timeline, pre-sales, and contact person.
Project management	Project name, technology, client name, tender name, start date, end date, cost, efforts, project contact person, and status.

Information source	Attributes
Resource capabilities/ information	Name, technologies, past experience, certifications, and current status.

Although these attributes distinguish information, the information source will carry a lot of unstructured data that will be difficult to separate out. However, that's never a problem because Solr does not require well-formed information, the indexes can be generated on text data, and the information can later be searched over Apache Solr. Defining the attributes helps us build new faceting capabilities to provide better browsing. Some of these attributes, for example client name and estimated efforts, are common between multiple information sources. Few attributes carry different naming, but they point to the same entity, that is, project contact person, pre-sales contact person, and so on. A detailed analysis of each attribute is necessary before writing the schema.xml file. The following table lists a sample subset of the overall listing:

Attribute	Type	Data source				Is mandatory	Storage needed	Multi-valued
		1	2	3	4			
Id	number	y	y	y	y	y	y	n
tender_name	text	y	n	n	n	n	y	n
client_name	text	y	y	y	n	n	y	n
technologies	text	y	y	y	y	y	y	y
bidding_cost	number	y	y	y	n	n	y	n
contact_person	text	y	y	y	y	y	y	y
ending_date	date	y	y	y	n	n	y	n

The data sources are as follows:

Data Source	Description
1	Tender information
2	Pre-sales repository
3	Project management repository
4	HR information

Once this information is decided, we can easily go ahead and create a schema.xml file to work on these types of data sources.

Integrating subsystems with Apache Solr

However, the inputs to Solr are continuous as new data gets generated every day. So, the following ways can be used for integration:

Resource	How it can be integrated with Solr
RSS feeds/ATOM	This can be done using `DataImportHandler`, as it supports RSS and ATOM. This can be a scheduled event.
Internal KM repository	There are various options, but let's say the KM repository mounted on Solr Server using DAV, then even simple SolrJ APIs can be used to upload this information through Solr Cell (`ExtractingRequestHandler`), that is, Apache Tika Rich documents processing. This can be a scheduled event.
ERP	Since there is no direct way to access ERP information, one can always build a simple web service client to access ERP information and push it to Apache Solr. Again, SolrJ can be used on the client side. This has to be a scheduled event since it's a service access.
Custom applications	Custom applications provide access to their database; a standard `DataImportHandler` with delta/full import can possibly be a good option to consider.

The overall enterprise search architecture may look like the following:

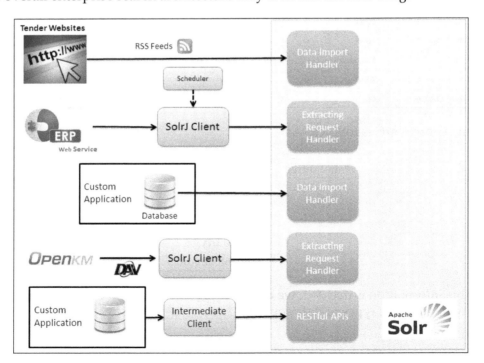

In the development/sandbox instance, we will configure a single instance of Solr — complete, configured, and ready to use. Based on the designs of each information source, further detailing on each component can be done. For example, for `DataImportHandler`, one may need to identify the tables and query pattern, and also make a provision for delta imports. Similarly, for RSS feeds, you will require `HttpDataSource` to connect, and a `data-config.xml` will look like the following:

```
<dataConfig>
  <dataSource type="HttpDataSource" />
  <document>
    <entity name="My Tender Site"
    pk="link"
    url="<your site-name>"
    processor="XPathEntityProcessor"
    forEach="/RDF/channel | /RDF/item"
    transformer="RegexTransformer,DateFormatTransformer">

      <field column="id" xpath="/RDF/channel/link"/>
      <field column="tender_name" xpath="/RDF/item/tender"/>
      <field column="client_name" xpath="/RDF/channel/from"/>

      <field column="technologies" xpath="/RDF/item/skills" />
      <field column="link" xpath="/RDF/item/link" />
      <field column="bidding_cost" xpath="/RDF/item/cost" />
      <field column="contact_person" xpath="/RDF/item/floated by" />
      <field column="ending_date" xpath="/RDF/item/date"
        dateTimeFormat="yyyy-MM-dd'T'hh:mm:ss" />
      ......
    </entity>
  </document>
</dataConfig>
```

We have already seen an example of how `DataImportHandler` can be used with relational databases. To connect with the knowledge management repository, a web service client can be created; the information can be extracted and fed to Solr.

Working on end user interface

Another aspect of designing the enterprise search solution is deciding upon the browsing and search experience. Apache Solr gives users many features. The following table lists some of the important features that can help us define the configuration for Apache Solr.

Feature	Description
Facets	Users need to decide what kind of browsing experience they need for their users. We have already seen facets and their configuration. Based on the attribute type, a facet can be applied.
More like this (similarity results)	More like this requires specific attributes on which it can perform more like this for end users. You can specify boosts as well.
Text highlighting	Highlighting can be performed on a common field that carries all the information and the size of the snippet, along with the highlighted text that can be defined.
Spell checking and autocomplete	These components can be enabled with various parameters.

There are additional components, although they do not really impact the user interface, but they do play a role in performance (for example, cache, size of buffer, and so on). This has to be decided in the later phase. Based on the data size, its growth, and the performance expectations, the clustering models can be applied. We will look at them in more detail in the next chapter. Similarly, performance is another aspect where one has to monitor instance performance and optimize it. Boosting your relevance ranking by index level boosting is another aspect of designing the Solr subsystem. In this case, possibly, HR-related recording will have lower boosts compared to tender, pre-sales repository. Many of these aspects play a role during development instance setup and testing. They can be configured accordingly.

Apache Solr provides its default application using Velocity templates. Its output can be consumed in clients directly through JSON and XML. Depending upon a customer's expectations, such UI design can take place.

Summary

In this chapter, we studied various aspects that need consideration while designing an enterprise level search solution. We tried to understand how one can try to gather the information regarding the current system landscape, and how a design can be carried out. We also went through design workflows supported by Apache Solr. Finally, we went through the case study of designing a search engine for software IT firms.

5
Integrating Apache Solr

The larger your IT landscapes, the more difficult it can be for its users to find what they need, even with the best navigation mechanisms. A search engine should be capable of integrating with multiple systems of this kind. In the last chapter, we have seen the different data integration patterns that are possible with Apache Solr. Apache Solr is capable of reading data from different data sources. The next level of enterprise search demands deeper integration with Apache Solr. For example, a search user interface in the application uses Apache Solr or the applications run Apache Solr in an embedded mode. These are just different possibilities to explore while moving into a deeper integration. Many organizations would like to retain the user interface and usability of their existing application, while moving the underlying processing layer on Apache Solr.

Apache Solr has an active development community, which means heavy usage of Solr based across different subsystems, enabling people to add different ways of integrating Solr with applications every day. To integrate Apache Solr with other systems, there are various options available. For example, in this chapter, we intend to understand various integration aspects of Apache Solr with other subsystems and technologies. The Apache Solr-based search can be embedded within your own application; it can also be used with other technologies, and most importantly, the major use case of Apache Solr is through integration of a **content management system** (CMS) with Solr. We will be looking at the following topics in more detail:

- Empowering Java Enterprise application with Solr search
- Integration with Content Management Systems (CMS)
- Integrating Apache Solr with client technologies
- Case study – Apache Solr with Drupal

Empowering the Java Enterprise application with Solr search

Since Apache Solr is a J2EE-based WAR file, it can be easily integrated with any other application. We have already seen how Apache Solr can be used on different J2EE application containers such as Tomcat and Jetty. For the applications that are developed on the J2EE platform, Apache Solr can be used in the following ways in your existing J2EE applications. While many Solr implementations go for HTML APIs with an XML/JSON request-response model from the client, the approaches discussed in the latter part of the chapter highlight a tighter integration with Apache Solr. HTML-based integration of Apache Solr demands consumer application to send HTTP requests to the Solr server, and accept responses in the XML/JSON format.

Embedding Apache Solr as a module (web application) in an enterprise application

Application servers such as JBoss and Weblogic support Java EE-based projects and the packaging. A typical enterprise archive (.ear) file contains many project-specific modules with interdependencies and these files contain the deployment descriptor for the complete enterprise archive. These modules can carry interdependencies, but each module runs either as a separate web application or a library. Apache Solr comes with a deployable web archive (solr.war) file. This WAR file can be combined with other applications, and together users can create a single enterprise archive file (.ear). The following screenshot depicts Oracle JDeveloper-based enterprise applications, which contain a Solr web archive along with our own projects. The deployment profile on the right-hand side depicts the enterprise deployment structure. Both the applications can co-exist and this kind of integration is loosely coupled. Consider the following screenshot:

Apache Solr can be accessed directly from your own web application through SolrJ (the `HTTPSolrServer` interface, `ConcurrentUpdateSolrServer`, or `EmbeddedSolrServer`) or other means.

> The `EmbeddedSolrServer` interface-based interaction does not require a transporting data over a network, thus reducing the additional overhead on data indexing and runtime queries. As `EmbeddedSolrServer` uses `solr.home` based path as the primary initialization parameter, its use in production-level usage itself is a big question, as it may not be able to offer us the flexibility and portability.

The following example shows a sample code on how `EmbeddedSolrServer` can be used to query and display results:

```
CoreContainer coreContainer = new CoreContainer("<put solr.home
path>");

for (String coreName : coreContainer.getCoreNames()) {
  System.out.println(coreName);//printing it
}
//here collection1 is my core
EmbeddedSolrServer server = new EmbeddedSolrServer(coreContainer,
"collection1");
//Prepare Solr Query, and get the response
SolrQuery solrQuery = new SolrQuery("*.*");
QueryResponse response = server.query(solrQuery);
SolrDocumentList dList = response.getResults();
//Print the key-value results
for (int i = 0; i < dList.getNumFound(); i++) {
  for (Map.Entry mE : dList.get(i).entrySet()) {
    System.out.println(mE.getKey() + ":" + mE.getValue());
  }
}
```

The preceding program simply prints all the indexed Solr attributes on `sysout` (your screen).

> From Apache Solr Version 4.4 onwards, if you get `SolrException` with the message **No such core**, you will be required to add another step of initializing `CoreContainer`: `coreContainer.load()`. This API loads the cores in the core container.

How to do it?

Once you have your IDE ready with your web application, follow the given steps. We will start with the assumption that you have downloaded the latest Apache Solr:

1. Create a new project from the WAR file by importing the `solr.war` file, and give it a name of your choice.

2. Create `application.xml` or `weblogic-application.xml` depending upon the container describing it. Your `application.xml` file will have different modules and their web URLs defined. Many times, the development studio generates this file automatically. Please find the sample `application.xml` file as follows:

    ```
    <?xml version = '1.0' encoding = 'windows-1252'?>
    <application xmlns:xsi="http://www.w3.org/2001/XMLSchema-
    instance" xsi:schemaLocation="http://java.sun.com/xml/ns/javaee
    http://java.sun.com/xml/ns/javaee/application_5.xsd" version="5"
    xmlns="http://java.sun.com/xml/ns/javaee">
      <display-name>solr-java-ee</display-name>
      <module>
        <web>
          <web-uri>SolrIntegratedApplication_
    MyApplicationViewController_webapp.war</web-uri>
          <context-root>SolrIntegratedApplication-
    MyApplicationViewController-context-root</context-root>
        </web>
      </module>
      <module>
        <web>
          <web-uri>solr.war</web-uri>
          <context-root>SolrIntegratedApplication-SolrWar-context-
    root</context-root>
        </web>
      </module>
    </application>
    ```

3. Package everything through Ant/build script or through your development studio; create the EAR package and deploy it on the container. Please remember that Solr requires a path to `solr.home` as we have seen in *Chapter 2, Getting Started with Apache Solr*. This can be provided as a JVM parameter as follows:

    ```
    -Dsolr.solr.home=SOLR_PATH
    ```

    `SOLR_PATH` gets the location on your filesystem where you copied the Solr configuration folder.

4. Now, you can use the same path with `EmbeddedSolrServer` while initializing the `CoreContainer` class in your application. You can get all the search results in your own bean/data-control/model layer, and render them as per your web application.

5. Configure your Solr instance, schema, and other configuration as per *Chapter 2, Getting Started with Apache Solr*, accordingly.

Running Solr with your application offers its own benefits and drawbacks. Since Apache Solr is a part of your application, you do not require a separate lifecycle to manage the instance and administer it; it can be done together. This works well with a single node configuration; as the demand grows, it becomes difficult to manage this configuration for clustered search.

Apache Solr in your web application

The previous approach works well when you intend to embed Apache Solr as a completely separate web application. When you have a requirement of adding search functionality in your existing application with a single deployment, the approach of adding Apache Solr as a separate web application does not really work. For these kinds of situations, Apache Solr runs as a part of the existing application. With this configuration, the overall system offers ample benefits due to the availability of Solr and Lucene APIs in the same code as a library import.

How to do it?

Apache Solr comes with its own web archive, with its entire configuration. Let's assume that we have our application's context root at `/myapplication`, and we would like to move all Solr components under `/myapplication/search`. Let's look at how it can be achieved:

1. Download Apache Solr, extract it, and prepare `schema.xml` and `solrconfig.xml` as per your requirements.

2. All the libraries that are part of `$SOLR_WAR/WEB-INF/lib` should be linked to your project, in libraries, and they should also be a part of your packaging depending upon your requirements.

3. The other folders of the `solr.war` file (as shown in the following screenshot), should be moved to your project's `public_html` folder or `web` folder. They contain information such as styling, css, administration, and so on.

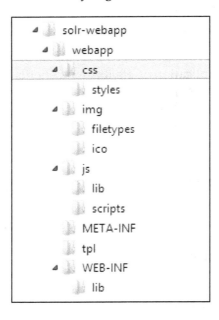

4. The next important task is to review the existing `web.xml` file. The default `SolrRequestFilter` runs through all the URLs, that is, `/*`; this has to be modified to specifics, which means `/search` is shown as follows:

```
....
<filter>
    <filter-name>SolrRequestFilter</filter-name>
    <filter-class>org.apache.solr.servlet.SolrDispatchFilter</
filter-class>

</filter>

<filter-mapping>
    <filter-name>SolrRequestFilter</filter-name>
    <url-pattern>/search/*</url-pattern>
</filter-mapping>
.....
```

Similarly, other URL patterns require to be modified appropriately. The `web.xml` file is provided in the code section of this book.

5. When a URL match is found, the Solr request / dispatch filter tries to perform the match with request handlers of `solrconfig.xml`, and delegates the response to the matched handler. However, since this URL pattern is out of sync with the current scenario, the system will not be able to find the matching request handler if it throws the **Not Found** error. So the next step is to fix all the request handler's URLs to pick up from their new location. To do that, we need to modify `solrconfig.xml` accordingly (please see the following example). This file is also available in the code section for reference.

```
.....
   <requestHandler name="/search/select" class="solr.
SearchHandler">
     <!-- default values for query parameters can be specified,
these will be overridden by parameters in the request -->
     <lst name="defaults">
       <str name="echoParams">explicit</str>
       <int name="rows">10</int>
       <str name="df">text</str>
     </lst>
.......
```

6. Put the `solr.home` path as explained in the previous section. Now, restart the container.

Once these changes are done, Apache Solr can run independently in a separate sub-URL of your application. With the current configuration, indexing and querying capabilities of Apache Solr can be utilized through SolrJ or any other means. Your application can run smoothly in a separate directory independently.

To use SolrJ, instead of copying the required JARs for usage, you can put a Maven dependency in your `pom.xml` file as follows:

```
<dependency>
  <artifactId>solr-solrj</artifactId>
  <groupId>org.apache.solr</groupId>
  <version>1.4.0</version>
  <type>jar</type>
  <scope>compile</scope>
</dependency>
```

This integration type offers unique benefits in terms of consumption of Apache Solr services. Due to the availability of Solr/Lucene APIs directly in your application, one can use these APIs directly, extend them, and provide more intuitive customized application-based search. The biggest drawback with this approach is whenever you upgrade Apache Solr, any changes that come from Solr's new release are required to be implemented carefully (as it requires merging of files) in your existing application. This adds overhead while upgrading your Solr-based solution.

Integration with client technologies

The typical IT landscape of any large-size organization comprises many different technologies. Apache Solr provides excellent ways to gather information from different types of sources; however, the business may demand integrating Apache Solr with non-J2EE-based technology. Although there are various technologies available in the market, the placement of an Apache Solr-like enterprise search engine in the broader picture of the organization's IT topology is always targeted for specific areas. This area is nothing but the end user web portals. Search engines are designed to provide information to end users, and they are expected to respond as fast as they can. Since they do not provide anything else beyond search, they always go in embedded mode with the applications. These applications mainly use various web-based technologies. In the previous section, we saw how Apache Solr can be used with different Java- and J2EE-based technologies and different integration techniques with J2EE-based applications. We will look at some other web-based technologies and how Apache Solr can be integrated with them.

Integrating Apache Solr with PHP for web portals

PHP (**Hypertext Preprocessor**) is one of the most widely used scripting languages that enables developers to create dynamic web content. PHP-based sites/portals are used by many; it is estimated that there are more than 32 million domains using PHP (refer to http://news.netcraft.com/archives/2013/01/31/php-just-grows-grows.html). Many of these sites are custom portals developed by organizations to address their specific requirements. Since Apache Solr and PHP are two different technologies, they have to run in different containers, and interact with each other.

Interacting directly with Solr

There are various ways to integrate Apache Solr in PHP-based web portals. Apache Solr provides PHP response directly through the wt parameter. You can simply try searching for some string (in this example, test) on your browser by typing the URL http://localhost:8983/solr/select?q=test&wt=php. The output of the search can be seen in the following screenshot:

Apache Solr returns a PHP array of responseHeader and response. You can easily extract content from this array directly. The following PHP code demonstrates the extraction of the document from the array:

```
<html>
  <head>
    <title>My Company Search</title>
  </head>
  <body>
    <?php
$code = file_get_contents('http://localhost:8983/solr /
select?q=No&wt=php');
eval("\$result = " . $code . ";");
?>
    <?php
      foreach ($result['response'] as $response) {
        foreach ($response as $doc) {
          foreach ($doc as $key => $value) {
            print_r($key);
            print_r('    :    ');
            print_r($value);
            print_r('<br/>');
          }
          print_r('<br/><br/>');
        }
      }
    ?>
  </body>
</html>
```

The sample PHP code simply reads arrays, and prints the results with the name-value pair in each line. A more detailed PHP file is available in the code section of this book.

> Additionally, you can also use the JSON format for interacting with your remote Apache Solr server. This can be done by changing `wt=json`; the URL looks like `http://localhost:8983/solr/select?q=test&wt=json`. The JSON format can be extracted using `json_decode()` in PHP, and convert the string into a PHP-based array. This is one of the recommended ways of using Apache Solr with PHP.

Using the Solr PHP client

The Solr PHP client library provides rich APIs for indexing and searching in remote Apache Solr. This was one of the robust and easiest implementations of APIs that can be used for integration; however, its development is stalled from 2011 (visit its Google code's home page at `http://code.google.com/p/solr-php-client/` for more details). The Solr PHP client has the following four classes:

Class	Description
`Apache_Solr_Document`	This class represents one Solr document. It holds key and value pairs of the elements in the document. The elements can be accessed by `for each` in PHP. This class also contains methods to get the boost of the fields. While indexing, one can add new field values and set boost on the document.
`Apache_Solr_Response`	This class represents the response from Apache Solr. It provides APIs to parse raw responses. It also returns the HTTP status.
`Apache_Solr_Service`	This class provides access to the Solr server. All the major functionalities, such as connecting to Solr, uploading the document for indexing, committing changes, optimizing the instance, and searching over the Solr instance are provided by this class.
`Apache_Solr_Service_Balancer`	This class provides you with a way to connect to multiple Solr servers. It provides APIs to add documents, delete them, commit, optimize, and search. It uses the `Apache_Solr_Service` class internally. It also provides APIs for reading and writing of services.

How to do it?

The Apache Solr PHP client provides one of the simplest ways of integrating Solr with PHP. To use the Solr PHP client, perform the following steps:

1. To work with the Solr PHP client, you need to download the latest ZIP file from `http://code.google.com/p/solr-php-client/downloads/list`.

2. Unzip the file in the folder at `web/php/html`. Remember its path.

3. Assuming that the Apache Solr instance is set up and running, create a PHP file and include `Service.php` from the `Solr` folder of the Solr PHP client. Remember to put a relative HTTP path to this file.

4. Now you can create a form, and the results page will search the API from the Solr PHP client directly. We have provided a sample code for reference, and the following is the output of that code:

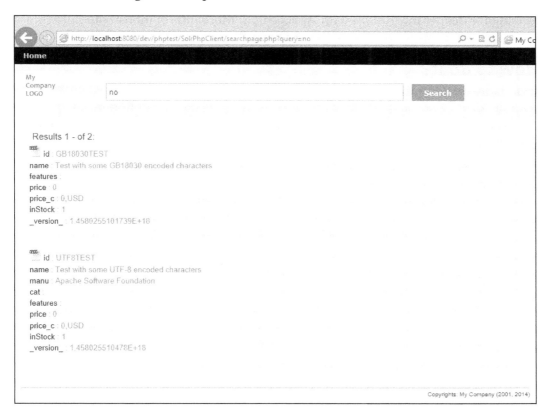

There is an enhanced `solr-php` client. It is based on this client that we work with the Solr 4.X Version (`https://github.com/Ramzi-Alqrainy/solr-php`). This client handles deprecated parameters.

Advanced integration with Solarium

Solarium is another open source initiative for integrating Apache Solr with PHP. Solarium provides support for Apache Solr's advanced features such as Solr facets of different types, indexing options with rich update queries, simple-advanced query building APIs, and so on. Solarium has dependency on PHP, and it does not carry any other dependencies, thereby making the installation of Solarium very easy. Solarium provides a readily available framework, through which PHP developers can build and customize enterprise search. Compared to other PHP integration options, Solarium provides the maximum features of Apache Solr to the PHP developers for consumption. Solarium is useful as a complete package for enterprises looking for deeper integration with Apache Solr. More information about Solarium can be read at `http://www.solarium-project.org/`.

How to do it?

Installation of Solarium is one of the easiest tasks. It ships with ample examples, with detailed example pages for each case, making the life of a PHP developer easy. All the examples can be found in the example directory of Solarium. Consider the following steps:

1. Download Solarium from GitHub by the accessing the URL `https://github.com/basdenooijer/solarium`. Before downloading, it is important to validate your PHP version with Solarium. Do read the requirements in the Solarium manual before deciding upon the version. Solarium 3+ has a minimum PHP version requirement of 5.3. All Solarium versions work with PHP5 and above.

2. Unzip the folder and include `library/Solarium/Autoloader.php` in your PHP to start using Solarium APIs.

3. To run the examples, go to the examples directory, edit the `config.dist.php` file, and enter the correct Solr instance information, that is, Solr instance location, port, relative path, and so on.

4. Try running examples directly from the `example` directory.

Here is a sample PHP file that runs on Apache Solr to get all indexes back to the web server.

```php
<?php
error_reporting(E_ALL);
ini_set('display_errors', true);//displays error
require('library/Solarium/Autoloader.php'); //put the web path the autoloader.php
Solarium_Autoloader::register();

$config = array(
    'adapteroptions' => array(
        'host' => 'localhost',
        'port' => 8983,
        'path' => '/solr/',
    )
);
$client = new Solarium_Client($config);
echo '<html><head><title>Solarium example</title></head><body>';
$query = $client->createSelect();
$resultset = $client->select($query);// this executes the query and returns the result

echo 'NumFound: '.$resultset->getNumFound();// display the total number of documents found by solr

foreach ($resultset as $document) {
    echo '<hr/><table>';
    foreach($document AS $field => $value)
    {
        if(is_array($value)) $value = implode(', ', $value);        // this converts multivalue fields to a comma-separated string
        echo '<tr><th>' . $field . '</th><td>' . $value . '</td></tr>';
    }
    echo '</table>';
}
echo '</body></html>';
?>
```

Integrating Apache Solr with JavaScript

JavaScript is used in many web technologies as the client-side script to interact with the server. Today, JavaScript along with AJAX and JQuery provides rich client Web 2.0 interfaces for web applications. Apache Solr provides CSV, XML, and JSON formats to interact with the clients. The developers can easily write the JavaScript-based code to query and then parse the outcomes and render them on the user screen in real time. Since JavaScript runs on client browsers, the access information to Solr is visible to the client applications and the user. However, developers can apply different code obfuscation techniques to make code readability difficult.

Using simple XMLHTTPRequest

JavaScript Object Notation (JSON) format is a simple and lightweight format, which provides much lesser message footprint while passing the data over a wire. Due to these unique features of JSON, it's becoming more and more popular for passing messages. To transfer search results between the Apache Solr server and the JavaScript client, use of AJAX and JSON together makes it simple to consume Solr information by modern Web 2.0 applications. Using the AJAX-based XMLHttpRequest API, clients can directly contact http://localhost:8983/solr/select?wt=json&q=No. The following code snippet shows how a request can be sent to Apache Solr server through the get method of XMLHTTPRequest:

```
function xmlhttpPost(strURL) {
  var xmlHttpReq = false;
  if (window.XMLHttpRequest) { // Mozilla/Safari
    this.xmlHttpReq = new XMLHttpRequest();
  }
  else if (window.ActiveXObject) { // IE
    this.xmlHttpReq = new ActiveXObject("Microsoft.XMLHTTP");
  }
  this.xmlHttpReq.open('GET', strURL, true);
  this.xmlHttpReq.setRequestHeader('Content-Type', 'application/x-www-
form-urlencoded');
  this.xmlHttpReq.onreadystatechange = function() {
    if (this.xmlHttpReq.readyState == 4) { //Holds the status of the
XMLHttpRequest.
      updatepage(this.xmlHttpReq.responseText);
    }
  }

  var params = getstandardargs().concat(getquerystring());
  var strData = params.join('&');
  alert(strURL + strData);
  this.xmlHttpReq.send(strData);
}
```

The function simply opens a connection; it composes the complete URL and sends the request to Apache Solr as a part of the request. The XMLHttpRequest implementation does not require any setup; it can be embedded in any HTML code. It is also supported by many applications.

Integrating Apache Solr using AJAX Solr

AJAX-Solr is an open source JavaScript AJAX-based library that provides rich APIs and widgets to bring Apache Solr's capabilities in the current application. This library also provides support for JQuery-based server interactions through a separate JQuery-based manager. Please access `https://github.com/evolvingweb/ajax-solr/wiki` to read more about AJAX-Solr. It provides rich UI functionality through UI widgets. The widget is nothing but small blocks of JavaScript that render a specific UI component. AJAX-Solr provides a benefit of providing both the UI component and straightforward API level access to process Solr requests. AJAX-Solr provides the following three major components:

- Manager — controller
- Parameter store or core — model
- UI widgets — view

The default installation comes with a pre-build demo in the `example` folder of AJAX-Solr and follows the same folder structure as the model-view-controller we described earlier:

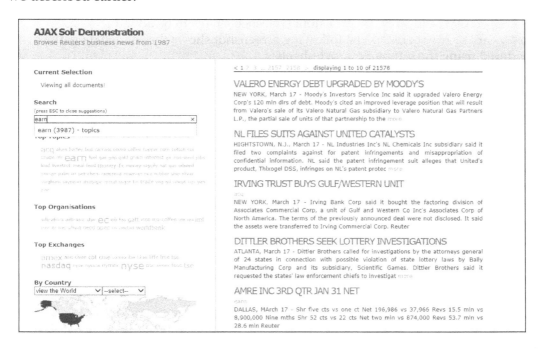

Although AJAX-Solr wins in terms of benefits with features such as API and pre-built widget, the widgets are in pretty basic shape, and they often require customizations to be built on top of it.

Parsing Solr XML with the help of XSLT

One of the results of the Apache Solr is the XML format; this can be retrieved by passing `wt=xml`. Traditionally, XML has been used at many places for data/message passing. Many applications still understand XML-based messaging, and it has been widely used in the service-oriented architecture. Applying **XSLT (XML stylesheet)** can create wonders and it can transform the data by itself. This is very useful for cases of legacy applications that do not use JSP- or PHP-based scripting language, and work on HTML or other custom scripting. This approach is most simple, and carries no library imports, or any other dependencies. The integration of Apache Solr with your application through XML-XSLT can be achieved using two approaches, which will be discussed shortly.

In the first approach, the stylesheet is uploaded on the Apache Solr server under `$SOLR.HOME/<corename>/conf/xsl`. You can introduce new stylesheets, and you can directly query them from your browser by passing the appropriate parameters. For example, `http://localhost:8983/solr/select/?q=apache&wt=xslt&tr=exa mple.xsl` request passes a parameter that allows clients to select the transformation. When we choose, the transformation takes place and the final HTML output is rendered back to the consumer. Apache Solr ships with some stylesheets, that is, RSS, ATOM, and so on. Any custom stylesheets have to be added to `$SOLR. HOME/<core>/conf/xslt`. The following screenshot shows the same data getting rendered using the inbuilt Solr stylesheets:

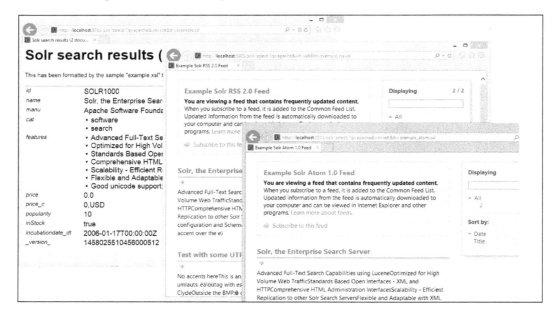

In the second approach, you can request the XML page from the remote location, and apply the local stylesheet here. We have provided an example where you can parse Solr results using local XSLT. It has two files mentioned in the following table:

File	Description
mypage.html	This page uses the MSXML2 DOM parser (works in Internet Explorer). First edit this page, update the appropriate Solr URL, and then open the mypage.html file in your browser.
example.xsl	This is the stylesheet that will be read by mypage.html to generate the XML + XSL outcome.

Case study – Apache Solr and Drupal

Apache Solr can be integrated with any subsystem given the technology integration feasibility. However, some of the subsystems provide additional plugins/modules through which such integration goes deeper. In this section, we will look at two different subsystems as a case study.

For any CMS, search is an integral part of the system. CMS contains most of the information that users are consistently updating every day. They also provide different versions of the same document, and many other features. However, many content management systems do not provide competitive search. This is mainly because the development focus of many CMSes have been around providing feature-rich, failsafe CMS for more practical usage. Besides web portal, CMSes are also widespread and many organizations use them heavily. Integrating Apache Solr Enterprise search with CMS brings the best of both worlds together. We will primarily look at the most popular open source CMS systems in the world.

Drupal is one of the most popular CMSes used today. Integrating Drupal with Apache Solr provides users with the access to a rich search interface. It also enables users to search for content dynamically at high speeds on CMS data. The unique Solr features such as facets and relevance ranking enable users to reach the information they were looking for at the earliest time, thus saving some time in their day-to-day work. Since Apache Solr never queries Drupal's database, it provides a scalable environment for both Drupal and Solr to grow. Apache Solr can be integrated with Drupal as a Drupal module. The integration between these two systems is beyond the normal information demand-sharing way. Drupal does a smart thing of performing batch indexing, keeping tracking of Solr server connectivity, and so on. This integration is at a deeper level.

How to do it?

Let's look at how Drupal and Apache Solr can be brought together to effectively use the capabilities of both these applications together:

1. First download Apache Solr and install it.

2. The next step is to download Drupal and install it. You will find installation instructions at `https://drupal.org/documentation/install`.

3. Once the two subsystems are available, the next step would be to make the **Apache Solr Search** module available in Drupal. To do that, first download the module from Drupal's site (`https://drupal.org/project/apachesolr`). Unzip it and put it in your sites module directory at, `sites/all/modules` or in the Drupal's module directory. You may also install the facet API (`https://drupal.org/project/facetapi`) and the Apache Solr framework modules along with this. If you use the Apache Solr framework, the facet API is a part of it.

4. Now enable Apache Solr Modules from Drupal administration. The modules are shown in the following screenshot:

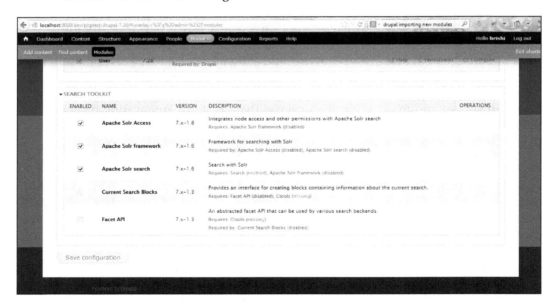

5. Since Drupal requires its own Apache Solr schema and configuration, it is recommended to create a separate domain (call it Drupal) and copy the schema from `$MODULE_HOME/solr-conf/<your-solr>/*` to your new core.

6. Restart Apache Solr and ensure everything works fine.

7. After enabling the modules in Drupal, go to the configuration of that module and click on the **SETTINGS** tab. Ensure the Solr URL is correct. You can also test the Solr connection by clicking on the localhost server as shown in the following screenshot:

8. Now create some data (pages) and add some content to them on Drupal.

9. Here, you have two options: either write a cron job (`http://<drupal-site>/cron.php`) or perform indexing manually. Drupal entities are indexed during a Drupal cron job. For now, visit the **DEFAULT INDEX** tab in the **Configure** module of the Apache Solr search, and try to run the index. Refer to the following screenshot:

The Apache Solr search module holds a pipeline of entities, which are processed into one or more documents. Each document object is then transformed into XML and sent to Solr for processing.

10. Validate on your Solr server to see whether data indexing has taken place. This can also be seen by simply running a search on Solr. Once this is verified, enable search blocks on the Drupal site. You can do this by navigating to **Module configuration | Page/Block**.

11. Verify the search results using the blocks.

On similar lines, you can extend the Apache Solr integration with Drupal in more advanced ways. Drupal provides a lot of interesting modules as shown in the following table:

Module	Description
Apache Solr attachment	This sends all the attachments to Tika and makes them searchable through Drupal.
Apache Solr multisite search	If you have multiple Drupal sites, they can be searched across a single Solr core.
Apache Solr sort	This adds support for the Solr grouping feature and adds a UI to enable/disable sort fields.
Facet APIs	This provides faceted search on top of the Drupal Solr basic search.

You can see a complete listing of these modules at `https://drupal.org/project/apachesolr`. We have seen the Drupal module for Solr; additionally, Acquia provides cloud-based Apache Solr search for Drupal customers. Similar to Drupal, many portals such as WordPress and Typo3 provides some way of integration:

Subsystem	Description
WordPress CMS	This is used through the WordPress plugin and is PHP-based (`http://wordpress.org/plugins/solr-for-wordpress/`).
OpenCMS	Previously, OpenCMS used to work with the `opencms-solr` project. From OpenCMS 8.0, it is integrated.
MongoDB	Solr cannot run on top of MongoDB; they can be parallely run with data sync. Sync can take place in the following ways:
	Replication feature of MongoDB
	Third-party MongoDB connectors
	JDBC-Solr DataImportHandler (`https://github.com/erh/mongo-jdbc`)
FOSWIKI (**Free and Open Source Wiki**)	It is used through the FOSWIKI Solr plugin (`http://foswiki.org/Extensions/SolrPlugin`).

Summary

In this section, we have understood how Apache Solr can be used for business, and the different ways of integration with applications and technologies. We looked at how Apache Solr can be integrated in enterprise and web-based applications. For non-J2EE-based applications, we studied different technological integration including PHP, JavaScript, and XSLT. Finally, we went through Apache Solr integration with CMS where we covered Drupal CMS.

6
Distributed Search Using Apache Solr

Traditionally, organizations have tried to optimize their business cost on information processing by limiting the information to smaller subsets based on business priority. This was mainly due to the exorbitant cost of storing and processing enterprise data in data stores such as relational databases. Today's technology advancements have reduced the overall cost of data processing through the use of low-cost hardware and open source software. It has also enabled organizations to go beyond smaller data subsets, demanding more data processing capabilities from these systems. Enterprise searches were no exception.

Since enterprise search applications work across multiple applications with different datasets across organizations, it requires lot of data storage and exceptional computation capabilities from the underlying hardware systems. Many organizations optimize cost by preferring to use low-cost distributed systems instead of purchasing high-end servers. Apache Solr provides excellent distributed processing capabilities for such consumers in many ways. In this chapter, we are going to look at distributed search using Apache Solr. We will be covering the following topics:

- Need for distributed search
- Distributed search and Apache Solr
- Setting up SolrCloud
- SolrCloud architecture
- Case study – distributed enterprise search server for ABC Corporation

Need for distributed search

At the beginning of the chapter, we have already seen some of the reasons leading to the need for distributed searches. Any search engine would have two important functions: firstly to index the data, and secondly to provide a real-time search. As the data grows, single node enterprise search applications face the following issues:

- There are times when an index on one machine is insufficient and it cannot accommodate enterprise information. This is mainly applicable for enterprises with growing data, which require the generation of large index sizes.

- As more and more users start using enterprise search, there is huge traffic for search operations. Single node searches have a limitation on the number of requests they can serve within a stipulated time, even if the data is not huge.

- For frequently changing data, the indexer has to index the data swiftly to avoid lagging and further delays. Often, index generation time is one of the primary expectations of enterprises. For example, many enterprises demand real-time or near real-time searches on their data.

- When complex user queries are run across the search index, the search response becomes slow at times. This slow response is the impact of multiple disk reads, and the complex computations demanded by the user queries.

These issues drive the need for distributed search support to be available for enterprise search applications. We have already seen different types of enterprise search data processing patterns in *Chapter 4, Designing Enterprise Search*. Typically, enterprises that go with distributed runtime search also generate indexes in a distributed manner; however, sometimes when complex indexes are to be generated on limited datasets, the distributed system is not required.

The decision to move to a distributed search from a standalone system should be driven by the needs of enterprises, because distributed search applications are not always efficient in terms of performance.

For smaller data sizes, standalone search architecture performances are better compared to distributed searches due to single index availability. With the growth in the data size, its performance degrades eventually. While designing a distributed search system, solution architects must take the following goals into consideration:

- Faster response to user queries.

- Number of queries responded by distributed search within the stipulated time.

- Amount of time required for indexing; similarly, time required for index updates across distributed search systems in case of document updation or deletion.

- High availability of distributed search. In case of failures of power, or nodes participating in the distributed search, the availability of the distributed search application is a must. The search must continue to perform as is with a performance degradation.

- Replication/backup should be one of the goals. In case of failures of the node holding shard, the replicated node (backup) must be able to recover in the shortest amount of time.

- Balancing of load (shards) across various nodes, to ensure optimal performance from the complete cluster.

- Query distribution across multiple nodes depending upon the availability.

Distributed search architecture

There are two important functions of any enterprise search: creation of indexes and runtime searching on indexes. Any or either of these functions can run in distributed mode, depending upon the requirements from an enterprise.

To utilize the distributed search, the indexing must be split into multiple shards and should be kept across multiple nodes of a distributed system. The shard is a complete index, and it can be queried independently. The search application has to be smart enough to query multiple nodes, collect and combine the results, and return to the client. The following architecture diagram depicts the overall scenario:

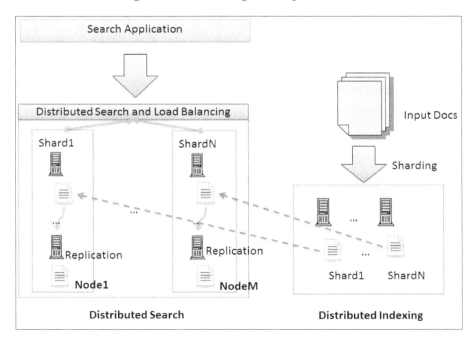

Based on the distributed architecture requirements, the following types of enterprise distributed search implementation scenarios can be found:

- **Master/Slave**: This is where there is one master and multiple slaves. The master is responsible for routing, and the slaves perform the search on the index shards.

- **Multinodes**: This is when all the nodes are masters, and the index is divided among them. The search is assigned to any one of the nodes, based on the load by balancer.

- **Multitenant**: This is used when multiple index/shards are part of the enterprise search application. This is used by the service that provides search capabilities to different tenants. This can use the multinode or master-slave approach.

Apache Solr and distributed search

By design, Apache Lucene and Solr are designed to support large-scale implementations. Apache Solr-based distributed environment is useful when:

- **Speeding up the search**: If Apache Solr is taking longer for the creation of indexes from data or for searching on a keyword across the index store, it is possibly the best candidate to run in a distributed environment.

- **Index generation time**: Incremental generation of indexes at faster speeds is an important aspect during the lifecycle of enterprise search. Distributed Solr can add faster performance.

- **Large indexes**: In cases when you have large indexes, a distribution of search index by means of partitioning adds a lot of value in terms of performance. An increase in index creates complexity.

At the same time, having your search distributed can address the following problems:

- No single point of failure for your search engine. With effective replication of indexes, this can be achieved. This requires ensuring additional systems, such as load balancer or DNS, to provide high availability on top of your search application. Commercial Amazon **ELB (Elastic Load Balancing)** provides such capabilities. More information is available at `http://aws.amazon.com/elasticloadbalancing/`.

- High availability of the system in spite of multiple nodes failing due to a high replication factor.

- Faster response time to searched data.

Apache Solr started support for distributed search since the release of 1.3. This approach had a straightforward way of creating shards and their replicas out of the document index, keeping it on different nodes in the distributed system, and finally running search with the parameter shards to run the search in a distributed manner. This system had its own limitations in terms of functionalities and feature support. We will not be covering the legacy distributed search support of Apache Solr here; the information about it can be found on the Solr wiki (`http://wiki.apache.org/solr/DistributedSearch` or `https://cwiki.apache.org/confluence/display/solr/Legacy+Scaling+and+Distribution`).

There have been efforts made to enable Apache Solr to work with the Apache Hadoop platform in the past. The integration between Hadoop and Solr is possible in the following ways:

- **Solr-1045 Patch**: This is used for generating the index through Apache Hadoop map task
- **Solr-1301 Patch**: This is used for generating the index through Apache Hadoop reduce task
- **Katta**: This is the open source software for distributed Hadoop and Solr
- **Solr on HDFS**: Running Solr on HDFS as a filesystem
- **SolBase**: This uses Apache Solr and HBase together

The Katta project is an open source project that enables you to store your data in a distributed manner without any failures. Although we do not see a lot of active development happening in the project, a lot of organizations have taken Katta and customized it to address their needs for distributed search. With Katta together with Hadoop and Solr, one can achieve distributed and replicated configuration of Apache Solr. There are two important tasks that can be deployed in the Hadoop framework with the help of Katta: indexing and searching. More information about Katta/Solr-1301 and Solr-1045 approaches can be found in the book *Scaling Big Data with Hadoop and Solr, Hrishikesh Karambelkar, Packt Publishing*.

Later, in October 2012, the Apache Solr community released Solr with the SolrCloud feature to enable direct support for distributed search from inside Solr. Many consumers use the old as well as new approach of supporting distributed search. Let's understand SolrCloud in more detail in the next section.

Understanding SolrCloud

SolrCloud provides a new way to enable distributed enterprise search using Apache Solr in enterprises. Previously, with the standard distributed Solr support, a lot of the manual work has been automated by SolrCloud. With the introduction of SolrCloud, the manual steps such as configuring `solr-config.xml` to talk with shards, adding documents to the shards, and similar type of work is automatic. Unlike the traditional approach of master- or slave-based distributed Solr, SolrCloud provides a leader-replica-based approach as its implementation. SolrCloud runs on top of Apache Zookeeper. First, let's understand Zookeeper.

Why Zookeeper?

SolrCloud contains a cluster of nodes, which talk with one another through Apache Zookeeper. Apache Zookeeper is responsible for maintaining coordination among various nodes. Besides coordinating among nodes, it also maintains configuration information, and group services to the distributed system. Due to its in-memory management of information, it offers distributed coordination at high speed.

 Apache Zookeeper itself is replicated over a set of nodes called ensemble. They all form a set called Zookeeper service. Each node that runs Zookeeper and stores its data is also called **znode**.

Each Zookeeper ensemble has one leader and many followers. The choice of the leader is on the start of the Zookeeper cluster. The Apache Zookeeper nodes contain information related to the distributed cluster, changes in the data, timestamp, **ACL** (**Access Control List**), as well as client-uploaded information. Zookeeper maintains a hierarchical metadata system unlike our conventional UNIX filesystem. The following figure depicts the structure of the Zookeeper in a distributed environment:

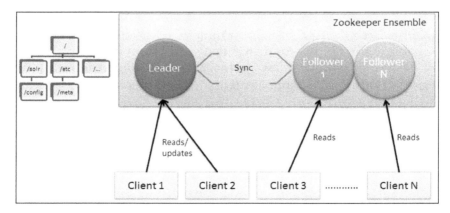

When the cluster is started, one of the nodes is elected as a leader. All others are followers. Each follower preserves the read-only copy of the leader's metadata in itself. The followers keep their metadata in sync with the leader by listening to the leader's atomic broadcast messages. A leader once broadcasted ensures the receipts by majority of the followers to commit the changes made and informs the client about transaction completion. This means that Apache Zookeeper ensures eventual consistency. The clients are allowed to upload their own information onto the Zookeeper and distribute it across the cluster. The clients can collect followers for reading the information. The Zookeeper maintains a sequential track of updates through its transaction logs; hence, it guarantees the sequential updates as they are received from different clients by the leader.

 Running Zookeeper in standalone mode is convenient for development and testing. But in production, you should run Zookeeper in replication. A replicated group of servers in the same application is called a **quorum**.

In case a leader fails, the next leader is chosen and the clients are expected to connect to the new leader. Apache Solr utilizes Zookeeper to enable distributed capabilities. By default, it provides the embedded Zookeeper along with its default installation. Apache Zookeeper was being used by many distributed systems including Apache Hadoop in the past.

SolrCloud architecture

We have already seen the concepts of shards and indexing in the earlier chapter. It is important to understand some terminologies used in SolrCloud. Unlike Apache Zookeeper, SolrCloud has a similar concept of leaders and replicas. Let's assume that we have to create a SolrCloud for the document database. Right now, the document database has a total of three documents, which are as follows:

```
Document [1] = "what are you eating"
Document [2] = "are you eating pie"
Document [3] = "I like apple pie"
```

The inverted index for these documents will be as follows:

```
what(1,1),are(1,2)(2,1),you(1,3)(2,2),eating(1,4)(2,3), pie(2,4)(3,4),
I(3,1),like(3,2), apple(3,3)
```

A collection is a complete set of indices in the SolrCloud cluster of nodes; in this case, it will be as follows:

```
what(1,1),are(1,2)(2,1),you(1,3)(2,2),eating(1,4)(2,3), pie(2,4)(3,4),
I(3,1),like(3,2), apple(3,3)
```

A shard leader in this case will be a piece of a complete index. A shard replica contains a copy of the same shard. Together, the shard leader and the shard replica form a complete shard index or slice. Let's say we divide the index into three shards; they will look like the following code:

```
Shard1: what(1,1),are(1,2)(2,1),you(1,3)(2,2)
Shard2: eating (1,4)(2,3), pie(2,4)(3,4)
Shard3: I (3,1),like(3,2), apple(3,3)
```

If we assume that all shards are replicated on three machines, each node participating in the SolrCloud will contain one or more shards / shard replicas of the index; the setup will look similar to the setup shown in the following table:

Machine/VM	Solr instance – Port*
M1	`M1:8983/solr/`: Solr Shard1
	`M1:9983`: Zookeeper Leader
	`M1:8883/solr/`: Solr Shard3-Replica
M1	`M1:8883/solr/`: Solr Shard2
	`M1:9983`: Zookeeper Follower
	`M1:8883/solr/`: Solr Shard1-Replica
M2	`M1:8983/solr/`: Solr Shard2-Replica
	`M1:9983/solr/`: Solr Shard3

* The follower/replica is decided automatically by Apache Zookeeper and Solr, by default.

A Solr core represents an instance of Apache Solr with complete configuration (including files, such as `solrconfig.xml`, schema files, stop words, and other essentials) that are required to run itself. In the preceding table, we can see a total of six Solr cores with each machine running two different cores.

The organization and interaction between multiple Solr cores and Zookeeper can be seen in the following system context diagram:

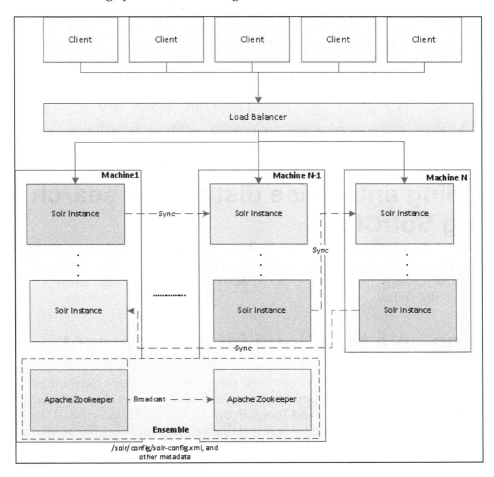

SolrCloud lets you create a cluster of Solr nodes, each of them running one or more collections. A collection holds one or more shards, which are hosted on one or more (in case of replication) nodes. Any updates to any nodes participating in SolrCloud can in turn sync with the rest of the nodes. It uses Apache Zookeeper to bring in distributed coordination and configuration among multiple nodes. This in turn enables near real-time searching on SolrCloud due to the active sync of indexes. Apache Zookeeper loads all the configuration files of Apache Solr in its own repository from the filesystem and allows nodes to access it in a distributed manner. With this, even if the instance goes away, the configuration will still be accessible to all other nodes. When a new core is introduced in SolrCloud, it registers with a Zookeeper server, by sharing information regarding core. SolrCloud may run one or more collections.

SolrCloud does index distribution to the appropriate shard; it also takes care of distributing search across multiple shards. Search is possible with near real time, after the document is committed. Zookeeper provides load balancing and failover to the Solr cluster making the overall setup more robust. Index partitioning can be done in the following ways using Apache Solr:

- **Simple**: This is done using the hashing function on a fixed number of shards.
- **Prefix based**: This involves partitioning based on the document ID, that is, `Red!12345`, `White!22321`. Red and White are prefixes used for partitioning.
- Custom: This is based on custom-defined partitioning, such as document creation time.

Building enterprise distributed search using SolrCloud

In this section, we will try to build a Solr cluster using Apache Solr's SolrCloud. SolrCloud can be built for development and for production. Development would contain an easy, smaller version whereas production would have a complex configuration.

Setting up a SolrCloud for development

The development environment typically does not require a fully fledged production-level landscape. Developers can simply set up a single machine proxy cluster of nodes on their development server. Each Solr instance can run on any J2EE container such as Jetty, Tomcat, and JBoss. In this mode, SolrCloud runs along with the internal Zookeeper provided by Solr installation. To start this, simply start your Jetty server using the following steps:

1. Download the latest version of Apache Solr from `http://lucene.apache.org/solr/downloads.html`.
2. Unzip the instance and go to `$SOLR_HOME/example`.
3. Now, run the following command:

   `$java -jar start.jar`

4. Stop the server. This step of running Solr in a non-Cloud mode is required to unpack the JAR files required for SolrCloud.

5. Modify the schema and other configuration files as per your requirements.

6. Now, start the Solr in cluster configuration with the following command:

```
java -DzkRun -DnumShards=2 -Dbootstrap_confdir=./solr/collection1/
conf -Dcollection.configName=solrconf -jar start.jar
```

Let's understand the different parameters in this process using the following table:

Parameter	Description
zkRun	This runs an instance of the embedded Zookeeper as a part of the Solr server. Run this on one of the nodes, which will serve as a central node for all the coordination.
collection.configName	This is used to set the configuration to be used for collection (optional).
bootstrap_confdir=<dir-name>	The given directory name should contain the complete configuration for SolrCloud, which will include all the configuration files such as solrconfig.xml, schema.xml. When Solr runs, the configuration is loaded in Zookeeper as the name given in collection.configName.
zkHost=<host>:<port>	This parameter points to the instance of the Zookeeper (Zookeeper ensemble) containing the cluster state and configuration.
numShards=<number>	Solr cloud can be run on one or multiple indexes; the number of shards denote the number of partitions to be carried out on these indexes.

You are required to run this command only for the first time, to push the necessary configuration on Zookeeper. The next time onwards, you can simply run the following:

```
java -DzkRun -jar start.jar
```

7. You will find on the console the Zookeeper selection for a leader, followed by all the configurations getting loaded in Zookeeper. Apache Zookeeper stores the metadata at `$SOLR_HOME/example/solr/zoo_data/`. Consider the following screenshot:

8. You can also validate the Solr configuration loaded in Zookeeper by going to `$SOLR_HOME\example\scripts\cloud-scripts` and running the following command to get `schema.xml` from the Zookeeper metadata store:

```
zkcli.bat -zkhost localhost:9983 -cmd get /configs/solrconf/
schema.xml
```

9. Now, create another Solr node, either by copying the `example` directory from `$SOLR_HOME` to `example1` under `$SOLR_CORE`, or creating another instance from the downloaded file `solr.zip`. You can do it on the same machine or on a different machine.

10. Now, run the following command:

```
java -Djetty.port=8888 -DzkHost=myhost:9983 -jar start.jar
```

11. This will start another node with shard. Now access `http://localhost:8983/solr/#/~cloud` and you will find the shards, with the collection and the way they are linked, as shown in the following screenshot:

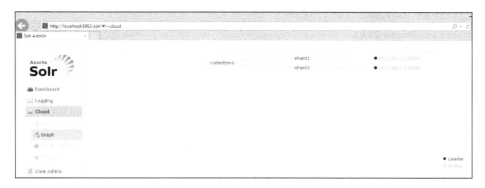

In the previous screenshot, Apache Solr administration user interface introspects among the nodes participating in the Cloud, and provides a graphical representation of leaders' active status. By default, the cluster continues in a round-robin fashion and adds shards, followed by replicas as and when a node is added. The round-robin algorithm ensures equal sharding for all the nodes that are participating. (More information can be found at `http://en.wikipedia.org/wiki/Round-robin_scheduling`.) Replicas are assigned automatically, unless their role is stated specifically by passing the `-DshardId=1` parameter.

Setting up a SolrCloud for production

To run a SolrCloud instance, with multinode, it is recommended to run it using a separate Zookeeper instead of going with the embedded Zookeeper. A fully distributed setup will require an Apache Zookeeper ensemble setup. Let's set up an Apache Zookeeper ensemble first using the following steps:

1. Download the latest version of Apache Zookeeper from `http://zookeeper.apache.org/releases.html#download`.

2. Copy and unzip it on all the nodes that are expected to participate in the Zookeeper ensemble.

3. Create a directory `zkdata` under `$ZK_HOME/`, and run the following command:

   $cat 1 > $ZK_HOME/zkdata/myid

   The number here denotes the ID of the server. Similarly, all the participating nodes should be assigned a unique identifier in this fashion.

4. Now, create $ZK_HOME/conf/zoo.cfg with the following entries:

```
dataDir=$ZK_HOME/zkdata
server.1=node1:2888:3888
server.2=node2:2888:3888
clientPort=2181
tickTime=2000
syncLimit=5
initLimit=10
```

A list of servers that participate in the Zookeeper service is provided by server.N. The ports 2888 and 3888 in case of server.1 denote the port for communication with peers and the port for leader selection, respectively. The initLimit variable is the maximum time in which Zookeeper in quorum should connect to the leader. The syncLimit variable denotes the maximum time of sync with the leader. While initLimit and syncLimit are units of tick, tickTime denotes the time of tick. In this case, tickTime is 2000 milliseconds, which means the server will have sync every 10000 ms. In this case, Zookeeper will run in a replicated mode, where node1 and node2 are replicated.

5. You need to make sure the node1 and node2 entries are the names of the nodes, and ensure your host or DNS resolves them to the appropriate IP addresses. You can find the host file at /etc/host in Unix, and in Windows, you will find it at %System Root%\system32\drivers\etc\hosts.

6. Run all Zookeeper nodes by running the following command:

```
$ZK_HOME/bin/zkServer.cmd or zkServer.sh
```

7. Check if the instance is available by connecting to the Zookeeper server. You can do this by running the following command:

```
bin\zkCli.cmd -server node1:2181
```

8. Now, connect to Zookeeper by running the following command:

```
[zk:] connect node1:2181
..............................
[zk: node1:2181(CONNECTED) 2]
```

9. Run the Zookeeper client commands such as `ls` (list directory) to validate the current metadata of Apache Zookeeper; you can do this in shell using the following code:

```
[zk: node1:2181(CONNECTED) 2] ls
```

You can also choose to configure logger for Zookeeper. This will in turn help you find out issues quickly for the initial start. Consider the following screenshot:

```
23    zookeeper.root.logger=INFO, CONSOLE
24    zookeeper.console.threshold=INFO
25    zookeeper.log.dir=/var/hrishi/zookeeper/log/
26    zookeeper.log.file=zookeeper.log
27    zookeeper.log.threshold=DEBUG
28    zookeeper.tracelog.dir=/var/hrishi/zookeeper/trace-log/
29    zookeeper.tracelog.file=zookeeper_trace.log
```

Now that your Apache Zookeeper ensemble is set up, we can configure Apache Solr in the recommended setup for production using Jetty. In case of Apache Tomcat or any other container, the parameters should be passed as per the container-specific parameter passing mechanism.

10. You need to follow steps similar to that of the development setup. Download and unzip the instance at every node that is participating in the SolrCloud.

11. Now identify the number of shards and accordingly set the parameters. Start with one of the nodes as follows:

```
java -DnumShards=2 -Dbootstrap_confdir=./solr/collection1/conf
-Dcollection.configName=testconf -DzkHost=node1:2181,node2:2181
-jar start.jar
```

Please note that all the Zookeeper nodes in the replicated phase have to be passed to the `-DzkHost` parameters in a comma-separated manner.

12. Once this server is up, the other nodes can be started using the following command:

```
java -Djetty.port=<your-choice-of-port> -DzkHost=<zkeeper-
leader>:2183 -jar start.jar
```

Once the nodes are started, you can validate it through the administration user interface. The Solr admin provides additional information. The Tree view provides directory browsing of Cloud-based configuration that is part of Zookeeper; you can access it by browsing `http://localhost:8983/solr/#/~cloud?view=tree`. Consider the following screenshot:

The admin UI shows information related to the cluster, the current shards along with the leaders, the status of a cluster, and the Solr cluster configuration. You can also use utility `zkCLI` (command line) to read/write the data to and from the Zookeeper store.

Adding a document to SolrCloud

To add a document in Solr, you can simply choose any node part of your cluster and run the following command:

```
curl http://node1:8983/solr/update/json -H 'Content-type:application/
json' -d
'
[
{"id" : "1", "text" : "This is a test document"},
]'
```

You can also load files from the example directory as shown in the following command:

```
curl http://node1:8983/solr/update/csv --data-binary @books.csv -H
'Content-type:text/plain; charset=utf-8'
```

The preceding command uploads the CSV file. Once this is complete, validate the uploaded document by running the query through the browser/administration window, or simply by typing `http://localhost:8983/solr/collection1/select ?q=*%3A*&wt=json&indent=true` in the browser.

Then, `node1` in the Solr cluster receives a request for indexing the document. If the document is a replica, it forwards it to the leader of the shard. Each leader performs hashing on the document ID, based on its prefix or automatically, and if the leader does not own the responsibility of that shard, it has to forward it to the leader of the shard. Once the correct leader receives the document, it updates its transactional log, and forwards the document to its replica for replication. While the document is received first, it is assigned the version ID. The leader first tries to see if it has a higher version; if it does, the leader will simply ignore the uploaded document.

> Solr transactional log is an append-only log of write operations per node in a cluster. Solr records all the write operations before the write commit, and marks it post commit. If the indexing process is stopped for some reason, the next time, Solr first reviews transaction logs, and then completes the pending indexing.

Creating shards, collections, and replicas in SolrCloud

You can create shards, collections, and their replicas on SolrCloud through the web-based handlers provided by Solr by uploading them using the CURL utility. Now, let us try an exercise of creating a distributed search index (shard) with replicas on one collection for SolrCloud. First, we need to start with the creation of a collection (that is, `clusterCollection`) assuming the replication of 3, and the maximum shards per node is 2, as shown in the following command:

```
curl 'http://node1:8983/solr/admin/collections?action=CREATE&name=clus
terCollection&numShards=3&replicationFactor=3&maxShardsPerNode=2'
```

This will create a collection with the name `clusterCollection` on Solr. We have already linked its configuration through Zookeeper earlier.

Now, let's create replicas of the shards by running the following command; this command has to run for each replica you intend to create in your Solr instance:

```
curl 'http://node1:8983/solr/admin/cores?action=CREATE&name=shardA-Replic
a1&collection=clusterCollection&shard=shardA'
```

```
curl 'http://node2:8983/solr/admin/cores?action=CREATE&name=shardB-Replic
a2&collection=clusterCollection&shard=shardA'
```

The following example shows how the admin UI will show the shard distribution of your indexes:

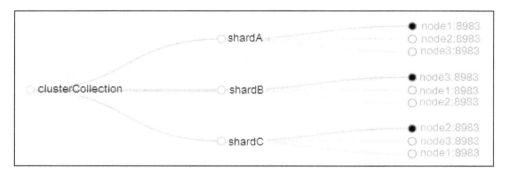

Now, the documents can directly be posted to any of the nodes hosting Solr index. The following example shows uploading of default documents shipped with Solr on this Cloud instance:

```
cd $SOLR_HOME/example/exampledocs/
java -Durl=http://node1:8983/solr/clusterCollection/update -jar post.
jar ipod_video.xml
java -Durl=http://node2:8983/solr/clusterCollection/update -jar post.
jar monitor.xml
```

You can simply verify it by accessing the Solr instance with a wildcard query as follows:

```
http://node1:8983/solr/clusterCollection/select?q=*:*
```

Common problems and resolutions

Now the installation is successful. Let's try to address some of the common problems and their solutions you may face during setup.

Question: I have been using SolrCloud for a long time. Now when I run it, it shows me some of the old nodes in the current cluster landscape. How do I fix it?

Answer: This can be fixed by cleaning the Zookeeper metadata; however, first you need to back up the existing Zookeeper metadata using the zkCLI command (the get/getfile calls). Once you back up the Zookeeper, shut down all the instances, and rename the zoo_data directory under $SOLR_HOME/example/solr to some other name, and then restart SolrCloud and Zookeeper. This will recreate the Zookeeper configuration again and add configuration directories. You can validate the new cluster configuration of Apache Zookeeper by running zkCLI with the following command:

```
[zk: node1:2181(CONNECTED) 4] get /clusterstate.json
```

This will show the complete details of the cluster. You can also validate this through the administration console by browsing the /clusterstate.json file as shown in the following screenshot:

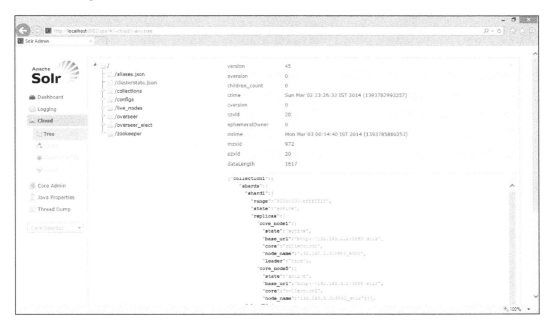

Question: I am getting a lot of exceptions from Solr with connection timeout as the error description. What should be done?

Answer: Since the connections are timing out, one possibility is that the leader himself is going down or the responses are slow due to network latency. This can be fixed by increasing the timeout of Apache Zookeeper. The Zoo.cfg file contains tick time (usually 2 seconds); this should not be touched; instead modify the zkClientTimeout property in solrconfig.xml to work with more ticks for Zookeeper.

Question: I have a single node Solr instance with information indexed as of now. Can I anyhow migrate this index to SolrCloud?

Answer: There is no support for this kind of problem in Apache Solr (Version 4.6), so in this case, you need to re-parse all the documents, and re-index them one more time.

Case study – distributed enterprise search server for the software industry

Let's look at one of the cases for building a SolrCloud for ABC Corporation. The company is multinational, and has offices in 10 different countries. The development centre for this company is in two countries. ABC Corporation has many functions, such as HR, accounting, project management, and so on. These functions exist at all offices. Now the company would like to build highly optimized, high availability, and reliable search for their organization. The company has the following data to be searched and analyzed across the organization:

- Human resource data comes from all offices
    - Resumes
    - Employee information
    - Files store (coming from knowledge management applications)
- Source code and documents related to products produced by the development centre
- Finance-related information comes from multiple software (all offices)

In this case, we will focus on the design aspects of the cluster, and skip the other aspects, such as knowledge management. We can create two different collections of data. This is because the development office requires access to additional information, which every other office does not require. So, /devcollection can focus on source code, and other development office specific artifacts, whereas / hrcollection can focus on the more global aspects of ABC Corporation, which covers HR and finance functions. A load balancer will be required to balance the amount of requests that get flooded on SolrCloud. Many times, read requests can be redirected to followers. Apache Zookeeper too can run in high availability replicated mode. The following schematic diagram shows the example architecture for a given problem:

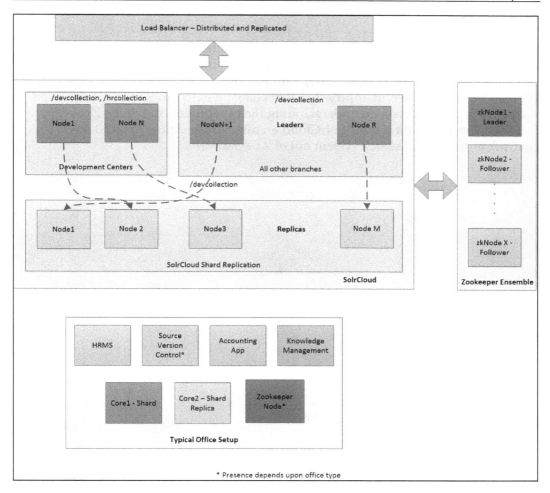

The figure also shows what a typical office setup would look like. Any single office landscape would have its own management set of software, along with the instance of the Zookeeper (depending upon how many are expected). This kind of configuration will ensure high availability in the context of any disasters and natural calamities since the setup is totally distributed across multiple offices. Since all offices are going to access the Solr-based enterprise search, they can go for localized cached Solr instance (replica) of the leader for all reads. So, a distributed load balancer can help detect the current office from the request, and redirect it to the respective Apache Solr.

Summary

In this chapter, we have gone through various aspects of distributed search. We started with understanding the needs behind distributed search, and how Apache Solr can enable your enterprise search with the distributed options that are available. We also looked at different approaches that enable you to run Solr in a distributed manner. We then focused on understanding the capabilities of Apache Zookeeper and SolrCloud. We studied the SolrCloud architecture and how to build an enterprise-distributed search system out of Apache Solr.

7
Scaling Solr through Sharding, Fault Tolerance, and Integration

In the previous chapters, we went through various aspects of Apache Solr, including its capabilities, features, and different case studies. In *Chapter 6*, *Distributed Search Using Apache Solr*, we looked at SolrCloud, which provides excellent scaling capabilities with features such as distributed Solr instances with replication for high availability. The capabilities of Apache Solr have enabled organizations to indulge themselves in Apache Solr-based solution development. This demand in turn triggered the need to integrate Apache Solr-based enterprise search to work with mature high-performance open source software available today to achieve the best of both worlds.

There are many parallel tracks that are going on along with the Apache Solr open source community. These tracks focus on enhancing the integration of Solr with different tools to overall achieve objectives of high-scale Solr. We are going to look at some of these aspects from this chapter onwards. This chapter does not only focus on scaling aspects of Apache Solr, but it also provides readers access to some of the advanced topics of Solr integration, such as result clustering. In this chapter, we will look at how Apache Solr can be further scaled with the help of different open source tools available today. In this chapter, we will be focusing on following aspects:

- Enable search result clustering through Carrot2
- Sharding and fault tolerance for SolrCloud
- Searching Solr documents in real time
- Solr and MongoDB
- Scaling Solr with Storm

All the examples provided in this chapter are tested on Apache Solr 4.7 releases.

Enabling search result clustering with Carrot2

Carrot2 is an application suite to provide document cluster on top of your dataset. It analyzes a set of documents and classifies them into multiple groups based on similarity. The similarities between the documents on various aspects can be used to cluster the documents in different groups. Cluster analysis is very useful, because it provides automatic categorization of your information so that users can browse a flat information model hierarchically.

 Cluster analysis techniques are useful in organization for statistical analysis. For example, a cluster analysis over the customer database enables an organization to classify the customers based on different patterns and plan the future strategies to improve upon the sales. Such analysis can be done using different algorithms research done by many statisticians. Among the famous ones are partitioning and hierarchy based.

Carrot2 is BSD licensed, and it can be utilized with any search engine such as Apache Lucene and Apache Solr. More information on Carrot2 can be found at http://project.carrot2.org/. There is also a live demo available at http://search.carrot2.org/stable/search, as shown in the following screenshot:

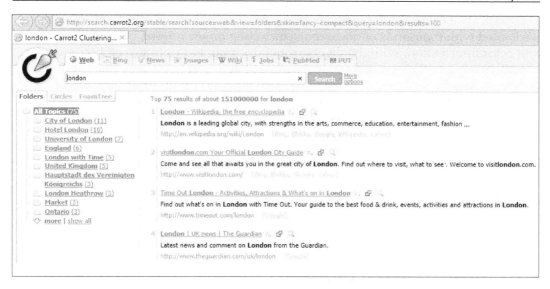

Why Carrot2?

Apache Solr can search across millions of documents and provide a subset of them as a matched search result to the end user. The results shown to end users are ordered based on the search result relevancy, which depends upon the TF-IDF algorithm used by Apache Solr. Besides these, Solr provides additional faceting for better browsing experience. Although these features provide users with a simplified manner of browsing, it is still questionable whether the results add a significant value in terms of logical grouping of information.

Apache Solr Facets are mainly based on schema element, whereas relevancy focuses on searched keywords and their occurrences in the results. The missing element here is the semantic proximity of each of the matched documents with the other so as to group them based on similarities.

Let's look at an example: the search engine is built on top of a movie database, and it's loaded with thousands of documents, including movie release, critics, ratings, and actor information. With the diverse set of documents, faceting itself becomes a challenging act. A user searches for "Nicholas Cage" and "John Travolta" on this database. Apache Solr-based search will match with thousands of documents, and it will parse them accordingly. Facets will provide static browsing experience based on the predefined schema element, as we have seen in earlier chapters. The relevancy scoring will render the documents based on the scoring of term frequency and inverse document frequency. The add-on value to this outcome will be a dynamic classification of search results, which will probably have classification types such as movies, award functions, and television series. In our example, a search for "John Travolta" will match with different database entities such as movies, videos, interviews, events, and films directed. Carrot2 will provide this classification dynamically. Using Carrot2 is feasible to get a dynamic classification with the help of clustering.

Enabling Carrot2-based document clustering

Apache Solr ships with Carrot2 libraries from Solr 4.0 onwards; however, due to library-licensing concerns, they are not added directly into `solr.war`. To enable Carrot2-based cluster for your Solr system, execute the following steps:

1. Download the latest version of Apache Solr from the Solr download page.

2. Unzip it, and run it once with the following command:

    `$java -jar solr.jar`

3. Let the instance start and access the following URL:
    `http://localhost:8983/solr/browse`.

4. Now, shutdown the instance, go to `$SOLR_HOME/contrib/clustering/lib`, and copy all JAR files to `$SOLR_HOME/example/solr-webapp/webapp/WEB-INF/lib` or to the container `lib` folder. In case you are running Tomcat or any other application container, you can open `solr.war`, copy these JAR files in `WEB-INF/lib`, and redeploy the application.

5. Now, add `-Dsolr.clustering.enabled=true` to your container startup file. In case of Jetty, start with the following command:

    `$ java -Dsolr.clustering.enabled=true -jar start.jar`

6. Once it is started, load your documents using either SolrJ, post utility, or through `dataImportHandler`.

7. Now, run the following query through the following browser: `http://localhost:8983/solr/clustering?q=*:*&rows=10`. You will find an additional XML component added to your response called "clustering", as shown in the following snippet:

```
<response>
  <lst name="responseHeader">
  </lst>
  <result name="response" numFound="32" start="0" maxScore="1.0">
...........................<snipped/>................................
  </result>
  <arr name="clusters">
    <lst>
      <arr name="labels">
        <str>Book</str>
      </arr>
      <double name="score">1.3174612693376382</double>
      <arr name="docs">
        <str>ISBN#1378</str><str>ISBN#1748</str><str>ISBN#1222<//
str>
      </arr>
    </lst>
  </arr>
</response>
```

This additional element can be parsed, and the user interface can be enhanced to support clustering-based facet in the user interface layer.

Understanding Carrot2 result clustering

The clustering component in Apache Solr was introduced as a part of JIRA SOLR-769 (more information is available at `https://issues.apache.org/jira/browse/SOLR-769`) to support Mahout- and Carrot2-based clustering for Solr results. Carrot2 in Solr understands the document title, its URL/location, and content. Titles carry more importance in terms of document clustering. Carrot2 analyzes each document snippet carefully, not just a token of words but even the sentences (for example, phrases). Hence, it can work on stored fields only.

In `solrconfig.xml`, the following entries demonstrate its current placement in default the Solr install:

```
<searchComponent name="clustering"
                 enable="${solr.clustering.enabled:false}"
                 class="solr.clustering.ClusteringComponent" >
    <lst name="engine">
        <str name="name">lingo</str>
        <str name="carrot.algorithm">org.carrot2.clustering.lingo.LingoClusteringAlgorithm</str>
        <str name="carrot.resourcesDir">clustering/carrot2</str>
    </lst>
    <lst name="engine">
        <str name="name">stc</str>
        <str name="carrot.algorithm">org.carrot2.clustering.stc.STCClusteringAlgorithm</str>
    </lst>
    <lst name="engine">
        <str name="name">kmeans</str>
        <str name="carrot.algorithm">org.carrot2.clustering.kmeans.BisectingKMeansClusteringAlgorithm</str>
    </lst>
</searchComponent>
<requestHandler name="/clustering"
                startup="lazy"
                enable="${solr.clustering.enabled:false}"
                class="solr.SearchHandler">
    <lst name="defaults">
        <bool name="clustering">true</bool>
        <bool name="clustering.results">true</bool>
        <str name="carrot.title">name</str>
        <str name="carrot.url">id</str>
        <str name="carrot.snippet">features</str>
        <bool name="carrot.produceSummary">true</bool>
        <bool name="carrot.outputSubClusters">false</bool>
        <str name="defType">edismax</str>
        <str name="qf">
          text^0.5 features^1.0 name^1.2 sku^1.5 id^10.0 manu^1.1 cat^1.4
        </str>
        <str name="q.alt">*:*</str>
```

If you intend to use clustering all the time, you can modify `searchComponent` of your `solrconfig.xml` to `enable=true`, as shown in the following screenshot:

Carrot2 has a separate request handler defined which is `/clustering`, the location where the clustered results can be accessed. More information on different types of parameters can be seen at `http://wiki.apache.org/solr/ClusteringComponent#Parameters`.

Additionally, each algorithm has its own parameters; the configuration files for these parameters can be found in the $SOLR_HOME/conf/clustering/carrot2 folder. The results have to be fetched in advance to provide better clustering experience instead of the usual set.

> Although Solr and Carrot2 together provide effective clustering through a uniform interaction, there is additional cost in terms of performance incurred by additional processing required by Carrot2. It also needs to pick up the results in advance to provide effective clustering. The performance impact can be minimized by reducing the amount of processing done by Carrot2 in run-time. This can be done by reducing the number of search results to some minimal count. Additionally, applying standard optimization techniques such as stop words and stemming, the performance of the subsystem can be enhanced further.
>
> More details can be read on Solr's clustering wiki at http://wiki.apache.org/solr/ClusteringComponent#Performance_impact.

Viewing Solr results in the Carrot2 workbench

The Carrot2 suite of applications comes with different subproducts. They are as follows:

- Carrot2 document clustering workbench: This is mainly used to observe the results that are GUI based

- Carrot2 APIs (C# and Java): This is used for integration; Solr uses these APIs

- Carrot2 document clustering server: The Carrot2 functionality can be exposed as RESTful service through this server

- Carrot2 command line interface (CLI): It allows invoking Carrot2 clustering from the command line directly

- Carrot2 web application: This provides rich web-based application for end users

To visualize the results in the Carrot2 workbench, you can download the Carrot2 workbench from the Carrot2 download page (described previously) and run it. Now, provide the source as Solr, algorithm, the query string, title field name and click on the **process** button. The following screenshot showcases the Solr clustering with Carrot2 rendered on the workbench with the default dataset shipped with Apache Solr:

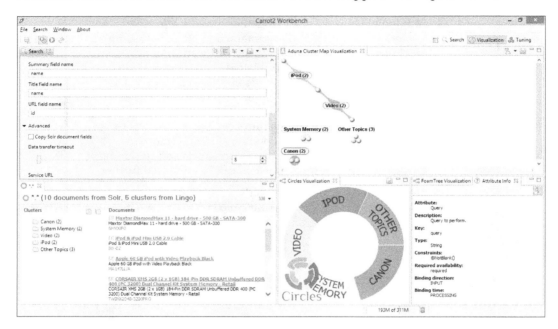

In the previous screenshot, it can be observed that out of 10 documents, five different clusters are created based on different document metadata. The placement of each cluster and how they are linked can be seen in the cluster map. As the graph renders, iPod and video are much closer as compared to system memory or canon.

FAQs and problems

Let's try to address some of the common problems, which you may face during the setup, and their solutions:

- I have followed the steps, and when I run my Solr server, I get `NoClassDefFoundException` in my console. What can I do?

  You need to make sure that all the JAR files are in the correct classpath (`/contrib/clustering`) of your Solr container so that they can be picked up by your container. In Apache Solr 3.X, the JAR files are different from 4.X. It is recommended that you make it part of your `solr.war`, so as to make it accessible only inside from Apache Solr.

- I am impressed by the Carrot2 clustered rendering; can I use it as my end user interface to render Solr results?

  It's possible to use Carrot2-based web application inside your web application. Carrot2 provides a demo application by default. You can use multiple integration strategies to integrate your Solr with Carrot2. To see the strategies, you can also visit the following link: `http://carrot2.github.io/solr-integration-strategies/carrot2-3.6.3/index.html`.

In this section, we have understood Carrot2 and how it can be worked with Apache Solr effectively. We will be focusing on sharding in the next chapter.

Sharding and fault tolerance

We have already seen sharding, collection, and replicas in *Chapter 6, Distributed Search Using Apache Solr*. In this section, we will look at some of the important aspects of sharding and how it plays a role in scalability and high availability. The strategy to create new shards is highly dependent upon the hardware and shard size. Let's say, you have two machines, A and B, of the same configuration, each with one shard. Shard A is loaded with 1 million index documents, and shard B is loaded with 100 documents. When a query is fired, the query response to any Solr query is determined by the query response of the slowest node (in this case, shard A). Hence, a shard with near to equal shard sizes can perform better in this case.

Document routing and sharding

We have seen the leader-selection process in *Chapter 6, Distributed Search Using Apache Solr*. Typically, when any enterprise search is deployed, the size of documents to be indexed keeps growing over time. As SolrCloud provides a way to create a cluster of Solr nodes that run on index shards, it becomes feasible to scale the enterprise search infrastructure with time. However, as the shard sizes grow, it becomes difficult to manage them on a single shard. SolrCloud can be started with numOfShards by controlling the number of shards that run in the cloud. To route the newly indexed documents, take a look at the following flowchart:

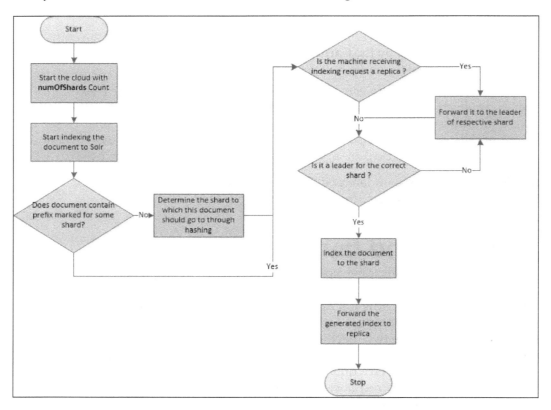

When a Solr instance is started, it first registers itself with Zookeeper, creating Ephemeral Node or z nodes. A Zookeeper provides a shared hierarchical namespace for processes to coordinate with each other. The namespace consists of registered data called znodes. Apache Solr provides you with two ways to distribute the Solr document across shards. Auto sharding distributes the documents automatically through its own hashing algorithm. Each shard is allocated with a range for hashing, and it can be seen in /clusterstate.json, as shown in the following screenshot:

```
{"collection1":{
    "shards":{
      "shard1":{
        "range":"80000000-ffffffff",
        "state":"active",
        "replicas":{"core_node1":{
            "state":"active",
            "base_url":"http://192.168.2.4:8983/solr",
            "core":"collection1",
            "node_name":"192.168.2.4:8983_solr",
            "leader":"true"}}},
      "shard2":{
        "range":"0-7fffffff",
        "state":"active",
        "replicas":{}}},
    "maxShardsPerNode":"1",
    "router":{"name":"compositeId"},
    "replicationFactor":"1",
    "autoCreated":"true"}}
```

Another way of distributing the document across a shard is to use custom sharding. With custom sharding, client applications that pass documents for indexing to Apache Solr are primarily responsible to place them in the shard. Each document has a unique ID attribute, and a shard key can be prefixed to this ID, for example, shard1!docId55. The ! operator acts as a separator. Custom sharding helps users in influencing the storage for their document indexes.

Users can choose various strategies to distribute the shards across different nodes for efficient usage. Similarly, a query can be performed on a specific shard (instead of complete index) by passing shard.keys=shard1!,shard2! as a query parameter. These features enable Apache Solr to work in a multitenancy environment or as regional distributed search. You can also spread tenants across multiple shards by introducing another prefix for the unique ID. The syntax for this is Shard_key/number!doc_id.

Shard splitting

The feature of Shard splitting was introduced in Apache Solr 4.3. It is designed to work with Apache Solr's auto-sharding. It allows users to split shards without breaking the search run-time or even the indexing. A shard can be split into two by running the following URL on your browser:

```
http://localhost:8983/solr/admin/collections?collection=collection1&s
hard=[shard_name]&action=SPLITSHARD
```

As you split the shards, the average query performance tends to slow down. The call to SPLITSHARD will create two new shards (shard1_1, and shard1_2 out of shard1), as shown in the following screenshot:

The numbers of documents are divided equally across these two subshards; once the split is complete, shard1 will be made inactive. The new subshards get created in construction state, and the index updates on shard start getting forwarded to new subshards. Once the splitting is complete, the parent shard becomes inactive. The old shard can be deleted by calling DELETESHARD in the following way:

```
http://localhost:8983/solr/admin/
collections?collection=collection1&shard=shard1&action=DELETESHARD
```

With large index sizes, the search performance can become slow. Auto-sharding in Solr lets you start with a fixed number of shards, and shard splitting offers an easy way to reduce the size of each shard across Solr cores as the index size grows.

 Although the parent shard is inactive, the Solr Admin UI does not become aware of the states and shows the parent shard in green (active state)..

Load balancing and fault tolerance in SolrCloud

SolrCloud provides built-in load-balancing capabilities to its clients. So, when a request is sent to one of the servers, it is redirected to the respective leader to get all the information. Fault tolerance in SolrCloud is the ability to continue in a degraded form in case of failure of Solr nodes. If your client application is Java-based, you can rely on the `CloudSolrServer` and `LbHttpSolrServer` (load-balanced HTTP server) classes of SolrJ to perform indexing and search across SolrCloud. `CloudSolrServer` will load balance queries across all operational servers automatically. The Java code through SolrJ for search on SolrCloud looks like the following:

```
CloudSolrServer server = new CloudSolrServer("localhost:9983");
server.setDefaultCollection("collection1");
SolrQuery solrQuery = new SolrQuery("*.*");
QueryResponse response = server.query(solrQuery);
SolrDocumentList dList = response.getResults();
for (int i = 0; i < dList.getNumFound(); i++)
{
for (Map.Entry mE : dList.get(i).entrySet())
{
        System.out.println(mE.getKey() + ":" + mE.getValue());
    }
}
```

Fault tolerance is the ability to keep the system functions working with degraded support, even in case of failure of system components. Fault tolerance in SolrCloud is managed at different levels.

As SolrCloud performs its own load balancing, a call to any one of the nodes participating in the cloud can be made. Applications that do not rely on Java-based client may require a load balancer to fire queries. The intent of load balancer is not to balance the load but to remove the single point of failure for the calling party. So, in case of the failure of node1, load balancer can forward the query to node2, thus enabling fault tolerance in Apache Solr.

When a search request is fired on SolrCloud, the request gets executed on all leaders of that shard (unless the user chooses shard in his query). If one of the nodes is failing to respond to a Solr query due to some error, the wait for the final search result can be avoided by enabling support for partial results. This support can be enabled by passing `shards.tolerant=true`. This read-side fault tolerance ensures that the system returns the results in spite of unavailability of the node.

Apache Solr also supports write-side fault tolerance, which makes the instance durable even in case of power failures, restarts, JVM crash, and so on. Each node participating in Solr maintains a transaction log that tracks all the changes to the node. This logging helps a Solr node to recover in case of failures or interruption during the indexing operation. We are going to look at write-side fault tolerance in the next section.

Searching Solr documents in near real time

Apache Solr performs indexing on the updated data, and the data is available for search. In many cases, the index-generation job is run during offline hours (late nights, weekends) to update the search with the newer data. Until this point, Apache Solr cannot search for documents added in the customer document repository. Many times, the demand is to make a document available for search as and when it is uploaded to the customer repository. Apache Solr can perform search on these documents in near real time. There is a delay to generate index for a document and to make it available for search; hence, Apache Solr can support near real-time search on documents.

Strategies for near real-time search in Apache Solr

In Apache Solr, a commit operation is required to enable the document to be made available for searching. Commit operation in Apache Solr involves Solr access transaction logs (or update logs), which pick the identifiers and sync the index files on the storage system, thus making the index store available, even in case of shutdown or restart. Considering the large index-loading scenario, the commit on huge index takes a longer time. During this time, the documents that are getting loaded on Apache Solr are not searchable.

In near real-time search, Apache Solr provides a way to enable soft commit. A soft commit in Apache Solr does not flush changes back to the underlying storage; instead, it makes it available in memory and persists it to the disk in the next hard commit. In case of a power failure or JVM crash, Apache Solr can remember the state of last hard commit. Although, soft commit does not guarantee indexing changes to be made persistent, they can be searched. Additionally, a transaction log in Solr can be enabled to ensure that there is no loss of indexing data. As all the commit operations are held in a queue waiting to be flushed to index files, soft commit offers a limit through the following parameters:

- Maximum number of documents (also called `maxDocs`)
- Maximum time (`maxTime` in milliseconds)

Apache Solr offers different commit strategies for clients to persist the changes in Solr repository. Let us look at these strategies.

Explicit call to commit from a client

A client can call explicit commit on its data changes, either soft or hard, directly by passing a set of parameters. The following `curl` example shows the call with explicit commit:

```
curl http://localhost:8983/solr/update?commit=true -H "Content-Type:
text/xml" --data-binary '<add><doc><field name="id">testdoc</field></
doc></add>'
```

In case of a soft commit, the command would be as follows:

```
curl "http://localhost:8983/solr/update?softCommit=true" -H
"Content-type:application/xml" --data-binary "<add><doc><field
name='id'>testcommit2</field><field name='name'>Hrishikesh
Karambelkar</field></doc></add>"
```

Similarly, in SolrJ, you can use `ContentStreamUpdateRequest` or `UpdateRequest`, as shown in the following snippet:

```
    UpdateRequest req = new UpdateRequest();
      req.add(mySolrInputDocument);
      ..........
      req.setAction(AbstractUpdateRequest.ACTION.COMMIT, true, false,
true); //Parameters: ACTION, waitFlush, waitSearcher, softCommit
      req.process(server);
```

solrconfig.xml – autocommit

Apache Solr provides automatic commit functionality to avoid clients from running explicit commit calls. Auto commit can be based on maximum time or maximum number of documents. To enable autocommit, you need to put entries for autoCommit and/or autoSoftCommit in solrconfig.xml as follows:

```
<autoCommit>
  <maxTime>10000</maxTime>
</autoCommit>

<autoSoftCommit>
  < maxDocs >1000</maxDocs>
</autoSoftCommit>
```

CommitWithin – delegating the responsibility to Solr

CommitWithin allows users to rely on Apache Solr to perform time-bound commit changes to every Solr document uploaded. CommitWithin offers an opportunity to perform uploads without commit, and Apache Solr can handle bulk commits on its own. The buffered document is committed before the minimum commitWithin time is reached. CommitWithin provides a soft commit. The following curl call to Solr to upload the data will ensure that commit happens within 20 seconds:

```
curl "http://localhost:8983/solr/update?commitWithin=20000" -H
"Content-type:application/xml" --data-binary "<add><doc><field
name='id'>testcommit2</field><field name='name'>Hrishikesh
Karambelkar</field></doc></add>"
```

Similarly, SolrJ provides the setCommitWithin call inside the UpdateRequest class to put the timeline for document update.

Real-time search in Apache Solr

Interestingly, Apache Solr 4.0 and higher versions allow users to peek inside the data that has been loaded in the Solr repository, but not yet committed. It works by running search through the transaction logs that record all the updates happening in Apache Solr. Although Solr supports real-time search, they cannot be used inside facets or any other components of Solr. To enable a real-time search, users must ensure that the update logging is enabled (by default, it's enabled in Solr) by verifying the following lines in solrcloud.xml:

```
<updateLog>
      <str name="dir">${solr.ulog.dir:}</str>
</updateLog>
```

The logs are stored in the `${solr.ulog.dir:}` directory. The real-time results cannot be retrieved with traditional response handlers of Solr. It provides a `RealTimeGetHandler` class to enable searching through the logfiles as well for the potential search results. This can be verified by accessing `solrconfig.xml` and looking for its handler, which looks like the following screenshot:

```
<requestHandler name="/get" class="solr.RealTimeGetHandler">
  <lst name="defaults">
    <str name="omitHeader">true</str>
    <str name="wt">json</str>
    <str name="indent">true</str>
  </lst>
</requestHandler>
```

You can try out near real-time `get` by loading the information without any commit through the `curl` utility. Run the following command on the default schema:

```
curl "http://localhost:8983/solr/update" -H "Content-type:application/
xml" --data-binary "<add><doc><field name='id'>scalingsolr</
field><field name='name'>Hrishikesh Karambelkar</field></doc></add>"
```

Once it runs successfully, you can access `http://localhost:8983/solr/get?id=scalingsolr` from your browse to see the output, as shown in the following screenshot:

As the real time is based on update logs, even restarts of Apache Solr would provide search over all the older uncommitted changes. Real-time `get` works seamlessly, until the point where there are limited update operations taking place. Real-time Solr is very useful in places where there is a search expectation on continuous data.

Solr with MongoDB

MongoDB is one of the popular NOSQL databases, just like Cassandra. It supports the storage of any random schemas in the document-oriented storage of its own. MongoDB supports JSON-based information pipe for any communication with the server. This database is designed to work with heavy data. Today, many organizations are focusing on utilizing MongoDB for various enterprise applications.

Understanding MongoDB

MongoDB provides high availability and load balancing. Each data unit is replicated, and a combination of data with its copes is called replica set. Replicas in MongoDB can be either primary or secondary. Primary is an active replica that is used for direct read-write operation; the secondary replica works like a backup for primary. MongoDB supports search by field, range queries, and regular expression searches. Queries can return specific fields of documents and also include user-defined JavaScript functions. Any field in a MongoDB document can be indexed. More information about MongoDB can be read at `https://www.mongodb.org/`.

The data on MongoDB is eventually consistent. Apache Solr can be used to work with MongoDB to enable database-searching capabilities on MongoDB-based data store. Unlike Cassandra, where the Solr indexes are stored directly through Solandra, MongoDB integration with Solr brings in the indexes in Solr-based optimized storage.

There are various ways in which the data residing in MongoDB can be analyzed and searched. MongoDB's replication works by recording all operations done on a database in a logfile, called the oplog. Many of the implementers suggest reading this logfile using standard file IO program to push the data directly to Apache Solr using CURL or SolrJ. As oplog is a collection of data with an upper limit on maximum storage, such kind of querying is feasible to enable sync with Apache Solr. Oplog also provides tailable cursors on the database. These cursors can provide a natural order of the documents loaded in MongoDB, thus preserving the order. We are going to look at a different approach. Let's look at the following schematic diagram:

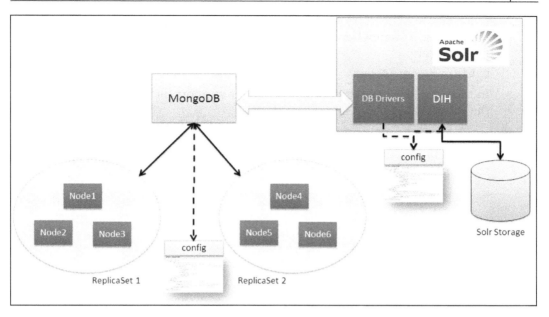

In this case, MongoDB is exposed as a database to Apache Solr through a custom database driver. Apache Solr reads MongoDB data through `DataImportHandler`; this in turn calls JDBC-based MongoDB driver to connect to MongoDB and run data import utilities. As MongoDB supports replica sets, it manages the distribution of data across nodes. It also supports sharding just like Apache Solr.

Installing MongoDB

To install MongoDB in your development environment, please follow the ensuing steps:

1. Download the latest version of MongoDB from `https://www.mongodb.org/downloads` for your supported operating system. Unzip the zipped folder at some place. MongoDB comes up with a default set of different command-line components and utilities. They are as follows:

    - `bin/mongod`: This is the database process
    - `bin/mongos`: This is the sharding controller
    - `bin/mongo`: This is the database shell (uses interactive JavaScript)

2. Now, create a directory for MongoDB to use it for user-data creation and management somewhere, and run the following command to start the single node server:

```
$ bin/mongod –dbpath <path to your data directory> --rest
```

In this case, the `--rest` parameter enables support for simple rest APIs to get the status.

3. Once the server is started, access `http://localhost:28017` from your favorite browser; you should be able to see the following administration status page:

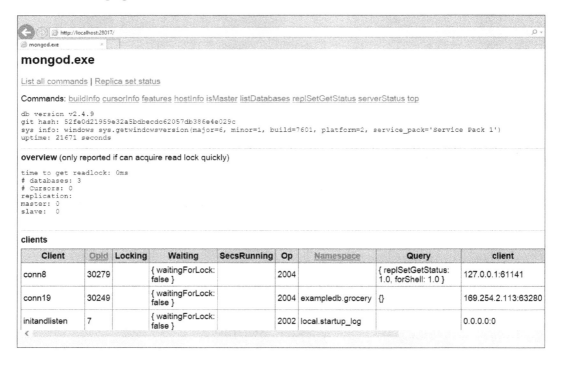

Now that you have successfully installed MongoDB, try loading a sample dataset from the book on MongoDB by opening a new command-line interface, changing the directory to `$MONGODB_HOME`, and then running the following command:

```
$ bin/mongoimport --db solr-test --collection zips --file "<file-dir>/
samples/zips.json"
```

You can see the stored data using MongoDB-based CLI by running the following set of commands from your shell:

```
$ bin/mongo
MongoDB shell version: 2.4.9
connecting to: test
Welcome to the MongoDB shell.
For interactive help, type "help".
For more comprehensive documentation, see
        http://docs.mongodb.org/
Questions? Try the support group
        http://groups.google.com/group/mongodb-user
> use test
Switched to db test
> show dbs
exampledb       0.203125GB
local   0.078125GB
test    0.203125GB
> db.zips.find({city:"ACMAR"})
{ "city" : "ACMAR", "loc" : [  -86.51557,  33.584132 ], "pop" : 6055,
"state" :"AL", "_id" : "35004" }
Congratulations! MongoDB is installed successfully
```

Creating Solr indexes from MongoDB

To run MongoDB as a database, you will need a JDBC driver built for MongoDB. However, Mongo-JDBC driver has certain limitations, and it does not work with Apache Solr DataImportHandler. So, I have extended Mongo-JDBC to work under Solr-based DataImportHandler. The project repository can be accessed with the following URL:

```
https://github.com/hrishik/solr-mongodb-dih.
```

Let's look at the setup steps to enable MongoDB-based Solr integration.

1. You may not require a complete package from the `solr-mongodb-dih` repository but just the JAR file. It can be downloaded from `https://github.com/hrishik/solr-mongodb-dih/tree/master/sample-jar`. This compiled `.jar` file is also available with this book for easy access. You will also need the following additional JAR files:

   ° `jsqlparser.jar`

   ° `mongo.jar`

   These JAR files are made available with the book, and you will find them in the `lib` directory of the `solr-mongodb-dih` repository.

2. In your Solr setup, copy these JAR files in the library path (`$SOLR_WAR_LOCATION/WEB-INF/lib folder`). Alternatively, point your container classpath variable to link them up.

3. Using simple Java source code, `DataLoad.java` (`https://github.com/hrishik/solr-mongodb-dih/blob/master/examples/DataLoad.java`), populate the database with some sample schema and tables that you will use to load in Apache Solr.

4. Now, create a data source file (`data-source-config.xml`) as follows:

```
<dataConfig>
  <dataSource name="mongod" type="JdbcDataSource" driver="com.
mongodb.jdbc.MongoDriver" url="mongodb://localhost/exampledb"/>
    <document>
      <entity name="nameage" dataSource="mongod" query="select name,
price from grocery">
        <field column="name" name="name"/>
        <field column="name" name="id"/>
        <!-- other files -->
      </entity>
    </document>
</dataConfig>
```

5. Copy `solr-dataimporthandler-*.jar` from your `contrib` directory to a container/application library path.

6. Modify `$SOLR_COLLECTION_ROOT/conf/solr-config.xml` with the DIH entry as follows:

```
<!-- DIH Starts -->
<requestHandler name="/dataimport" class="org.apache.solr.
handler.dataimport.DataImportHandler">
    <lst name="defaults">
        <str name="config"><path to config>/data-source-config.xml</
str>
    </lst>
</requestHandler>
  <!-- DIH ends -->
```

7. Once this configuration is done, you are ready to test it out; access `http://localhost:8983/solr/dataimport?command=full-import` from your browser to run the full import on Apache Solr. You will see that your import handler has successfully ran and it has loaded the data in the Solr store, as shown in the following screenshot:

8. You can validate the content created by your new MongoDB DIH by accessing the admin page and running a query, as shown in the following screenshot:

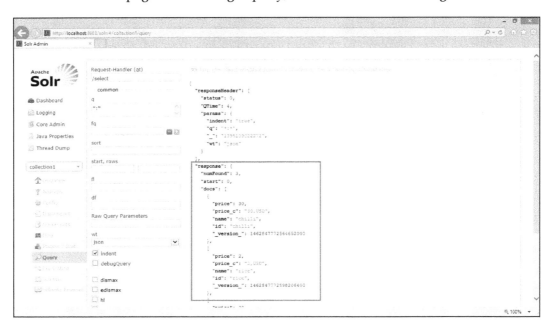

Using this connector, you can perform operations for full import on various data elements. As MongoDB is not a relational database, it will not support joined queries. However, it supports selects, order by, and so on.

Scaling Solr through Storm

Apache Storm is a real-time distributed computation framework. It processes with humongous data in real time. Recently, Storm has been adapted by Apache as an incubating project and for the development of Apache Storm. You can read more information about Apache Storm features at `http://storm.incubator.apache.org/`.

Apache Storm can be used to process massive streams of data in a distributed manner. So, it provides excellent batch-oriented processing capabilities for time-sensitive analytics. With Apache Solr and Storm together, organizations can process Big Data in real time. For example, Apache Solr and Storm can be used if industrial plants would like to extract information from their plant systems that are emitting raw data continuously and process it to facilitate real-time analytics such as identifying the top problematic systems or look for recent errors/failures. Apache Solr and Storm can work together to get this batch processing for Big Data in real time.

Apache Storm runs in a cluster mode where multiple nodes participate in performing computation in real time. It supports two types of nodes: master node (also called Nimbus) and a worker node (also called a slave). As the name describes, Nimbus is responsible to distributing code around the cluster, assigning tasks to machines, and monitoring for failures, whereas a supervisor listens for work assigned to its machine and starts and stops worker processes as necessary, based on what Nimbus has assigned to it. Apache Storm uses Zookeeper to perform all the coordination between Nimbus and supervisor. The data in Apache Storm is ready as a stream, which is nothing but a tuple of name value pairs as follows:

```
{id: 1748, author_name: "hrishi", full_name: "Hrishikesh Karambelkar"}
```

Apache Storm uses the concept of spout and bolts. Any work is executed in an Apache Storm topology. The following diagram shows the Storm topology with an example of word count:

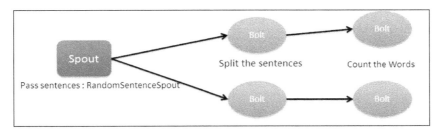

Spouts are data inputs; this is where data arrives in the Storm cluster. Bolts process the streams that get piped into it. They can be fed data from spouts or other bolts. The bolts can form a chain of processing, with each bolt performing a unit task. This concept is similar to map-reduce that we are going to look at in the following chapters.

Getting along with Apache Storm

Let's install Apache Storm and try out a simple word count example using the following steps:

1. You will require Zookeeper to be downloaded first, as both Nimbus and supervisor have dependencies on them. Download it from `http://zookeeper.apache.org/` and unzip it at some place. Copy `zoo.cfg` from the book's codebase or rename `zoo_sample.cfg` to `zoo.cfg` in your code.

2. Start the zookeeper using the following command:

    ```
    $ bin/zkServer.sh
    ```

3. Make sure Zookeeper is running. Now, download Apache Storm from `http://storm.incubator.apache.org/downloads.html`.

4. Unzip it, and go to the `$STORM_HOME/conf` folder. Edit `storm.yaml` and put the correct Nimbus host. You can use the configuration file provided along with the book. In case you are running it in a cluster environment, your `nimbus_host` needs to point to the correct master. In this configuration, you may also provide multiple Zookeeper servers for failsafe.

5. Now, set `JAVA_HOME` and `STORM_HOME` as follows:

   ```
   $ export STORM_HOME=/home/hrishi/storm
   $ export JAVA_HOME=/usr/share/jdk
   ```

6. Start master in a separate terminal by running the following command:

   ```
   $ $STORM_HOME/bin/storm nimbus
   ```

7. Start workers on machines by calling the following command:

   ```
   $ $STORM_HOME/bin/storm supervisor
   ```

8. Start the web interface by running the following command:

   ```
   $ $STORM_HOME/bin/storm ui
   ```

9. Now, access the web user interface by typing `http://localhost:8080` from your browser. You should be able to see the following screenshot:

10. Now, the Storm cluster is working fine; let's try a simple word count example from `https://github.com/nathanmarz/storm-starter`. You can download the source and compile or take a precompiled JAR from the book's source code repository.

11. You also need to install Python on your instances where Apache Storm is running, to run this example. You can download and install Python from `http:// www.python.org/`. Once Python is installed and added in the path environment, you can run the following command to start the word count task:

```
$ bin\storm jar storm-starter-0.0.1-SNAPSHOT-jar-with-dependencies.jar storm.starter.WordCountTopology WordCount -c nimbus.host=<host>
```

In the word count example, you will find different classes being mapped to different roles, as shown in the following screenshot:

```
                                                            WordCountTopology.java
public static void main(String[] args) throws Exception {

  TopologyBuilder builder = new TopologyBuilder();

  builder.setSpout("spout", new RandomSentenceSpout(), 5);

  builder.setBolt("split", new SplitSentence(), 8).shuffleGrouping("spout");
  builder.setBolt("count", new WordCount(), 12).fieldsGrouping("split", new Fields("word"));

  Config conf = new Config();
  conf.setDebug(true);


  if (args != null && args.length > 0) {
    conf.setNumWorkers(3);

    StormSubmitter.submitTopology(args[0], conf, builder.createTopology());
  }
  else {
```

Solr and Apache Storm

Apache Solr can use the capabilities of Apache Storm to generate the indexes for data stream that is getting populated in Storm. Using Storm, Apache Solr can access data from real-time distributed applications for searching. The near real-time indexing and searching can be made possible through Apache Storm. There is already an initiative to provide extended implementation of the IRichBolt interface of Storm (`https://github.com/arianpasquali/storm-solr`). It provides a `SimpleSolrBolt` class that extracts tuples from Apache Storm inputs and pushes them to Solr by connecting them, as shown in the following diagram:

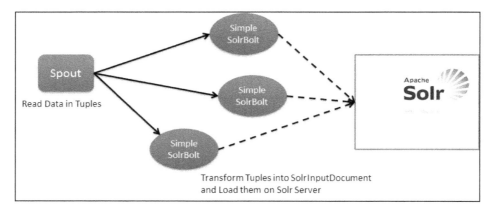

It adds value if Apache Solr is working in a SolrCloud mode. Apache Storm together with Apache Solr can help parse large index size. Besides indexing, Apache Storm can play a role in querying the Apache Solr instance. The bolts in Storm allow users to put their custom code, using the one that can fire a query on the Solr database directly.

Summary

In this chapter, we focused mainly on working with big databases that work on large datasets for processing and how Apache Solr can add value to them. We also looked at some of the implementations to integrate Apache Solr with MongoDB, Apache Cassandra, and Apache Storm. We also looked at some of the advanced topics such as clustering the outcomes/results from Apache Solr using Carrot2. In the next chapter, we will be focusing on optimizing Apache Solr for high performance.

8
Scaling Solr through High Performance

In the last chapter, we looked at how effectively Apache Solr can be used with advanced capabilities. Apache Solr can work on low-cost hardware, thereby making it a strong candidate for adaption at various organizations looking at cutting costs. Besides cutting costs, an important aspect of any enterprise search implementation is to get optimal performance out of the existing hardware and search infrastructure. This is one of the challenging domains, because with the inflow of more and more data, the search indexing as well as real-time search on these indexes slows down. In such cases, the need for distributed instances comes into the frame. At the same time, the unit of performance does not scale linearly with the number of CPU cores or memory; hence, at times, even if you increase the memory after certain limits, the performance does not improve. Therefore, it makes sense to optimize the Solr instance for high performance to ensure maximum utilization of available resources.

In this chapter, we will look at various ways of optimizing the Solr instance while scaling the instance for higher capabilities. We will be covering the following topics:

- Monitoring the performance of Solr
- Tuning of Solr JVM and the container server
- Optimizing Solr schema and indexing
- Speeding Solr through Solr cache
- Improving search runtime of Solr
- Optimizing SolrCloud

Monitoring performance of Apache Solr

An Apache Solr-based search runs on a J2EE container. Just like any other application management, the requirement for monitoring search beyond the standard application management is needed to ensure search is highly optimized and running within the limits. Monitoring is a critical part of any enterprise search production system. There are some interesting case studies of Spunk implementations and monitoring available at http://www.splunk.com/view/customer-case-studies/SP-CAAABB2#case_study.

What should be monitored?

Apache Solr is the application on top of the Java container, which has its own database for storing indexes. Solr supports three major workflows (indexing, search, and administration). At each layer, different parameters can be monitored for performance metrics. Monitoring can happen at various levels, which could be at the operating system, JVM, or at the Apache Solr search level. You can use various tools for this purpose. While monitoring, it is important to first identify the different variables you will be required to monitor on a continuous basis or periodically.

Hardware and operating system

Operating system and hardware play a major role in determining performance. Apache Solr uses a standard filesystem to store its data/index and it relies on the underlying operation system APIs for all operations through JVM. Many of these parameters can be measured through standard operating system tools, and you do not require anything specific for its measurement.

Measures	Description
CPU load	This parameter tells you the amount of CPU utilized by Apache Solr. It would be better if a CPU core idle/load time can be measured. Many operating systems do provide that. And the average CPU time would reveal the load on the enterprise search system. This has to be measured frequently.
IO waits	Excess IO wait cycle reveals that the CPU is waiting for the disk and as of now, the disk is the bottleneck. The IO wait cycle can be reduced through various ways. This can be measured periodically.
RAM or memory used/ free	If RAM is not available, the search becomes not scalable, and the query cache of Apache Solr cannot grow; this means a poorer performance. This can be measured periodically, based on the data loading and searching frequency.

Measures	Description
Swap space and OS paging	This parameter works in combination with the memory used. If there is a lot of swapping happening, it's going to be because of the disk slowing your search, and you may even consider adding some memory. This can be measured if free memory is less.
Disk space	If you are low on disk space, Apache Solr cannot scale. You would be measuring this infrequently.

Java virtual machine

Apache Solr accesses hardware and software resources through JVM, so measuring this becomes an important task. These parameters can be measured through JConsole/SolrAdmin and other such tools that we are going to discuss in the next section. Apache Solr exposes **Java Management Extensions (JMX)** beans. JMX is a J2EE technology used in the Java application to expose different application control parameters to the administrators in a standardized format. The following parameters can be monitored through JVM:

Measures	Description
Heap size	This has to be optimal to ensure Java does not work hard to make more memory available, or to unnecessarily hog the memory even if it's not required.
Thread count	Each thread takes certain memory, and wants to use some CPU processing time. The greater the number of threads is a warning for performance bottleneck due to a lack of hardware resource. This should be monitored continuously.
Garbage collection	Each GC, when executed, makes your search slow. It is because GC, when run, eats most of your resources. The need for GC cleanup is mainly due to the memory getting full. This has to be monitored periodically based on the usage pattern and indexing pattern. There are different parameters under GC that can be monitored such as GC run timings, and full GC versus runtime percentage.

Apache Solr search runtime

Apache Solr search runtime is what many consumers are concerned with. It's mainly because it relates to the performance of your search. Apache Solr specific parameter monitoring can be done through JMX. If you have an existing MBeanServer, JMX can be exposed to it via Apache Solr by modifying `solrconfig.xml` with the following change:

```
<jmx agentId="myAgent" serviceUrl="service:jmx:rmi:///jndi/rmi://
localhost:9999/solrjmx" />
```

The `agentId` parameter will match with your existing MBeanServer, and `serviceURL` is where you can provide the specific URL directly. Now, you can run your Jetty with the following code to enable the JMX server for remote access:

```
java -Dcom.sun.management.jmxremote -jar start.jar
```

All the Solr-specific JMX beans are available under `solr/` as the root in the JMX browser.

Measures	Description
Response time	This is one of the most important measurement parameters. It is the time taken for Solr to search, rank, and return the results to the client. It can be measured as average, or worst N responses for certain queries. It can be found on the following JMX bean: `"solr/<corename>:type=standard,id=org.apache.solr.handler.StandardRequestHandler"`, `totalTime`, `requests`.
Query rate	This parameter identifies the number of queries that your instance is running per unit time. It can be **Queries Per Second (QPS)**.
Cache hit ratio	Apache Solr uses an internal cache to avoid unnecessary computations for queries that are rerun. The cache is at various levels, and we are going to look at them in the next section. A higher cache ratio means faster responses.

Apache Solr indexing time

Apache Solr indexing is another aspect in which different parameters can be monitored for ensuring speedy index creation.

Measures	Description
Number of document/ index size	The number of documents for indexing play an important role when considering performance; as the documents grow, the performance degrades.
Number of updates	Similarly, the number of updates run on Solr indexing are also critical; too many updates can potentially slow the instance, and you may be required to identify a strategy for indexing.
Segment merge	Apache Solr stores its index information in segments; when the segment exceeds the count, it tries to merge the segments and enlarge them. This is a significant time consumption process, and the maximum segment count and time for merging can hog resources, thereby slowing the search performance. We are going to look at it in more detail when understanding Solr indexes.
Time taken after running the optimize command	Solr provides you with a way to run merged over index segments through an optimized call. This call is expensive and may slow your regular searches.

SolrCloud

When run in the SolrCloud mode, you may need to observe additional parameters for performance monitoring besides standard Apache Solr measures:

Measures	Description
Network trace/ ping time	It is the time taken to ping the server when multiple nodes are run.
Zookeeper latency and throughput	Since SolrCloud uses Apache Zookeeper, you may be required to monitor its latency with different data loads. There are some sites that publish these statistics, such as `https://ramcloud.stanford.edu/wiki/display/ramcloud/ZooKeeper+Performance` and `http://wiki.apache.org/hadoop/ZooKeeper/Performance`.

Tools for monitoring Solr performance

We have looked at different parameters that can be measured; let's look at different tools that you would use to monitor your Solr instance.

Solr administration user interface

Apache Solr administration user interface provides a nice UI to monitor Solr statistics over the Web. It supports Solr-based JMX MBeans, and provides a browser for browsing the beans. The following screenshot demonstrates the Solr admin user interface:

It provides different parameters that can be observed through the web console. The details of each page and what it reveals is listed in the following table:

Measures	Description
Thread dump	You can see a list of all threads in enterprise search at `http:// <host>:<port>/solr/#/~threads`.
Logs access	You can also access the log, the log level, and the detail of each log message through the user interface at `http:// <host>:<port>/solr/#/~logging`.
Heap/segment information	Apache Solr provides information regarding the current configured segment size and heap size at `http://<host>:<port>/solr/#/<collection-name>`. `http:// /<host>:<port>/solr/#/` shows the dashboard with the memory consumption graph.
JMX MBeans	You can directly browse JMX MBeans through the MBean browser of the Apache Solr administration user interface at `http://<host>:<port>/solr/#/<collection-name>/plugins/`.

JConsole

JConsole is a tool that is shipped with the Java Development Kit, and it provides instant access to primary monitoring parameters such as memory and CPU usage consumed by JVM. JConsole that can be found at `$JDK_HOME/bin` `$JDK_HOME` is your JDK installation directory:

```
$ jconsole <process-id optional>
```

Once you run JConsole, you can see the graphical user interface to select a JVM process you wish to monitor. The process can be a local process or remote JMX URL that can be specified. Once JConsole connects to the process, you will start seeing a graphical user interface as shown in the following screenshot:

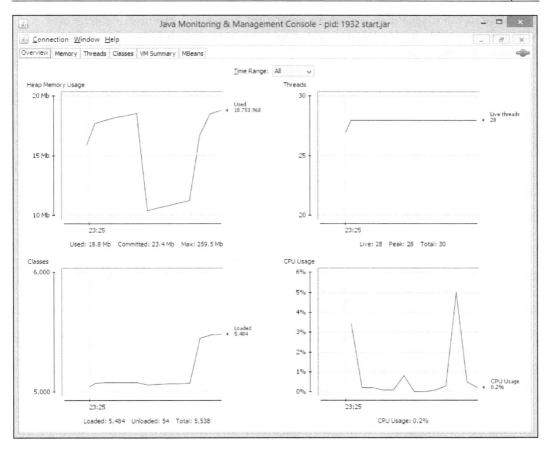

It shows the **Overview** tab with the summary information of important attributes of JVM such as thread count, heap memory, CPU, and a number of classes loaded with the *x* axis showing time. JConsole provides different tabs; the **Memory** tab displays information about the memory usage with different heap spaces (Eden Space, Survivor Space, Tenured Generation, and so on), and you can also run a garbage collector from here. The **Threads** tab shows the threads' chat with time, along with active threads and their information. It also shows if there are any deadlocking threads in JVM. The **Classes** tab shows information about classes loaded in memory along with the total count. The **VM Summary** tab shows a summary of the existing JVM with detailed information on threads (live, daemon, peak, and so on), JVM details, memory (heap, GC, and so on.), classes, system uptime, operating system, environment variables, and so on.

The **MBean** tab displays information regarding registered MBeans. Apache Solr MBeans are visible in this tab if you connect to Jetty through JConsole as shown in the following screenshot:

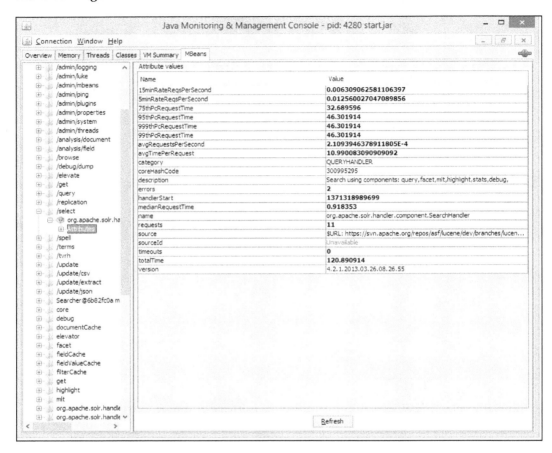

MBeans in JConsole are displayed in a tree format, with name-value pairs. You can also fire operations on MBean through a JConsole GUI. You can visit `http://docs.oracle.com/javase/6/docs/technotes/guides/management/jconsole.html` for JConsole documentation.

SolrMeter

SolrMeter is a tool that allows users to perform stress testing of their Solr instance. Besides running stress tests, SolrMeter provides statistics on the Solr instance for different key performance indexes such as queries and the time taken to run them, documents added, and commit and optimize measures. SolrMeter can be downloaded from `http://code.google.com/p/solrmeter/downloads/list/solrmeter-<version>.jar` on your machine. Now we will call the following command:

```
java -jar solrmeter-<version>.jar
```

After running the preceding command, the system opens a SolrMeter GUI, as shown in the following screenshot:

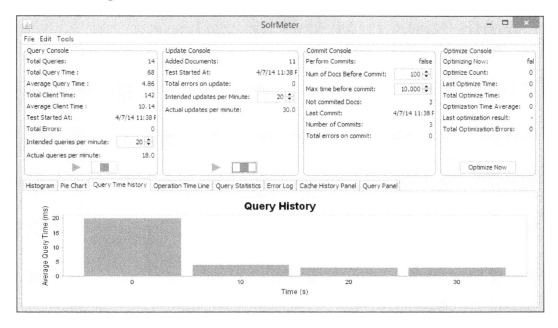

By pressing the play button, SolrMeter starts monitoring your Solr process. SolrMeter provides the following performance measurements:

- **Query Console**: This console shows information related to the total queries, errors, average time per query, and intended/actual query comparison

- **Update Console**: This console provides information on documents updated in the Solr instance; it also shows errors and intended/actual documents per minute

- **Commit Console**: This console talks about the commit made by the process while loading the documents; it provides statistics related to the errors, last commit, number of documents that are collected without commit, and so on

- **Optimize Console**: This console provides a way to run an optimize command on Solr, it also shows statistics regarding the time taken by Solr to complete optimize, last optimize runtime, and so on

The performances are displayed in a graphical manner with histogram, pie chart, and so on. Through SolrCloud, error logs can be accessed directly. SolrMeter allows you to replay the logs so you can perform a load testing to your application. You can visit the SolrMeter tutorial at https://code.google.com/p/solrmeter/wiki/Tutorial.

Tuning Solr JVM and container

Apache Solr runs on the underlying JVM in the J2EE container. While scaling Solr for processing more requests and indexing data, it becomes important that the underlying JVM is capable of scaling and is optimized well. Choosing the right JVM is an important factor. There are many JVMs available in the market today that can be considered such as Oracle Java HotSpot, BEA JRockit, and Open JDK (the list is available at http://en.wikipedia.org/wiki/List_of_Java_virtual_machines).

Some of these JVMs are commercially optimized for production usage; you may find comparison studies at http://dior.ics.muni.cz/~makub/java/speed.html. Some of the JVM implementations provide server versions, which would be more appropriate than normal ones.

Since Solr runs in JVM, all the standard optimizations for applications are applicable to it. It starts with choosing the right heap size for your JVM. The heap size depends upon the following aspects:

- Use of facets and sorting options
- Size of the Solr index
- Update frequencies on Solr
- Solr cache

Heap size for JVM can be controlled by the following parameters:

Parameter	Description
-Xms	This is the minimum heap size required during JVM initialization, that is, container
-Xmx	This is the maximum heap size up to which the JVM or J2EE container can consume

Deciding heap size

Heap in JVM contributes as a major factor while optimizing the performance of any system. JVM uses heap to store its objects, as well as its own content. Poor allocation of JVM heap results in Java heap space OutOfMemoryError thrown at runtime crashing the application. When the heap is allocated with less memory, the application takes a longer time to initialize, as well as slowing the execution speed of the Java process during runtime. Similarly, higher heap size may underutilize expensive memory, which otherwise could have been used by the other application.

JVM starts with initial heap size, and as the demand grows, it tries to resize the heap to accommodate new space requirements. If a demand for memory crosses the maximum limit, JVM throws an Out of Memory exception. We have already seen the parameters in the previous section with which you can specify the heap size. The objects that expire or are unused, unnecessarily consume memory in JVM. This memory can be taken back by releasing these objects by a process called garbage collection. Although it's tricky to find out whether you should increase or reduce the heap size, there are simple ways that can help you out. In a memory graph, typically, when you start the Solr server and run your first query, the memory usage increases, and based on subsequent queries and memory size, the memory graph may increase or remain constant. When garbage collection is run automatically by the JVM container, it sharply brings down its usage. If it's difficult to trace GC execution from the memory graph, you can run Solr with the following additional parameters:

```
-Xloggc:<some file> -verbose:gc
-XX:+PrintGCTimeStamps  -XX:+PrintGCDetails
```

If you are monitoring the heap usage continuously, you will find a graph that increases and decreases (sawtooth); the increase is due to the querying that is going on consistently demanding more memory by your Solr cache, and decrease is due to GC execution. In a running environment, the average heap size should not grow over time or the number of GC runs should be less than the number of queries executed on Solr. If that's not the case, you will need more memory.

Features such as Solr faceting and sorting requires more memory on top of traditional search. If memory is unavailable, the operating system needs to perform hot swapping with the storage media, thereby increasing the response time; thus, users find huge latency while searching on large indexes. Many of the operating systems allow users to control swapping of programs.

How can we optimize JVM?

Whenever a facet query is run in Solr, memory is used to store each unique element in the index for each field. So, for example, a search over a small set of facet value (an year from 1980 to 2014) will consume less memory than a search with larger set of facet value, such as people's names (can vary from person to person). To reduce the memory usage, you may set the term index divisor to 2 (default is 4) by setting the following in `solrconfig.xml`:

```
<indexReaderFactory name="IndexReaderFactory"
                    class="solr.StandardIndexReaderFactory">
    <int name="setTermIndexDivisor">2</int>
</indexReaderFactory >
```

From Solr 4.x onwards, the ability to set the min, max (term index divisor) block size ability is not available. This will reduce the memory usage for storing all the terms to half; however, it will double the seek time for terms and will impact a little on your search runtime.

One of the causes of large heap is the size of index, so one solution is to introduce SolrCloud and the distributed large index into multiple shards. This will not reduce your memory requirement, but will spread it across the cluster.

You can look at some of the optimized GC parameters described at `http://wiki.apache.org/solr/ShawnHeisey#GC_Tuning` page. Similarly, Oracle provides a GC tuning guide for advanced development stages, and it can be seen at `http://www.oracle.com/technetwork/java/javase/gc-tuning-6-140523.html`. Additionally, you can look at the Solr performance problems at `http://wiki.apache.org/solr/SolrPerformanceProblems`.

Optimizing JVM container

JVM containers allow users to have their requests served in threads. This in turn enables JVM to support concurrent sessions created for different users connecting at the same time. The concurrency can, however, be controlled to reduce the load on the search server.

If you are using Apache Tomcat, you can modify the following entries in `server.xml` for changing the number of concurrent connections:

```
69          -->
70          <Connector port="10080" protocol="HTTP/1.1"
71                    connectionTimeout="20000"
72                    redirectPort="10443" acceptCount="100"/>
73          <!-- A "Connector" using the shared thread pool-->
```

Similarly, in Jetty, you can control the number of connections held by modifying `jetty.xml`:

```
48      <!-- This connector is currently being used for Solr because it
49              showed better performance than nio.SelectChannelConnector
50              for typical Solr requests.  -->
51      <Call name="addConnector">
52        <Arg>
53          <New class="org.eclipse.jetty.server.bio.SocketConnector">
54            <Set name="host"><SystemProperty name="jetty.host" /></Set>
55            <Set name="port"><SystemProperty name="jetty.port" default="8983"/></Set>
56            <Set name="maxIdleTime">50000</Set>
57            <Set name="lowResourceMaxIdleTime">1500</Set>
58            <Set name="Acceptors">20</Set>
59            <Set name="statsOn">false</Set>
60          </New>
61        </Arg>
62      </Call>
63
```

Similarly, for other containers, these files can change appropriately. Many containers provide a cache on top of the application to avoid server hits. This cache can be utilized for static pages such as the search page. Containers such as Weblogic provide a development versus production mode. Typically, a development mode runs with 15 threads and a limited JDBC pool size by default, whereas, for a production mode, this can be increased. For tuning containers, besides standard optimization, specific performance-tuning guidelines should be followed, as shown in the following table:

Container	Performance tuning guide
Jetty	`http://wiki.eclipse.org/Jetty/Howto/High_Load`
Tomcat	`http://www.mulesoft.com/tcat/tomcat-performance` and `http://javamaster.wordpress.com/2013/03/13/apache-tomcat-tuning-guide/`
JBoss	`https://access.redhat.com/site/documentation/en-US/JBoss_Enterprise_Application_Platform/5/pdf/Performance_Tuning_Guide/JBoss_Enterprise_Application_Platform-5-Performance_Tuning_Guide-en-US.pdf`

Container	Performance tuning guide
Weblogic	`http://docs.oracle.com/cd/E13222_01/wls/docs92/perform/WLSTuning.html`
Websphere	`http://www.ibm.com/developerworks/websphere/techjournal/0909_blythe/0909_blythe.html`

Apache Solr works better with the default container it ships with, Jetty, since it offers a small footprint compared to other containers such as JBoss and Tomcat for which the memory required is a little higher.

Optimizing Solr schema and indexing

Apache Solr schema can also be optimized for reducing the overall footprint of your index and to speed up the search. Let's take a look at some of the possible optimizations.

Stored fields

The `schema.xml` file also provides a configuration to define whether a field needs to be stored as an optional attribute (`stored=true/false`). Typically, the fields are stored so that their values can be displayed as search results in the search results page. However, if the size of the fields is large, it unnecessarily increases the size of the index, eating up Solr's memory. For large fields, it is better to store their identifiers and let the search client be responsible for rendering the result; fire a query to another system (database or filesystem) to gather the required field information as a part of the result. This will not only reduce the load on Solr but will also ease the management of the field in another store (like relational databases) which are optimized for standard querying.

Indexed fields and field lengths

The size of the index is being impacted by the number of fields that are marked for indexing in `schema.xml`. So, it is always recommended to monitor and control the schema fields that should be indexed by Solr. It can be done by specifying `indexed=true` or `indexed=false` appropriately for each schema attribute. For example, out of the five fields marked for indexing, if you reduce one field, it is roughly a 20 percent reduction in the size of index, although it depends upon the field type, size, and data. It is recommended to avoid indexing unnecessary fields that you do not intend to use in search.

Fields with a larger size take more memory and consume a sufficient block of memory. Hence, if the fields are not truncated, it may impact the performance. Apache Solr provides the `maxFieldLength` attribute, which allows users to specify the maximum size of the field to help users reduce the size of the fields.

Copy fields and dynamic fields

A `copyField` declaration will take any field you tell it to and copy it into another field. For example, look at the following code:

```
<copyField source="*_name" dest="all_names"/>
```

The preceding code will copy all the fields ending with _name to all_names. Apache Solr also ships with default `copyFields`, which may not suit your requirements, so it is better to get rid of as many `copyFields` as we can. This can offer major speed improvements in your searches, especially for large index sizes.

For best index size and searching performance, set the index to `false` for all general text fields. Use `copyField` to copy them to one text field, and use that for searching.

Dynamic fields allow users to run Solr in a schemaless mode. In schemaless, users do not have to define a schema for application. For example, please look at the following dynamic field definition:

```
<dynamicField name="*_integer" type="pint"    indexed="true"
stored="true"/>
```

This means that the user can pass any document with fields ending with _integer, and they will all be indexed under the given dynamic field. This feature provides excellent schemaless capabilities to the end user. However, it adds an overhead. The Apache Solr default schema ships with plenty of dynamic fields. So, the removal of unused dynamic fields can reduce the overall index size.

Fields for range queries

Apache Solr provides optimized fields for range queries. These are `tint`, `tlong`, `tdate`, `tdouble`, and `tfloat` and they index each value at various levels of precision. Although it increases the index size, the range queries are faster than normal integer, float, date, double, and long. The precisions and position increment gap can be changed by the user by modifying the following fields in `schema.xml`:

```
<fieldType name="tint" class="solr.TrieIntField" precisionStep="8"
positionIncrementGap="0"/>
    <fieldType name="tfloat" class="solr.TrieFloatField"
precisionStep="8" positionIncrementGap="0"/>
```

```
    <fieldType name="tlong" class="solr.TrieLongField"
precisionStep="8" positionIncrementGap="0"/>
    <fieldType name="tdouble" class="solr.TrieDoubleField"
precisionStep="8" positionIncrementGap="0"/>
```

Index field updates

Whenever Solr index requires an update, many users perform removal and insert of the Index field. However, Apache Solr supports index updation, which includes adding new attributes to the current data, modifying the existing attribute value, and so on. This operation performs faster than the remove-create route. We will now look at some examples about how it can be done. Load the data with some document to be indexed as follows:

```
curl http://<host>:<port>/solr/update?commit=true -H "Content-Type:
text/xml" --data-binary "<add><doc><field name='id'>1748</field><field
name='name'>Scaling Solr</field><field name='features'>Apache Solr,
Lucene</field></doc></add>"
```

Now, modify the value of the field name using the following CURL command:

```
curl http://<host>:<port>/solr/update?commit=true -H "Content-Type:
text/xml" --data-binary "<add><doc><field name='id'>1748</field><field
name='name' update='set'>Scaling Solr by packtpub Karambelkar</
field></doc></add>"
```

You can add a new attribute as follows:

```
curl http://<host>:<port>/solr/update?commit=true -H "Content-Type:
text/xml" --data-binary "<add><doc><field name='id'>1748</field><field
name='popularity' update='set'>100</field></doc></add>"
```

The update also supports multivalued attributes, and they can be added as shown in the following code:

```
curl http://<host>:<port>/solr/update?commit=true -H "Content-Type:
text/xml" --data-binary "<add><doc><field name='id'>1748</field><field
name='features' update='add'>Java, J2EE</field></doc></add>"
```

Synonyms, stemming, and stopwords

It is highly possible that enterprise search results get influenced by the number of common words that appear in unstructured data. For example, the, a, an, may, and more; these words not only distort the search result but also unnecessarily appear on top of all the results (due to heavy occurrences). Apache Solr provides the user with a way to stop indexing of these words by means of the stopwords feature. The stopwords can be listed in the file, and schema.xml can point to this file.

Stemming is a process of reducing any word into its shorter form. For example, talked, talker, talks would reduce to a base form, talk. Similarly, a synonym would match talk with chat, conversation, and so on. Apache Solr provides support for both. These features not only save your search time but also improve search query performance.

There are different stemming algorithms supported by Apache Solr; it also allows users to define their own algorithm. The following table describes different algorithms for stemming:

Algorithm	Description
Porter	This is a rule-based algorithm that transforms any form of the word in English into its original word (stem). For example, talking and walked are marked as walk and awesome is marked as awe.
KStem	This algorithm is similar to Porter, but it returns words instead of truncated word forms. For example, amplification->amplify.
Snowball	Snowball is a language for creating stemming (in the domains of Information Retrieval or IR). Using Snowball, you can define your own stemming algorithm. Please visit `http://snowball.tartarus.org/`for more details.
Hunspell	Open Office dictionary-based algorithm. It works with all languages. More information on Hunspell is available at `http://hunspell.sourceforge.net/`

Overall, the workflow and the mandatory fields mapping is shown in the following section. The true value indicates the presence of this attribute while defining the field.

Tuning DataImportHandler

`DataImportHandler` in Solr is often used to connect with a relational database and to perform full/delta imports. It is designed to stream rows one by one. It also supports other types of databases, hence, it becomes important to ensure it runs in an optimized manner.

`DataImportHandler` allows users to create different entities for SQL queries. It also supports inner entities to write complex SQL queries. Each entity can take a SQL query as a parameter in case of a relational database. Inner entities should be avoided wherever possible. It is because many times, SQL queries can be combined resulting in the database performing faster joins than the Apache Solr JDBC layer doing it.

In database configuration for `DataImportHandler`, Solr allows you to write your own transformers, which can be regular expressions, JavaScript, and so on. Each transformer call will execute on each row of your resultset. Many of them can directly be performed in the relational database query itself on the data. So, it is effective to avoid them wherever possible, and move them in the database layer. This way, the RDBMS query optimizer can provide an overall query plan in a more optimized manner.

When you are running a complex query with multiple inner joins, it is often found that the bottleneck for these inner joins stay with databases, such as Solr `DataImportHandler`. If the joins are based on unique IDs recognized by Apache Solr schema, these can be reduced to separate entities, and an index merge can be performed.

For inner entities that are unavoidable, `CachedSqlEntityProcessor` can be used for faster indexing. `CachedSqlEntityProcessor` caches SQL row and avoids running SQL queries again.

In the `DataImportHandler` configuration, the default batch size for each fetch block is 500; it can be tuned based on the database updates that are taking place in the database. It can be defined as follows:

```
<dataSource type="JdbcDataSource" name="MyJDBC" driver="oracle.
jdbc.OracleDriver" url="jdbc:oracle:thin:@//myhost:1521/orcl"
batchSize="100" user="scott" password="tiger"/>
```

Speeding up index generation

Theoretically, Apache Solr does not have any limit on the maximum number of documents that can be loaded on its search indexing while running in a distributed mode. Apache Lucene has an upper cap on the size of index (approximately to 2 billion documents).

While indexing, Apache Solr pushes the newly generated index into a segment. Each segment is equally sized. The `solrconfig.xml` provides the `<mergeFactor>10</mergeFactor>` parameter to optimize the index storage on the filesystem. The `mergeFactor` count represents the maximum number of segments Apache Solr can have at any point in time. While indexing, if the Apache Solr segment count equals the merge factor count, the segments are merged into one segment, and the process continues. In addition to `mergeFactor`, there are other configuration parameters in `solrconfig.xml` that can be set. The `maxMergeDocument` count indicates that all segments containing more documents than its value won't be merged.

Committing the change

When documents are getting indexed, the Apache Solr memory usage grows until a commit operation. Commit in Solr ensures all the changes done with Solr indexing are persisted on the disk. With Solr, you can perform commit in the following different ways:

- Automatic commit (hard and soft)
- Manual commit

  ° Soft commit
  ° Hard commit

Apache Solr writes the Solr document automatically to the underlying storage when the user enables the automatic commit option. Automatic commit provides hard and soft options. A soft commit does not commit the changes, but they are made available for searching, whereas a hard commit will replicate the indexes across Solr nodes in case of a cluster. Users can specify a limit on soft commit with the maximum time (`maxTime`) or maximum documents (`maxDocs`) after which a commit should take place.

The value for maximum time/document should be decided cautiously because it can potentially impact the performance of the Solr instance. Choosing these values is driven by the actual Solr use case. For example, if the Solr instance is deployed at a place where there are frequent update operations, the value can be low to avoid large data waiting for the commit process to happen. When a commit is run on a large document list, it slows the other processes by eating the CPU and memory of Solr, resulting in the end users experiencing a slow response. Similarly, if the insert/updates are not frequently done, these values can be higher, to avoid any overhead of unnecessary insert/update run by the Solr instance. Solr writes an update log, and the size of the update log can be specified in the Solr instance. Specifying the hard commit size limit based on the size of the update log will enable maximum utilization of the available resources in the Solr setup.

We have already seen soft commit and hard commit earlier in the context of near-real-time search capabilities of Solr in the previous chapter.

Limiting indexing buffer size

When a Solr document is indexed in a streaming manner, the commit does not take place with every document. Solr holds it in its memory buffer also called the RAM buffer. Once the size of the documents exceed the Solr buffer size, Apache Solr creates a new segment if there is no existing segment with a smaller size, or merges the current document into existing segments. The complete operation is run in the batch mode. Apache Solr allows users to specify the size of the RAM buffer with the following parameter in `solrconfig.xml`:

```
<ramBufferSizeMB>100</ramBufferSizeMB>
```

The default value of the RAM buffer size is 100 MB (Solr 1.4 onwards). Apache Solr also provides the user with an option to specify the number of documents to buffer during the indexing operation with the following parameter:

```
<maxBufferedDocs>1000</maxBufferedDocs>
```

At any point of time during the indexing operation, if Solr encounters the size of memory in MB, or the number of documents exceeding the maximum size specified in the configuration, the in-memory Solr documents are flushed to the underlying storage.

Solr also provides an option to control the maximum number of threads that can be used while indexing the document. Having a sufficient number of threads of Solr processes, the underlying hardware can be effectively utilized as follows:

```
< maxIndexingThread>8</ maxIndexingThread >
```

The default value for indexing the thread is 8; however, based on the indexing requirement, this can be changed. To utilize the threading effectively, Apache SolrJ provides the `ConcurrentUpdateSolrServer` class, which utilizes the existing cloud system to upload the data using threads.

SolrJ implementation classes

When working with SolrJ, the documents for indexing can be uploaded through the following `SolrServer` class implementations:

- `CloudSolrServer`: This is meant to work with SolrCloud and internally uses `LBHttpSolrServer`

- `ConcurrentUpdateSolrServer`: This buffers all the added documents and writes them into open HTTP connections. This class is thread safe

- `HttpSolrServer`: This class is used to upload the content to Solr

- `LBHttpSolrServer`: This is a load balancing wrapper around `HttpSolrServer`
- `EmbeddedSolrServer`: This connects to the local Solr Core directly to create indexes

Among these implementations, `ConcurrentUpdateSolrServer` allows a concurrent update of documents for indexing in Solr over remote access.

Speeding Solr through Solr caching

Many times, the queries that are run on search are repetitive in nature. In such cases, the presence of a cache brings down the average response time for search results. Apache Solr provides a caching mechanism on top of the index data. This cache, unlike a normal cache, does not carry any expiry (persistent cache). It is associated with `IndexWriter`. The following are the three different types of cache supported by Solr:

- `LRUCache`: This is Least Recently Used (based on synchronized LinkedHashMap) (default)
- `FastLRUCache`: This is a newer form of cache and is expected to be faster than all the others
- `LFUCache`: This is Least Frequently Used (based on `ConcurrentHashMap`)

The following are the common parameters for the cache in `solrconfig.xml`:

Parameter	Description
`class`	You can specify the type of cache you wish to attach, that is, `LRUCache`, `FastLRUCache`, or `LFUCache`.
`size`	This is the maximum size a cache can reach.
`initialSize`	This is the initial size of the cache when it is initialized.
`autowarmCount`	This is the number of entries to seed from the old cache. We will look at this in the next section.
`minSize`	This is applicable for `FastLRUCache`; after the cache reaches its peak size, it tries to reduce the cache size to minSize. The default value is 90 percent of the size.
`acceptableSize`	If `FastLRUCache` cannot reduce to `minSize` when the cache reaches its peak, it will at least touch to `acceptableSize`.

The filter cache

The filter cache provides a caching layer on top of filter queries. For any query that is fired as a filter query, Solr first looks into the cache for search results. If not found, it gets fired on the repository, and the results are moved to the cache. Each filter is cached separately; when queries are filtered, this cache returns the results and eventually, based on the filtering criteria, the system performs an intersection of them. If a search is using faceting, use of the filter cache provides better performance. This cache stores the document IDs in an unordered state.

The query result cache

As the name suggests, this cache is responsible for caching the query results. This way, repeated requests for similar searches does not require complete search, but instead it can return the results from the cache. This cache will store the top N query results for each query passed by the user. It stores an ordered set of document IDs. This cache is useful where similar queries are passed again and again. You can specify the maximum number of documents that can be cached by this cache in `solrconfig.xml`. Consider the following snippet:

```
<queryResultMaxDocsCached>200</queryResultMaxDocsCached>
```

The document cache

The document cache is responsible for storing Solr documents into the cache. Once a document is cached, it does not require a fetch request on the disk thereby reducing the disk IOs. This cache is part of Apache Solr and it is different from the disk cache that operating systems provide. This cache works on IDs of a document, so the autowarming feature does not really seem to bring any impact, since the document IDs keep changing as and when there is a change in index.

 The size of the document cache should be based on your size of results and size of the maximum number of queries allowed to run; this will ensure there is no re-fetch of documents by Solr.

The field value cache

Field value cache provides caching of Solr fields. It can provide sorting on fields, and it supports multivalued fields. This cache is useful when you have extensive use of Solr faceting. Since faceting is a field-based caching of fields, this cache is used mainly for faceting. You can monitor the status of the field value cache through the Apache Solr Administration console, and it provides information pertaining to hit ratio, number of hits, load on cache, and so on.

The warming up cache

Cache autowarming is a feature by which a cache can pre populate itself with objects from old search instances/cache. This property can be set in `solrconfig.xml`. Whenever the user commits new documents for Solr index, Apache Solr starts a new searcher, and it copies the cache from the previous searcher. A cache can be preloaded by explicitly running frequently run queries. This way Solr does not start with no cache. Having a prepopulated cache helps in that any query run after Solr is up will utilize the pre populated cache content. The following snippet from `solrconfig.xml` shows an example of autowarming of Solr cache on a new search initialization:

```
<listener event="newSearcher" class="solr.QuerySenderListener">
    <arr name="queries">
      <!-- seed common sort fields -->
      <lst> <str name="q">java books databases</str></lst>
    </arr>
</listener>
```

The autowarming count determines Solr startup time, so for frequently updated indexes it is better to keep this count low. The count can be set by adding the attribute to your cache element in `solrconfig.xml`. The following is an example of this:

```
<filterCache class="solr.FastLRUCache"
              size="512"
              initialSize="512"
              autowarmCount="0"/>
```

Improving runtime search for Solr

To speed up the querying and rendering of results, it is important to optimize the runtime of Apache Solr. The optimization of Solr runtime can be achieved in various ways, which will be discussed shortly.

Pagination

A typical search screen provides results on a single page with pagination. Apache Solr provides support for pagination at the search level, thereby enabling search responses. When Solr fetches results for the queries passed by the user, Apache Solr allows users to limit the fetching of the result to a certain number by specifying the rows attribute in the search queries. For example, the following query will return 10 rows of results from 10 to 20:

```
q=Sudarshan&rows=10&start=10
```

The pagination parameters can also be specified in `solrconfig.xml` as `queryResultWindowSize`. By having a minimum page size, the response of a search over Apache Solr becomes fast, since it does not have to wait until all results are captured.

Reducing Solr response footprint

Apache Solr can provide search results in different formats. The response can be a simple `.txt`, `.csv`, `.xml`, or `.json` format. A Solr response contains information about matched results. It also provides information-related facets, highlighted text, and many other things that are used by the client (by default, a velocity-template-based client provided by Solr). This in turn is heavy response and it can be optimized by providing a compression over result. Standard JSON response has a smaller footprint over other formats, and can be parsed easily using JSON APIs in different languages.

Using filter queries

The difference between normal query and filter query is that a normal query on Solr will perform the search, and then it applies a complex scoring mechanism to determine the relevance of the document with the search results, whereas a filter query on Solr will perform the search and apply the filter; this does not apply any scoring mechanism. So, filter queries provide faster responses compared to normal queries because filter queries do not require additional processing time for scoring. For higher speeds, it is recommended to go with filter queries. A normal query can easily be converted into a filter query, as shown in the following code snippet:

```
Normally: q=publisher:packtpub AND tag:bigdata
Filter Query: q=*:*&fq=publisher:packtpub&fq=tag:bigdata
```

The scoring is no more applicable with filter queries; if the same query is passed again and again, the results are returned from the filter cache directly.

Search query and the parsers

A query parser is responsible for parsing the queries passed by users. Solr allows different types of parsers, including custom parsers as well. Among them, the `DisMax` parser is one of the simplified parsers. The parsers should be used based on the requirements of search. Overall, some of the widely used parsers are explained in the following table:

Parser	Description
Standard (Lucene)	This is the default parser that provides wildcard, math, range queries support, and filter queries.
DisMax	This parser supports plain searches without any additional field required in search criteria or without heavy syntax, such as AND, OR, boosting, and so on. The search is executed across fields.
NestedQuery	This supports complex nested queries: `{!query defType=func v=$q1}`; if the `q1` parameter is price then the query would be a function query on the price field.
Extended DisMax	`DisMax` + features such as multiplicative boost function.

More information on parsers can be read at `http://wiki.apache.org/solr/QueryParser`. At times while writing search queries, if you are using a DisMax parser, it may end up searching across all the fields spending significant time to match the search string. In such cases, you may consider using standard parser filter queries to reduce the result returned by Solr.

Lazy field loading

By default, Apache Solr reads all stored fields and then filters the ones that are not needed. This becomes a performance overhead if there are a large number of fields defined by the user. Solr also provides lazy field loading with which users can choose to delay the loading of the fields as and when it is needed, that is, lazily. This lazy field loading feature in Solr can be enabled by setting the following flag in `solrconfig.xml`:

```
<enableLazyFieldLoading>true</enableLazyFieldLoading>
```

This offers a significant improvement over speed of search. This can be done by setting the following flag in `solrconfig.xml`. In addition to these options, you can also define your cache implementation.

Optimizing SolrCloud

In any distributed system, if a user has fired a query across multiple nodes, the waiting time will be dependent upon the average performance of the slowest nodes. This concept is called "laggard problem" for indexes of your instance. This problem states that the response to your search query, which is an aggregation of results from all the shards, is controlled by the following formulae:

```
QueryResponse = avg(max(shardResponseTime))
```

If you have distributed search in shards, a shard node that has the slowest response time will impact your query response time, and it will start increasing. Similar to the laggard problem, a distributed search also faces limitations. For example, each document uploaded on the distributed Big Data must have a unique key, and that unique key must be stored in the Solr repository, To do that, Solr schema.xml should have stored=true against the key attribute. This unique key has to be unique across all shards. It enables Apache Solr to distribute the indexes across shards, and to clearly identify each Solr document through unique IDs.

Another problem among Apache Solr is the issue of Distributed Deadlock. When a query is passed to a shard, it can make subqueries to all the other shards. This is a common problem of resources waiting for other resources to complete. In this case, it is shard nodes. When the work is assigned to shards, and if they wait for each other to complete the response, they will get stuck forever. For example, if there are two shards and each of them has a job to process, now they create subtasks that are then assigned to each other's threads. Both the requests are waiting for other shards to complete the task.

 SOLR-5216 JIRA was targeted to address this problem. If you are using Apache Solr beyond 4.6, you may not face this issue.

Solr Cloud relies heavily on Apache Zookeeper. So, if there are any operations that are taking a longer time than zkClientTimeout (default 15 seconds), it becomes a concern. Since Zookeeper expects a faster read/write, the metadata stored in Zookeeper's own database should effectively use OS level cache, and must be on a high-speed disk. Sometimes even having a dedicated machine for multiple Zookeeper nodes can help. A Zookeeper that is replicated requires a minimum of three hosts, or two active hosts. Zookeeper requires a majority $(n/2)+1$ of hosts to be active to maintain quorum.

We have already seen Document Routing for SolrCloud in the previous chapter. SolrCloud supports sharding based on automatic as well as user-defined document routing. Similarly, the querying can be enhanced to search and return results from one or more shards that are passed along with search query using the shard.keys parameter. For higher optimization, instead of relying on SolrCloud-based sharding and search queries, clients can understand their enterprise search requirements; design optimized sharding and document routing strategy for efficient information retrieval and optimal performance.

Summary

In this chapter, we started with different parameters that can be used to monitor the health of the Solr system; we then looked at different open source tools available in the market; and, finally, we have gone through different ways of optimizing your Solr instance to perform high-speed data search and analysis.

Solr and Cloud Computing

In the last chapter, we have seen how Apache Solr can be optimized for better performance on a single node as well as a cluster of nodes. Apache Solr can be scaled horizontally or vertically. Horizontal scaling focuses on adding additional nodes for better distribution of search over multiple machines. Vertical scaling involves adding more resources to the current node setup, such as CPU cores, RAM, or other hardware components. Solr can be scaled in both cases. The IT industry today is keen to look for a way to increase capacity or add capabilities on the fly without investing in new infrastructure, or licensing new software. This requirement highlights the importance of Cloud computing, which provides a subscription-based or pay-for-usage-based service to enable the IT industry to explore new horizons at minimal cost.

In this chapter, we are going to look at how Apache Solr can work with Cloud computing in detail. We will cover the following topics:

- Understanding Cloud deployments for search
- Solr on Cloud strategies
- Running Solr on Cloud (IaaS and PaaS)
- Running Solr on Cloud (SaaS)

Enterprise search on Cloud

In this section, we are going to understand more about Cloud computing, and how it can be used for deployment of an enterprise search, which is Apache Solr search.

Models of engagement

The Cloud computing service provides different models of engagement with consumers, and together it forms a Cloud infrastructure. The following image shows different ways of interacting with an enterprise search using Cloud:

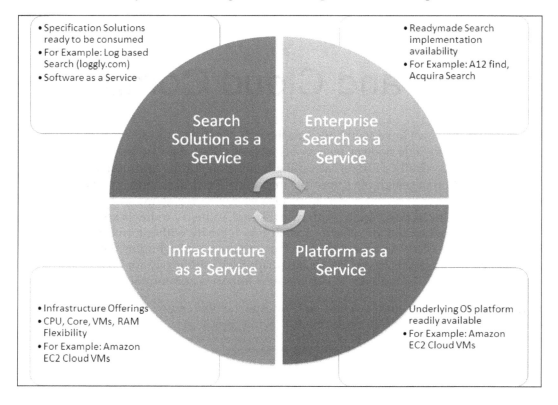

The figure explains the following services:

- **Infrastructure as a Service (IaaS)**: This model provides the complete infrastructure of Cloud to its consumers, which covers CPU cores, RAM, disk, cluster nodes, and so on. Amazon EC2 and other Cloud providers provide IAAS-based services.

- **Platform as a Service (PaaS)**: This model provides an underlying platform along with hardware to its customer. The platform includes a preconfigured operating system, database, container/server, programming environment, and so on. Amazon EC2 Cloud provides a preconfigured environment for different requirements.

- **Software as a Service (SaaS)**: This model provides application software to its customers over Cloud. This covers underlying hardware, platform to run the software, and preconfigured software. For example, Amazon EC2 ships with elastic search VMs, which can be configured to work with the latest version enterprises directly.

- **Search solution as a service**: In this service model, the ready-made solution for an enterprise search is available for consumption readily and the consumer does not really need to put any effort into building a solution on top of an enterprise search for indexing and search. One of the most famous examples of this is Loggly (`https://www.loggly.com/`). Loggly provides a Cloud-based log management solution and searches for users directly.

Enterprise search Cloud deployment models

In the last section, we have seen different types of Cloud service models that can be used by organizations. Enterprise search applications can be deployed on different types of Cloud configuration. However, the most widely used are public Cloud and private Cloud.

Private Cloud is mainly used by a single organization across multiple offices. This type of deployment can be built on campus or off campus. Private Clouds are created mainly due to security, better control, and utilization of on-campus resources. The following diagram depicts what a private Cloud looks like:

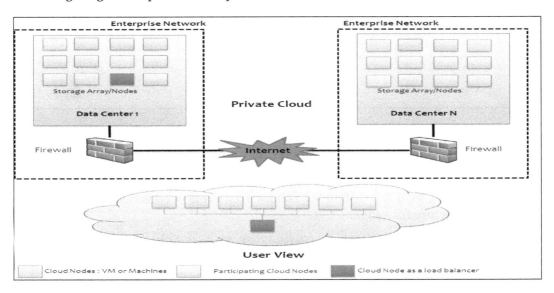

Public Clouds are hosted remotely and are managed by different vendors. The organization can register and subscribe to their services. These Clouds provide all three kinds of services and they are most commonly used for Cloud deployment. There are different public Cloud providers, such as Amazon, A2, and so on. The following diagram shows what the actual public Cloud system looks like:

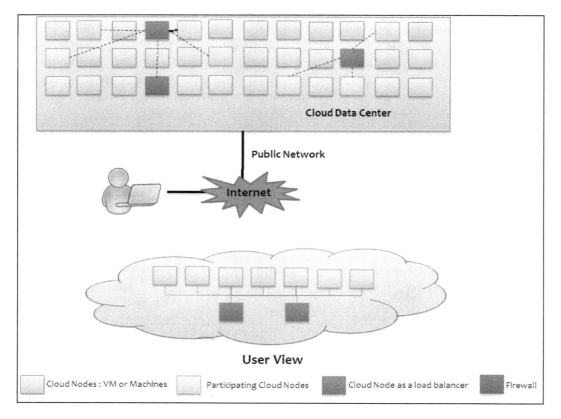

It is also possible to deploy applications on public and private Clouds together. It's called a hybrid Cloud. A hybrid Cloud consists of two or more Clouds.

Based on the needs of the system, the enterprise search can be deployed on a private or public Cloud. The following factors play a role in considering the Cloud infrastructure for usage:

- Many enterprises find it an expensive affair to set up the distributed search infrastructure, and maintain it with a team of dedicated administrators
- The enterprise search on the Cloud provides a reusable, off-the-shelf solution, which can be used with multiple clients based on the requirement

- The cost of ownership is clearly defined and predictable, as compared to the number of unknowns involved

- During the initial phase of setup, Cloud infrastructure provides the try-and-use test bed for a minimum investment

- Professionally managed infrastructure and well-defined **service level agreements (SLA)** can keep the enterprise at peace with respect to the post-implementation phase

- Due to the support for virtualization, the Cloud-deployed applications are portable to be migrated from one location to another, making them device and location independent

The Cloud with search enabled has definitely proven to be beneficial for applications and many search solution providers are prospering through it.

Solr on Cloud strategies

Solr provides its own distributed setup called SolrCloud. We have studied details of SolrCloud in the past chapters. Before deployment of Solr on a Cloud computing stack, a Cloud strategy must be decided to identify the right Solr-based search support deployment in different forms. Cloud-based instances are meant to achieve a high degree of multitenancy. We will look at some of the popular strategies.

Scaling Solr with a dedicated application

One of the simplest strategies is to have Apache Solr deployed as a separate instance for each client. It is as good as Apache Solr instances running completely independently. They can be managed independently. The installation steps for this configuration are standard installation instructions of the Apache Solr installation, as explained in the previous chapters. This approach, although naive, offers the following advantages and disadvantages.

Advantages

It has completely independent instances, enabling each client to control its instance separately from one another. Unlimited levels of customization are possible without impacting the other instances.

Disadvantages

The cost of having a separate instance per client is too high. It is very difficult to manage the upgrades, patching, and so on across instances for administrators. We need to perform repetitive tasks for each client.

Scaling Solr horizontal as multiple applications

Apache Solr can be deployed as an application on any standard J2EE container. One of the strategies is to have a separate Solr-based application for each group of users/clients so as to achieve multitenancy in a way. As Cloud supports virtualization, one can build a virtual machine with high CPU and memory for this multi-application scenario. With this strategy, Cloud will have a single container, with Apache Solr being deployed as an application for each user. Since each application is independent of one another, it can be customized in its own way, requiring separate storage and configuration. These applications share resources such as CPU load, RAM, and so on with one another. Let's try building the Solr multi-application on Tomcat. We will try building two different Solr applications, that is, `solr1` and `solr2` for now. You need to perform the following steps to achieve multiple Solr applications on a server:

1. Download the Tomcat server from `http://tomcat.apache.org/`.

2. Similarly, download the latest Apache Solr instance from `https://lucene.apache.org/solr/`.

3. Extract the ZIPs in your preferred folder.

   If you are going to use Tomcat in a service mode on Windows 64-bit machines, you may need to follow the `http://stackoverflow.com/questions/211446/how-to-run-tomcat-6-on-winxp-64-bit` page for workarounds.

4. Now, you need a separate configuration for each file, so you will need separate configuration folders, that is, `solr1` and `solr2` to be created at some place.

5. Copy the content of `$SOLR_HOME/example/solr` to your `solr1` and `solr2` configuration storage locations. We will try with the basic configuration.

   Based on your configuration, you may also be required to copy library JAR files from `$SOLR_HOME/contrib` to the respective Solr application's `WEB-INF/lib` folder or a common shared library folder in `$TOMCAT_HOME/lib`. You may require files such as sl4j logger, velocity template library, and so on.

6. Now, you need to copy `solr.war` into the `$TOMCAT_HOME/webapps` folder as `solr1.war` and `solr2.war`.

7. The next step is to point the respective Solr instances to the correct configuration, so you need to create files with the same name as your application, that is, `solr1.xml` and `solr2.xml` in the `$TOMCAT_HOME/conf/Catalina/localhost` folder. You will be required to put the following content to it:

   ```
   <Context docBase="<path to solr1.war>/solr1.war" debug="0"
   crossContext="true" >
   ```

```
<Environment name="solr/home" type="java.lang.String"
value="<path of solr1 configuration>\solr1" override="true" />
</Context>
```

8. Now, go to `$TOMCAT_HOME/conf/tomcat-users.xml` and provide access of the Tomcat manager UI to user `Tomcat`:

```
<tomcat-users>
  <user username="tomcat" password="tomcat" roles="manager-gui"/>
</tomcat-users>
```

9. Once this is complete, you can start the Tomcat instance and try accessing `http://localhost:8080/solr1/admin` and `http://localhost:8080/solr2/admin`.

10. Now, go to the Tomcat manager UI by accessing `http://localhost:8080/manager/html`, and you should see both the Solr applications listed, as shown in the following screenshot:

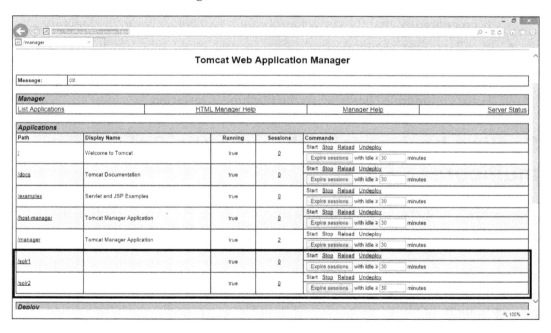

This type of configuration has its own advantages and disadvantages.

Advantages

The advantages of scaling Solr horizontal as multiple applications are as follows:

- It is easy to upgrade the container since it's common; it requires less effort and has less amount of server downtime
- It facilitates better utilization of resources among multiple Solr applications, since the resources, specifically the CPU and memory, are shared across applications
- It is easy to monitor, since it has one place for all the applications due to them being deployed on a common container

Disadvantages

The disadvantages of scaling Solr horizontal as multiple applications are as follows:

- It is difficult to implement container-level memory optimizations, since there is no guarantee that the correct application will get access to the memory
- It still requires a separate application for each client, which is unnecessary
- It cannot perform certain activities at will such as restarting the container for any changes in the Solr configuration, and there needs to be an agreement between multiple clients when the machine is restarted

Scaling horizontally through the Solr multicore

Scaling horizontally with Apache Solr through the Solr multicore has two approaches. The first approach allows a direct replication of Apache Solr in the master-slave configuration, whereas the second approach provides multicore capabilities through Apache Zookeeper.

Scaling horizontally with replication

Solr replication for multicore has been a traditional approach, which has existed since the older versions of Apache Solr. In this approach, the Apache Solr nodes participate in a master-slave manner. The master needs to define a replication handler in `solrconfig.xml`. Consider the following code snippet:

```
<requestHandler name="/replication" class="solr.ReplicationHandler" >
  <lst name="master">
    <!--Replicate on 'startup' and 'commit'. 'optimize' is also a
valid value for replicateAfter. -->
```

```
    <str name="replicateAfter">commit</str>
    <!--Create a backup after 'optimize'. Other values can be
'commit', 'startup'. It is possible to have multiple entries of this
config string.  Note that this is just for backup, replication does
not require this. -->
    <!-- <str name="backupAfter">optimize</str> -->
    <!--If configuration files need to be replicated give the names
here, separated by comma -->
    <str name="confFiles"> schema.xml,mapping-ISOLatin1Accent.
txt,protwords.txt,stopwords.txt,synonyms.txt,elevate.xml</str>
    <!--The default value of reservation is 10 secs.See the
documentation below . Normally , you should not need to specify this
-->
    <str name="commitReserveDuration">00:00:10</str>
  </lst>
  <!-- keep only 1 backup.  Using this parameter precludes using the
"numberToKeep" request parameter. (Solr3.6 / Solr4.0)-->
  <!-- (For this to work in conjunction with "backupAfter" with Solr
3.6.0, see bug fix https://issues.apache.org/jira/browse/SOLR-3361
)-->
  <str name="maxNumberOfBackups">1</str>
</requestHandler>
```

Slave, on the other hand, needs to point to the master URL in `solrconfig.xml`:

```
<requestHandler name="/replication" class="solr.ReplicationHandler" >
  <lst name="slave">
    <str name="masterUrl"> http://${MASTER_CORE_URL}/${solr.core.
name}</str>
    <str name="pollInterval">${POLL_TIME}</str>
  </lst>
</requestHandler>
```

Variables ($POLL_TIME $MASTER_CORE_URL) can be defined in a `solrcore.properties` file for each core. The master can serve any number of slaves, but the performance goes down as the number of slaves increases, so there may be a need to set up the repeater. More information about the Solr replication approach is available at `http://wiki.apache.org/solr/SolrReplication`. The site provides information about performance statistics for replication using `rsync`, built-in replication, and so on.

Scaling horizontally with Zookeeper

Apache Solr supports multitenancy directly through the use of its unique composite ID route. This feature was released in Apache Solr 4.1. When the Solr instance is started, the `numOfShards` parameter determines how many shards Apache Solr is going to work with. Since each document ID is unique in Apache Solr, the new functionality enables users to use `compositeId` instead of a unique document ID. So if a document is a book with the ISBN number 1748, you may specify it as `book!isbn1748`. The `book!` separator acts as a scope or tenant. This tenant is used to hash the document for a particular shard, and the routing is done accordingly. Documents with IDs sharing the same prefix/ tenantId/domain, will be routed to the same shard, allowing efficient querying. The following screenshot of the `/clusterstate.json` file shows the hashing range for each shard and default router set by Apache SolrCloud to be the composite ID:

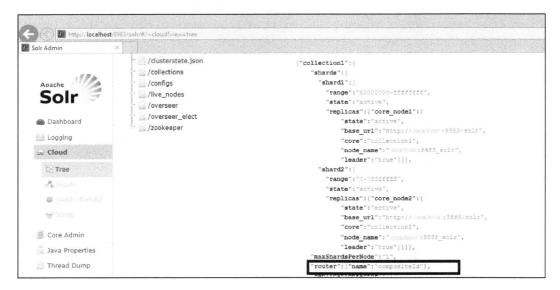

Let's try to create a simple cluster of two nodes with multitenancy using Jetty. Please perform the following steps:

1. Download the latest version of Apache Solr from the Solr distribution (`http://lucene.apache.org/solr/downloads.html`).

2. Unzip the instance, and go to the `$SOLR_HOME/example` directory.

3. Now, run the following command:

```
$java -jar start.jar
```

4. Stop the server. This step of running Solr in a non-Cloud mode is required to unpack the JAR files required for SolrCloud.

5. Now, start Solr in a cluster configuration with the following command:

```
java -DzkRun -DnumShards=2 -Dbootstrap_confdir=./solr/collection1/
conf -Dcollection.configName=solrconf -jar start.jar
```

6. Next, create another Solr node, either by copying the `$SOLR_HOME/example` directory to `$SOLR_CORE/example1`, or by creating another instance from the downloaded `solr.zip` file. You can do it on the same machine, or a different machine.

7. Now, run the following command:

```
java -Djetty.port=8888 -DzkHost=myhost:9983 -jar start.jar
```

8. This will start another node with shard. Now, access `http://localhost:8983/solr/#/~cloud` and you will find the shards with the collection and see how they are linked.

9. Now, let's index simple documents to test the tenancy; execute the following curl commands from the command prompt. This will load four sample entries: two for books and two for movies:

```
curl http://localhost:8983/solr/update?commit=true -H
"Content-Type: text/xml" --data-binary "<add><doc><field
name='id'>book!gandhi</field></doc></add>"
```

```
curl http://localhost:8983/solr/update?commit=true -H
"Content-Type: text/xml" --data-binary "<add><doc><field
name='id'>book!predators</field></doc></add>"
```

```
curl http://localhost:8983/solr/update?commit=true -H
"Content-Type: text/xml" --data-binary "<add><doc><field
name='id'>movie!predators</field></doc></add>"
```

```
curl http://localhost:8983/solr/update?commit=true -H
"Content-Type: text/xml" --data-binary "<add><doc><field
name='id'>movie!maverick</field></doc></add>"
```

10. The tenants are created for books and movies. As you can see, the ID is composite ID with tenant IDs.

You can read more about them here: `http://docs.aws.amazon.com/AWSEC2/latest/UserGuide/get-set-up-for-amazon-ec2.html`. Let's create our first Apache Solr instance on Amazon:

1. Access `https://console.aws.amazon.com/console/home`, and log in with your credentials.

2. Click on EC2, as shown in the following screenshot:

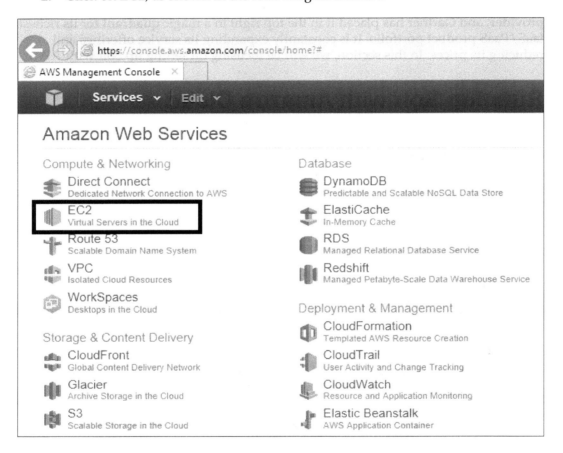

3. Once you visit the EC2 console, you will first be required to create a new instance, so simply click on **Launch Instance**:

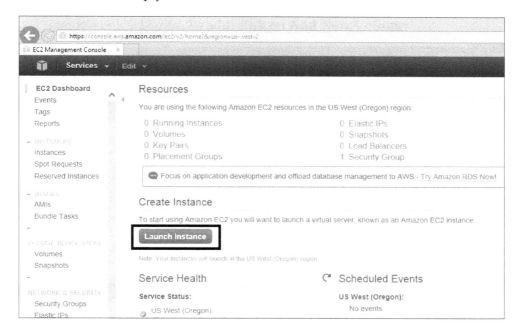

4. Choose AMI. You can choose your own operating system. We will use Ubuntu for our instance creation:

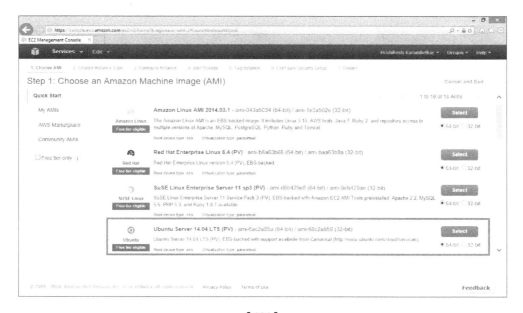

9. Now, put some tags for your instance so that it can be searched:

10. The next step is defining a security group, if you will require SSH access for the instance. You will also need Solr instance accessibility through the Jetty port (or whichever is applicable). If you are going to use Solr in the SolrCloud mode, you may also specify the port for the Apache Zookeeper ensemble:

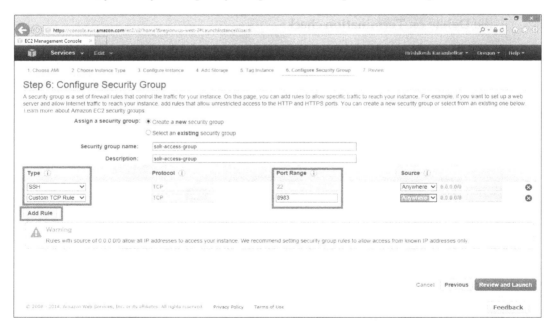

11. The next step is to create a key-value pair for encryption, download the key, and keep it safe so that it is not lost:

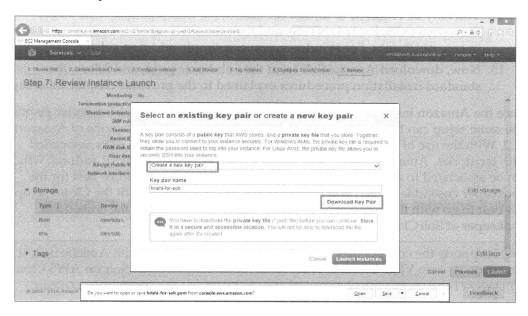

12. Now, launch the instance; the console shows you your instance. You can connect to your instance through SSH. You can also enable VNC or other desktop-sharing software:

The instance also allows you to change the configuration, access different errors, browse data, and run data imports through a common collections manager, as shown in the following screenshot:

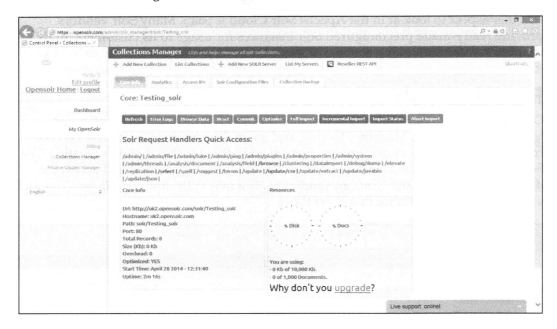

It provides users with different analytics, such as top 20 queries, slowest 20 queries, and so on. You can take a backup of your instance. The default free Solr server runs on port 8180. The new features are published in the OpenSolr blog (`https://www.opensolr.com/blog/`).

5. In the next screen, you will see a summary of the entire configuration. Click on the **Confirm** button to create a CloudSearch instance.

6. Now, the instance is ready to be used just like Amazon EC2. More information is available at `https://aws.amazon.com/cloudsearch/details/`.

Drupal-Solr SaaS with Acquia

Acquia (`http://www.acquia.com/`) provides Apache Solr-based Cloud search with easy integration of Drupal. It is an SaaS-based service on top of Amazon EC2. The integration with Drupal can take place by enabling the extension in Drupal directly. This service is particularly useful for online Drupal sites looking for enhancing search capabilities beyond what Drupal offers. Acquia provides standard Apache Solr 3.5-based features, such as faceted search, result sorting, and weighting. Additionally, it supports multisite search, advanced geospatial search, search relevancy-based recommendations, as well as provides search statistics to its customers.

Summary

In this chapter, we have gone through the Apache Solr in Cloud capabilities. We have understood the Cloud infrastructure and different models of engagement. We also looked at different types of deployment profiles and Cloud strategies. Then, we went through some examples of Solr with Cloud enabled through IaaS, PaaS, SaaS, and finally the enterprise search on Cloud.

10
Scaling Solr Capabilities with Big Data

In today's world, organizations produce gigabytes of information every day from various applications that are actively utilized by employees for various purposes. The data sources can vary from application software databases, online social media, mobile devices, and system logs to factory-based operational subsystem sensors. With such huge, heterogeneous data, it becomes a challenge for IT teams to process it together and provide data analytics. In addition to this, the size of this information is growing exponentially. With such variety and veracity, using standard data-processing applications to deal with large datasets becomes a challenge and the traditional distributed system cannot handle this Big Data. In this chapter, we intend to look at the problem of handling Big Data using Apache Solr and other distributed systems.

We have already seen some information about NOSQL databases and CAP theorem in *Chapter 2, Getting Started with Apache Solr*. NOSQL databases can be classified into multiple types: key-value based stores or columnar storage, document-oriented storage, graph databases, and so on. In key-value stores, the data gets stored in terms of key and values. Key is a unique identifier that identifies each data unit, and value is your actual data unit (document). There are further subtypes to this store: hierarchical, tabular, volatile (in-memory) and persistent (storage). NOSQL databases provide support for heavy data storage such as Big Data, unlike standard relational database models. Recently, Gartner (`http://www.gartner.com/newsroom/id/2304615`) published an executive program survey report, which reveals that Big Data and analytics are among the top 10 business priorities for CIOs; similarly, analytics and BI stand top priority for CIO's technical priorities.

Big Data presents three major concerns of any organization: the storage of Big Data, data access or querying, and data analytics. Apache Hadoop provides an excellent implementation framework for the organizations looking to solve these problems. Similarly, there is other software that provides efficient storage and access to Big Data, such as Apache Cassandra and R Statistical. In this chapter, we intend to explore the possibilities of Apache Solr in working with Big Data. We have already seen scaling search with SolrCloud in the previous chapters. In this chapter, we will be focusing on the following topics:

- Apache Solr and HDFS
- Using Katta for Big Data search
- Solr 1045 patch: map-side indexing
- Solr 1301 patch: reduce-side indexing
- Apache Solr and Cassandra
- Advanced Analytics with Solr

Apache Hadoop is designed to work in a completely distributed manner. The Apache Hadoop ecosystem comprises two major components, which are as follows:

- The MapReduce framework
- **Hadoop Distributed File System (HDFS)**

The MapReduce framework splits the input data into small chunks that are forwarded to a mapper, followed by a reducer that reduces them and produces the final outcome. Similarly, the HDFS filesystem manages how the datasets are stored in the Hadoop cluster. Apache Hadoop can be set up in a single proxy node or in a cluster node configuration. Apache Solr can be integrated with the Hadoop ecosystem in different ways. Let's look at each of them.

Apache Solr and HDFS

Apache Solr can utilize HDFS to index and store its indices on the Hadoop system. It does not utilize MapReduce-based framework for indexing. The following diagram shows the interaction pattern between Solr and HDFS. You can read more details about Apache Hadoop at http://hadoop.apache.org/docs/r2.4.0/.

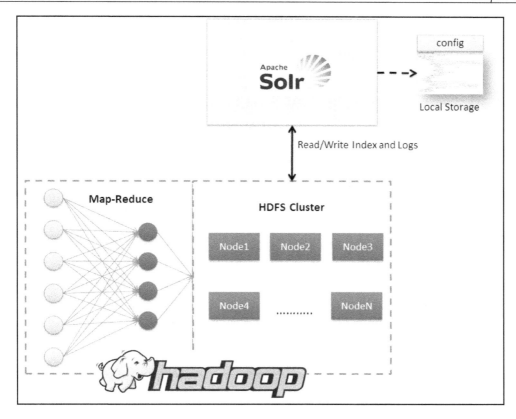

Let's understand how this can be done:

1. To start with, the first and most important task is getting Apache Hadoop set up on your machine (proxy node configuration) or setting up a Hadoop cluster. You can download the latest Hadoop tarball or ZIP from `http://hadoop.apache.org`. The newer generation Hadoop uses advanced MapReduce (also known as yarn).

2. Based on the requirement, you can set up a single node (`http://hadoop. apache.org/docs/r<version>/hadoop-project-dist/hadoop-common/ SingleCluster.html`) or a cluster setup (`http://hadoop.apache.org/docs/ r<version>/hadoop-project-dist/hadoop-common/ClusterSetup.html`).

3. Typically, you will be required to set up the Hadoop environment and modify different configurations (`yarn-site.xml`, `hdfs-site.xml`, master, slaves, and so on). Once it is set up, restart the Hadoop cluster.

4. Once Hadoop is set up, verify the installation of Hadoop by accessing `http://host:port/cluster`; you would see the Hadoop cluster status, as shown in the following screenshot:

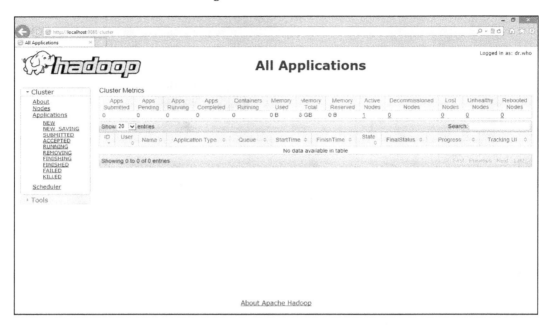

5. Now, using the following HDFS command, create a directory in HDFS to keep your Solr index and Solr logs:

```
$ $HADOOP_HOME/bin/hdfs.sh dfs -mkdir /solr

$ $HADOOP_HOME/bin/hdfs.sh dfs -mkdir /solr-logs
```

This call will create directories on the / root folder on HDFS. You can verify these by running the following command:

```
$ $HADOOP_HOME/bin/hdfs.sh dfs -ls /

Found 2 items

drwxr-xr-x   - hrishi supergroup          0 2014-05-11 11:29 /solr

drwxr-xr-x   - hrishi supergroup          0 2014-05-11 11:27 /
solr-logs
```

You may also browse the directory structure by accessing `http://<host>:50070/`

6. Once the directories are created, the next step will be to point Apache Solr to run with Hadoop HDFS. This can be done by passing JVM arguments for DirectoryFactory. If you are running Solr on Jetty, you can run the following command:

```
java -Dsolr.directoryFactory=HdfsDirectoryFactory -Dsolr.lock.
type=hdfs -Dsolr.data.dir=hdfs://<host>:19000/solr -Dsolr.
updatelog=hdfs:// <host>:19000/solr-logs -jar start.jar
```

You can validate Solr on HDFS by accessing the Solr admin UI. Consider the following screenshot:

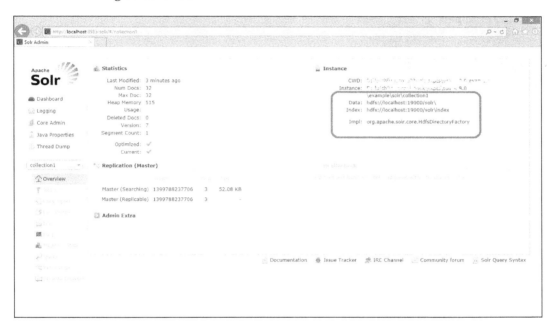

7. In case you are using Apache SolrCloud, you can point `solr.hdfs.home` to your HDFS directory and keep the data and logs on the local machine:

```
java -Dsolr.directoryFactory=HdfsDirectoryFactory -Dsolr.lock.
type=hdfs -Dsolr.hdfs.home=hdfs://<host>:19000/solrhdfs -jar
start.jar
```

Big Data search on Katta

Katta provides highly scalable, fault-tolerant information storage. It is an open source project and uses the underlying Hadoop infrastructure (to be specific, HDFS) to store its indices and provide access to it. Katta has been in the market for the last few years. Recently, development on Katta has been stalled; yet, there are many users who go with Solr-Katta-based integration for Big Data search. Some organizations customize Katta as per their needs and utilize its capabilities for highly scalable search. Katta brings Apache Hadoop and Solr together, enabling search supported by distributed MapReduce cluster. You can read more information about Katta on `http://katta.sourceforge.net/`.

How Katta works?

Katta can primarily be used with two different functions: first is to generate the Solr index, and the second is to run search on the Hadoop cluster. The following diagram depicts what the Katta architecture looks like:

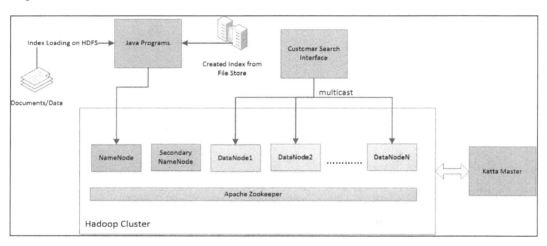

Katta cluster has a master node called Katta master. All other nodes are participants and are responsible for storing the data in their own local store using HDFS or any other filesystem (if Katta is not used with Hadoop). Katta concepts are similar to Hadoop; each index is divided into multiple shards, and these shards are stored on participating nodes. Each node also contains a content server to determine which type of shard is supported by a given Katta-participating node.

Katta master is responsible for communicating with nodes. Apache Zookeeper communicates a channel between Katta master and other participating nodes. Now, all the nodes share a common directory (virtual directory) as supported by Apache Zookeeper. This is where all the participating nodes keep updated status of each node. This way, Katta cluster does not require heartbeats, which are typically used by Zookeeper clients to keep the status of each node. Katta cluster provides a blocking queue through which the overall work is divided among the nodes. Each node holds one queue, and the work is pushed to this queue. When the node completes a task, it looks at its own queue for the next assignment. Operations such as shard deployment are supported by these queues.

Katta uses multicasting concept for search. Multicasting scope is determined by Katta master based on the placement of shards, so when a search is requested, the client multicasts the query to selected nodes, through the use of the Hadoop **Remote Procedure Calls** (**RPC**) mechanism for faster direct communication. Each node then runs the query on its own shard and provides results matched along with scores. The scores are calculated across Katta cluster by each node and the results are merged together across all nodes based on their ranks. They are then returned to the client application.

Setting up Katta cluster

Setting up Katta cluster requires you to either download the distribution from `http://sourceforge.net/project/showfiles.php?group_id=225750` or build the source available on `http://katta.sourceforge.net/documentation/build-katta/`. If you are building the source, you need to run the following commands once you untar the source on Apache Ant Version 1.6:

```
ant dist
```

The source will compile. Once it is completed, you will find the distribution created at the `$KATTA_ROOT/build` directory. You need to untar and copy `katta-core-VERSION.tar.gz` to all the participating nodes as well as to the master node. Once copied, validate the deploy policy in the `katta.master.properties` file. Similarly, update the `katta.zk.properties` file as per your Zookeeper configuration (ensemble or embedded). For embedded Zookeeper, you will need to modify the `zookeeper.servers` attribute for all nodes. You need to point to the master node. Now, you can start the master by running the following command:

```
bin/katta startMaster
```

This will start the master at first. You should start the individual nodes on all machines using the following command:

```
bin/katta startNode
```

Once all the nodes are started, you can start adding indexes to Katta.

Creating Katta indexes

Using Katta, you can create either a Hadoop map files-based index or use Lucene index; you can also create your own type of shard. Lucene index can be loaded on HDFS using the import of index in the Hadoop cluster. This is applicable for the indexes that are already generated or exist.

You can alternatively use Hadoop's MapReduce capabilities to create an index out of normal documents. This is feasible by first transforming your data into Hadoop's sequential format with the help of the `net.sf.katta.indexing. SequenceFileCreator.java` class. You can also use Katta's sample creator script (`http://katta.sourceforge.net/documentation/how-to-create-a-katta-index`). Note that Katta runs on older versions of Hadoop (0.20). Once the index is created, you may deploy them using the `addIndex` call as follows:

```
bin/katta addIndex <index-name> hdfs://<location-of-index>
```

Once index is created, you can validate the availability of index by running a search with the following command:

```
bin/katta search <index-name> <field:search-string>
```

Katta also provides a web-based interface for monitoring and administration purpose. It can be started by running the following command:

```
bin/katta startGui
```

It provides masters, nodes' information, shards, and indexes on the administration UI. This application is developed using the Grails technology.

Although Katta provides completely Hadoop-based distributed search, it lacks the speed, and many times, users have to customize the Katta code as per their requirements. Katta provides excellent failover for master and slaves nodes, which are replicated, thereby making it eligible for enterprise-level Big Data search. However, the search cannot be used in real time, due to limits on speed. Katta is also not actively developed by the users. Apache Solr's development community initially tried to incorporate Katta in Solr, but due to focus and advancements in SolrCloud, it is not merged with Apache Solr. Apache Solr had created a JIRA to integrate Katta in Solr (`https://issues.apache.org/jira/browse/SOLR-1395`).

Using the Solr 1045 patch – map-side indexing

The Apache Solr 1045 patch provides Solr users a way to build Solr indexes using the MapReduce framework of Apache Hadoop. Once created, this index can be pushed to Solr storage. The following diagram depicts the mapper and reducer in Hadoop:

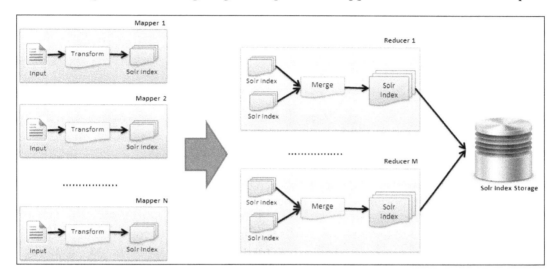

Each Apache Hadoop mapper transforms input records into a set of (key-value) pairs, which then gets transformed into `SolrInputDocument`. The Mapper task ends up creating an index from `SolrInputDocument`.

The focus of reducer is to perform de-duplication of different indexes and merge them if needed. Once the indexes are created, you can load them on your Solr instance and use them to search. You can read more about this patch on `https://issues.apache.org/jira/browse/SOLR-1045`.

The patch follows the standard process of patching up your label through SVN. To apply a patch to your Solr instance, you first need to build your Solr instance using source. The instance should be supported by the Solr 1045 patch. Now, download the patch from the Apache JIRA site (`https://issues.apache.org/jira/secure/attachment/12401278/SOLR-1045.0.patch`). Before running the patch, first do a dry run, which does not actually apply the patch. You can do it with the following command:

```
cd <solr-trunk-dir>
svn patch <name-of-patch> --dry-run
```

If `dry-run` works without any failure, you can apply the patch directly. You can also perform `dry-run` using a simple `patch` command:

```
patch <name-of-patch> --dry-run
```

If it is successful, you can run the patch without the `-dry-run` option to apply the patch. On Windows, you can apply the patch with a right-click:

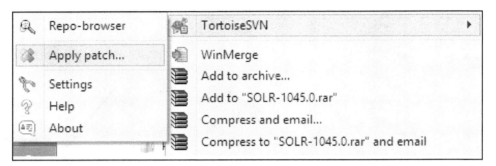

On Linux, you can use the SVN path as shown in the previous example. Let's look at some of the important classes in the patch. The `SolrIndexUpdateMapper` class is responsible for creating create new indexes from the input document. The `SolrXMLDocRecordReader` class reads Solr input XML files for indexing. The `SolrIndexUpdater` class is responsible for creating a MapReduce job and running it to read the document and for updating Solr instance.

> Although Apache Solr patch 1045 provides an excellent parallel mapper and reducer, when the indexing is done at map side, all the `<key, value>` pairs received by the reducer gain equal weight/importance. So, it is difficult to use this patch with data that carries ranking/weight information.

This patch also provides a way for users to merge the indexes in the reducer phase of the patch. This patch is not yet part of the Solr label, but it is targeted for the Solr 4.9/5.0 label.

Using the Solr 1301 patch – reduce-side indexing

The Solr 1301 patch is again responsible for generating an index using the Apache Hadoop MapReduce framework. This patch is merged in Solr Version 4.7 and is available in the code line if you take Apache Solr with 4.7 and higher versions. This patch is similar to the previous patch (SOLR-1045), but the difference is that the indexes that are generated using Solr 1301 are in the reduce phase and not in the map phase of Apache Hadoop's MapReduce. Once the indexes are generated, they can be loaded on Solr and SolrCloud for further processing and application searching. The following diagram depicts the overall flow:

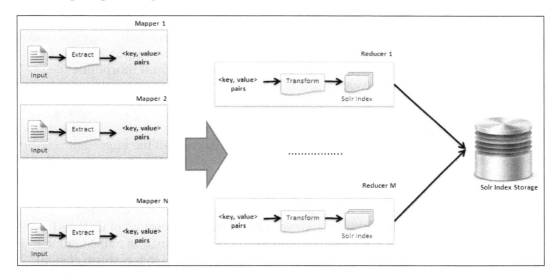

In case of Solr 1301, a map task is responsible for converting input records to the pair of `<key, value>`; later, they are passed to the reducer. The reducer is responsible for converting and publishing `SolrInputDocument`, which is then transformed into Solr indexes. The indexes are then persisted on HDFS directly, which can later be exported on the Solr instance. In the latest Solr instance, this patch is part of the `contrib` module under `$SOLR_HOME\contrib\map-reduce` folder. The `patch/contrib map-reduce` parameter provides a MapReduce job that allows the user to build Solr indexes and merge them in the Solr cluster optionally.

You require the Hadoop cluster to run the Solr 1301 patch. The Solr 1301 patch is merged in Solr Version 4.7, and it is part of the Solr contrib already. Once Hadoop is set, you can run the following command:

```
$HADOOP_HOME/bin/hadoop --config $HADOOP_CONF_DIR jar $SOLR_HOME/
contrib/dist/solr-map-reduce-*.jar -D 'mapred.child.java.opts=-Xmx500m'
--morphline-file readAvroContainer.conf --zk-host 127.0.0.1:9983
--output-dir hdfs://127.0.0.1:8020/outdir --collection collection1
--log4j log4j.properties --go-live --verbose "hdfs://127.0.0.1:8020/
indir"
```

In the preceding command, the `config` parameter requires the configuration directory path of the Hadoop setup. The `mapred.child.java.opts` parameter passes the parameters to MapReduce programs. The `zk-host` parameter points to the Apache Zookeeper instance; `output-dir` is where the output of this program should be stored; `collection` points to the collection in Apache Solr; `log4j` provides pointers to log. The `go-live` option enables the merging of the output shards of the previous phase into a set of live customer facing Solr servers, and morphline file provides a configuration of Avro-based pipe.

This will run mapper and reducer to generate a Solr index. Once the index is created through the Hadoop patch, it should then be provisioned to the Solr server. The patch contains the default converter for CSV files. Let's look at some of the important classes that are part of this patch. The `CSVDocumentConverter` class takes care of converting the output of a mapper (key-value) to `SolrInputDocument`. The `CSVReducer` class provides the reducer implementation of the Hadoop reduce cluster. The `CSVIndexer` class should be called from the command line to run and create indexes using MapReduce; similarly, the `CSVMapper` class provides an introspection of CSV and extracts key-value pairs. It will require additional parameters such as paths to pint and output to store shards. `SolrDocumentConverter` is responsible to transform custom objects into `SolrInputDocument`. The class transforms (key-value) into data that resides in HDFS or locally. The `SolrRecordWriter` class provides extension over the MapReduce record writer. It divides the data into multiple pairs; these pairs are then transformed into the `SolrInputDocument` form.

To run this patch, perform the following steps:

1. Create a local directory with configuration, `conf`, which contains Solr configuration (`solr-config.xml`, `schema.xml`), and the library directory, the `lib` folder, which contains library.

2. `SolrDocumentConverter` provides abstract class to write your own converters. Create your own converter class that implements `SolrDocumentConverter`; this will be used by `SolrOutputFormat` to convert output records to the Solr document. If required, override the `OutputFormat` class provided in Solr by your own extension.

3. Write a simple Hadoop MapReduce job in the configuration writer, as shown in the following code:

```
SolrOutputFormat.setupSolrHomeCache(new File(solrConfigDir),
conf);
conf.setOutputFormat(SolrOutputFormat.class);
SolrDocumentConverter.setSolrDocumentConverter(<your classname>.
class, conf);
```

4. Zip your configuration, and load it in HDFS. The ZIP file's name should be `solr.zip` (unless you change the patch code).

5. Now, run the patch; each of the jobs will instantiate `EmbeddedSolrInstance`, which will in turn do the conversion, and finally, `SolrOutputDocument`(s) get stored in the output format.

With the generation of an index of smaller size, it is possible to preserve the weights of documents, which can contribute while performing a prioritization during the search query.

Merging of indexes is not possible like in Solr 1045; the indexes are created in the reduce phase. Reducer becomes the crucial component of the system due to a major task being performed in the reducer.

Apache Solr and Cassandra

Cassandra is one of the most widely used and distributed, fault-tolerant NOSQL database. Cassandra is designed to handle Big Data workloads across multiple nodes without a single point of failure. There are some interesting performance benchmarks published at planet Cassandra (`http://planetcassandra.org/nosql-performance-benchmarks/`), which places Apache Cassandra as one of the fastest NOSQL database among its competitors in terms of throughput, load, and so on. Apache Cassandra allows schemaless storage of user information in its store called column families pattern. For example, look at the data model for sales information, which is shown as follows:

Customer Id	Name	Address	Contact Number	Designation	Revenue	Domain	Company Name
222	John C	1234, ABC Main, CA	9983988973				
123	David Alba		123434559		155 Billion		MyHome Corporation
432	Sunder Vishwanathan	6676, Park Avenue, IL				Energy Sector	
687			23444566	Architect			

When this model is transformed for the Cassandra store, it becomes columnar storage. The following image shows how this model would look using Apache Cassandra:

As one can see, the key here is the customer ID, and value is a set of attributes/columns, which vary for each row key. Further, columns can be compressed, so reduce the size of your data footprint. The column compression is highly useful when you have common columns with repetitive values (for example, year or color). Cassandra partitions its data using multiple strategies. All the nodes participating in the Cassandra cluster form a ring of nodes called Cassandra ring. Column family data is partitioned across the nodes based on the row key. To determine the node where the first replica of a row will live, the ring is walked clockwise until it locates the node with a token value greater than that of the row key. The data is partitioned based on hashing or ordered partitions, and it is distributed across a cluster of nodes.

With the heavy data, users cannot live with a single Solr node-based approach, and they move to a cluster approach. While Apache Solr provides an inbuilt SolrCloud, which seems to be capable of dealing with a huge dataset, many organizations still consider going for other options. This is because Big Data processing has multiple objectives beyond a pure search and querying. It is used for data analysis and predictions. Apache SolrCloud provides highly optimized index storage, specifically for search, and it cannot be easily used for any other purpose. Apache Cassandra is an open store that supports Hadoop-based MapReduce programs to be run on its datasets, and it can easily be integrated with any standard application in a much easier way. The cases where there are data usages beyond search and basic analysis, Apache Cassandra can server as a single data store for multiple applications. Another reason to go ahead with Cassandra-Solr combination is Cassandra is scalable and a high-performance database.

Working with Cassandra and Solr

There are two major approaches one can go ahead with to integrate Cassandra with Solr. The first one is based on an open source application called Solandra, and the second one is based on DataStax Enterprise Search built using Cassandra and Solr. There are differences between these two approaches in terms of integration with Solr. Solandra uses Cassandra instead of flat file storage to store indexes in the Lucene index format. The DSE allows users to have their data in Apache Cassandra and generate index using Cassandra's secondary index API, thus enabling other applications to consume the data for Big Data processing.

Solandra, on the other hand, uses legacy-distributed search support from Apache Solr, and allows the usage of standard Apache Solr-based APIs, by hiding the underlying Cassandra-based distributed data storage. All the queries are fired through Apache Solr's distributed search support and Cassandra instead of a flat file. Similarly, the indexing too goes through the same overridden APIs.

We will be looking at the open source approach primarily; for integration using **DataStax Enterprise (DSE)**, please visit http://www.datastax.com/download.

Single node configuration

Solandra comes with inbuilt Solr and Cassandra embedded, which can be used for the purpose of development/evaluation. It also has a sample dataset that can be loaded into Cassandra for initial testing. Although the active development of Solandra was stopped almost 2 years back, it still can be used, and it can be extended to work with the latest Apache Solr instance. Let's go through the steps:

1. Download Solandra from https://github.com/tjake/Solandra.

2. Unzip the ZIP file; you will require Java as well as Ant build scripting. You can download and unzip Ant from https://ant.apache.org/bindownload.cgi.

3. Put a path of the $ANT_HOME/bin folder in your shell paths so that you would be able to run Ant directly from the command line anywhere. Try running it from any directory, and you will see something like this:

```
$ ant -v
Apache Ant version 1.7.1 compiled on June 27 2008
Buildfile: build.xml does not exist!
Build failed
```

4. You will also require Apache Ivy to resolve the Ivy dependency. You can download Ivy from https://ant.apache.org/ivy/ and add it in PATH.

5. Now, go to $SOLANDRA_HOME/solandra-app/conf and open the cassandra.yaml file as shown in the following image. Modify the paths to point to your temporary directory.

   In the case of Windows, it will be the DRIVE:\tmp\cassandra-data folder. DRIVE is the name of the drive your Solandra is installed in. The Cassandra.yaml file is responsible for storing information on cluster of nodes. As you can see, it uses random partitioning algorithm, which applies a hashing to each data element and places it in the appropriate node in a Cassandra cluster.

```
49  # - ByteOrderedPartitioner orders rows lexically by key bytes.  BOP allows
50  #   scanning rows in key order, but the ordering can generate hot spots
51  #   for sequential insertion workloads.
52  # - OrderPreservingPartitioner is an obsolete form of BOP, that stores
53  # - keys in a less-efficient format and only works with keys that are
54  #   UTF8-encoded Strings.
55  # - CollatingOPP colates according to EN,US rules rather than lexical byte
56  #   ordering.  Use this as an example if you need custom collation.
57  #
58  # See http://wiki.apache.org/cassandra/Operations for more on
59  # partitioners and token selection.
60  partitioner: lucandra.dht.RandomPartitioner
61
62  # directories where Cassandra should store data on disk.
63  data_file_directories:
64      - /tmp/cassandra-data/data
65
66  # commit log
67  commitlog_directory: /tmp/cassandra-data/commitlog
68
69  # Maximum size of the key cache in memory.
70  #
71  # Each key cache hit saves 1 seek and each row cache hit saves 2 seeks at the
72  # minimum, sometimes more. The key cache is fairly tiny for the amount of
73  # time it saves, so it's worthwhile to use it at large numbers.
```

Now, when Ant runs from $SOLANDRA_HOME, it will create additional directories.

6. Once Ant is complete, go to Solandra-app and run the following command:

   `$ bin/solandra`

7. This will start your server with Apache Solr and Cassandra together on one JVM.

8. You can load a sample data for reuters by going to $SOLANDRA_HOME/reuter-demo.

9. Download the sample dataset by executing the following command:

   `$ 1-download-data.sh`

10. Load it in Solandra (Solr) by executing the following command:

```
$ 2-import-data.sh
```

This script first loads reuter's schema using curl to access `http://localhost:8983/solandra/schema/reuters`, followed by data loading through Solandra's data loader (`reutersimporter.jar`).

Once this is done, you can run a select query on the router by calling `http://localhost:8983/solandra/reuters/select?q=*:*` from your browser to see the data coming from the embedded Solr-Cassandra-based single node Solandra instance. On similar lines, you can load your own schema on Solandra and use data importer to import the data onto the Apache Solr instance. You can access the Solr configuration in the `$SOLANDRA_HOME/solandra-app/conf` folder.

The current Solandra version available for download uses Apache Solr 3.4, and it can be upgraded by modifying the library files of your Solr instance in `$SOLANDRA_HOME/solandra-app/lib` along with the configuration. In the configuration, Solandra uses its own index reader, `SolandraIndexReaderFactory`, by overriding the default index reader as well as a search component (`SolandraQueryComponent`).

Integrating with multinode Cassandra

To work with fully working Apache Cassandra, you will need to perform the following steps:

1. First, download Apache Cassandra from `http://cassandra.apache.org/`; if you already have a running Cassandra, you may skip the following steps.

2. Unzip Cassandra and copy the library files of Solandra in `solandra-app/lib` to Cassandra's library folder (`$CASSANDRA_HOME/lib`), the `/bin` folder to `$CASSANDRA_HOME/bin`, and Solr configuration core files to the `$CASSANDRA_HOME/conf` folder. You can also run the following Ant task:

```
ant -Dcassandra={unzipped dir} cassandra-dist
```

3. You can now start Solr within Cassandra using the `$CASSANDRA_HOME/bin/solandra` command. Cassandra now takes two optional properties: `-Dsolandra.context` and `-Dsolandra.port` for the context path and the Jetty port, respectively. With the latest Cassandra version, you may get incompatible class exception, and you may have to compile the Solandra source against newer libraries, or go back to an older Cassandra version (Version 1.1).

Advanced analytics with Solr

Apache Solr provides excellent searching capabilities on the metadata. It is also possible to go beyond a search and faceting through the integration space. As the search industry grows to the next generation, the expectations to go beyond basic search have led to Apache Solr-like software that is capable of providing excellent browsing and filtering experience. It provides basic analytical capabilities. However, for many organizations, this is not sufficient. They would like to bring in capabilities of business intelligence and analytics on top of search engines. Today, it's possible to compliment Apache Solr with such advanced analytical capabilities. We will be looking at enabling Solr integration with R.

R is an open source language and environment for statistical computing and graphics. More information about R can be found at `http://www.r-project.org/`. Development of R started in 1994 as an alternative to SAS, SPSS, and other proprietary statistical environments. R is an integrated suite of software facilities for data manipulation, calculation, and graphical display. There are around 2 million R users worldwide, and it is widely taught in universities. Many Corporate Analysts know and use R. R provides hundreds of open source packages to enhance productivity. Some of the packages are as follows:

- Linear and nonlinear modeling
- Classical statistical tests
- Time-series analysis
- Spatial statistics
- Classification, clustering, and other capabilities
- Matrix arithmetic, with scalar, vector, matrices, list, and data frame (table) structures
- Extensive library functions (more than 2000) for different graphs/charts

Integrating R with Solr provides organizations access to these extensive library functions to perform data analysis on Solr outputs.

Integrating Solr and R

As R is analytical engine, it can work on top of Apache Solr to perform direct analysis on the results of Apache Solr. R can be installed directly through executable installers (`.exe/.rpm/bin`) that can be downloaded from cran mirrors (`http://cran.r-project.org/mirrors.html`) for any *nix, Windows, or Mac OS. R can connect to Apache Solr through the CURL utility built in as library RCURL in R packages. R also provides a library called Solr to use Solr capabilities to search over user data, extract content, and so on. To enable R with Solr, open the R console and run the following:

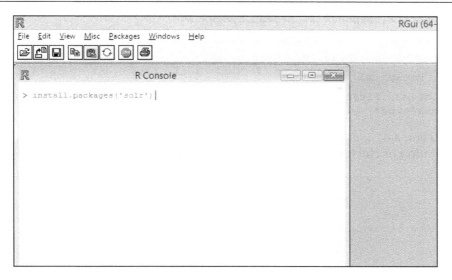

Now, to test it, fire a search on your Solr server:

```
> library(solr)
```

To test analytics, let's take a simple use case. Assume that there is a multinational recruitment firm, and they are using Apache Solr built on top of candidate resumes. They provide facets such as technical capabilities, country, and so on. Now, using Apache Solr, they would like to decide which countries to focus their business on for a certain technology (let's say Solr). So, they would like to classify the countries based on the current available resource pool for Apache Solr. R provides various clustering algorithms, which can provide different clusters of data based on the characteristics. One of the most widely used algorithms is K-Means clustering (http://en.wikipedia.org/wiki/K-means_clustering). To use K-Means in R and plot the graph, you will be required to install package cluster by calling the following command:

```
> install.packages('cluster')
```

After the installation of the cluster package, get the facet information using Solr package of R, and process it for K-Means. Run the following R script on the console to get the cluster information:

```
> library(cluster)
> library(solr)
> url <- 'http://localhost:8983/solr/select'
> response1 <- solr_group(q='*:Solr', group.field='Country', rows=10, group.limit=1, base=url)
```

```
> m2 <- matrix(response1$numFound,byrow=TRUE)
> rownames(m2) <- response1$groupValue
> colnames(m2) <- 'Available Workforce';
> fit <- kmeans(m2, 2)
> clusplot(m2, fit$cluster, color=TRUE, shade=TRUE,labels=2, lines=0,
xlab="Workforce", ylab="Cluster", main="K-Means Cluster")
```

Once you run a `clusplot()` function, you should be able to get a graphical representation of cluster, as shown in the following screenshot:

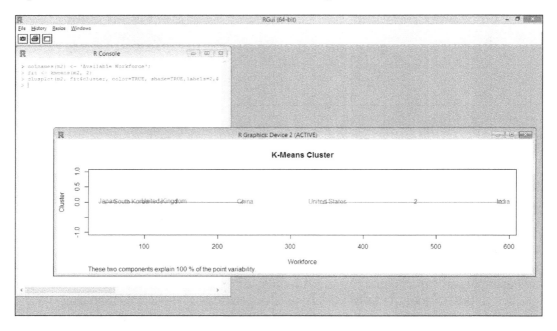

The cluster plot in the preceding screenshot demonstrates how Apache Solr search analytics can be used for further advanced analytics using the R statistical language.

Summary

In this chapter, we have understood the different ways in which Apache Solr can be scaled to work with Big Data/large datasets. We looked at different implementations of Solr Big Data such as Solr HDFS, Katta, Solr 1045, Solr 1301, Apache Solr with Cassandra, and so on. We also looked at advanced analytics by integrating Apache Solr with R.

Sample Configuration for Apache Solr

Let's look at some of the real configuration files. We are only going to look at additions or changes to these files.

schema.xml

Broadly, `schema.xml` contains the following information:

- Different types of field names of schema, and data types (`<fields>`...`<field>`)
- Definition of user/seeded defined data types (`<types>`...`<fieldTypes>`)
- Dynamic fields (`<fields>`....`<dynamicField>`)
- Information about unique key to define each document uniquely (`<uniqueKey>`)
- Information regarding query parser for Solr (`<solrQueryParser>`)
- Default search field to be used when the user does not pass the field name (`<defaultSearchField>`)
- Information about copying the field from one field to another (`<copyField>`)

In the *Configuring the Apache Solr for enterprise* section of *Chapter 2, Getting Started with Apache Solr*, we have already explained the important attributes of schema.xml. The following is a sample of the schema.xml file; the fields will look like the ones shown in the following screenshot:

```
448
449    <fields>
450        <!-- My Schema -->
451        <field name="id" type="string" indexed="true" stored="true" required="true"/>
452        <field name="text" type="text_general" indexed="true" stored="true" multiValued="true" termVector="true"/>
453        <field name="date" type="date" indexed="true" stored="true"/>
454        <field name="q" type="text_general" indexed="true" stored="true"/>
455        <field name="class" type="string" indexed="true" stored="true"/>
456        <field name="method" type="string" indexed="true" stored="true"/>
457        <field name="Action" type="string" indexed="true" stored="true"/>
458        <field name="Level" type="string" indexed="true" stored="true"/>
459        <field name="ApplicationName" type="string" indexed="true" stored="true"/>
460        <field name="User" type="string" indexed="true" stored="true"/>
461        <field name="Path" type="string" indexed="true" stored="true"/>
462        <field name="Hits" type="string" indexed="true" stored="true" multiValued="true"/>
463        <field name="IP" type="string" indexed="true" stored="true"/>
464        <field name="Status" type="string" indexed="true" stored="true" multiValued="true"/>
465        <field name="QTime" type="string" indexed="true" stored="true" multiValued="true"/>
466        <field name="Parameters" type="string" indexed="true" stored="true" multiValued="true"/>
467        <field name="URL" type="string" indexed="true" stored="true"/>
```

You can remove all copy fields, if not needed. The unique key is used to determine each document uniquely; this will be required unless it is marked as required=false. The default search field provides a field name that Solr will use for searching when the user does not specify any field. The specific unique key and the default search is shown in the following screenshot:

```
509    -->
510    <uniqueKey>id</uniqueKey>
511
512    <!-- field for the QueryParser to use when an explicit fieldname is absent -->
513    <defaultSearchField>text_general</defaultSearchField>
514
```

solrconfig.xml

The *Configuring the Apache Solr for enterprise* section of *Chapter 2, Getting Started with Apache Solr*, of this book explains solrconfig.xml in detail. We will look at the sample configuration in this section for log management. In the Solr configuration, the interesting part will be the introduction of facets. For log management, you may consider the following facets to make the overall browsing experience interesting:

Facet	Description
Timeline-based	With this facet, users will be able to effectively filter their search based on the time. For example, options such as the past 1 hour and the past 1 week.
Levels of log	Levels of log provide you the severity. For example, SEVERE, ERROR, and Information.

Facet	Description
Host	Since this system provides a common search for multiple machines, this facet can provide filtering criteria if an administrator is looking for something specific.
User	If the administrator knows about the user, extracting user information from the log can add better filtering through the user facet.
Application	Similar to the host, administrators can filter the logs based on the application using this facet.
Severity	Severity can be another filtering criterion. Most severe errors can be filtered with this facet.

In addition to this, you will also use features for highlighting logs, spelling correction, suggestions (more like this), master-slave, and so on. The following screenshot shows a sample facet sidebar of Apache Solr to get us a better understanding of how it may look:

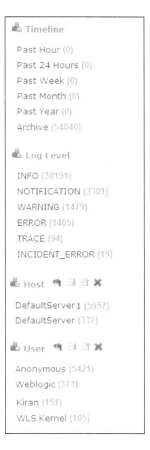

The following sample configuration for Solr shows different facets and other
information when you access/browse:

```
806      <requestHandler name="/browse" class="solr.SearchHandler">
807          <lst name="defaults">
808              <str name="echoParams">explicit</str>
809
810              <!-- VelocityResponseWriter settings -->
811              <str name="wt">velocity</str>
812              <str name="v.template">browse</str>
813              <str name="v.layout">layout</str>
814              <str name="title">My Log Management Server</str>
815
816              <!-- Query settings -->
817              <str name="defType">dismax</str>
818              <!--str name="qf">
819                  text^0.5 features^1.0 name^1.2 sku^1.5 id^10.0 manu^1.1 cat^1.4
820              </str-->
821              <!--str name="qf">text</str-->
822              <str name="q.alt">*:*</str>
823              <str name="rows">10</str>
824              <str name="fl">*,score</str>
825
826              <!-- Faceting defaults -->
827              <str name="facet">on</str>
828              <!--str name="facet.field">class</str>
829              <str name="facet.field">method</str-->
830              <str name="facet.field">Level</str>
831              <str name="facet.field">ApplicationName</str>
832              <str name="facet.field">IP</str>
833              <str name="facet.field">User</str>
834              <!--str name="facet.field">Path</str>
835              <str name="facet.field">Hits</str>
836
837              <str name="facet.field">Status</str>
838              <str name="facet.field">QTime</str-->
839              <str name="facet.mincount">1</str>
840              <str name="facet.limit">10</str>
841              <!--str name="facet.pivot">Level,class,User</str-->
842              <str name="facet.range.other">after</str>
```

Similarly, the following configuration shows timeline-based facets, and features such as highlighting and spell check:

```
842        <str name="facet.range.other">after</str>
843
844        <str name="facet.date">date</str>
845        <str name="facet.date.end">NOW</str>
846        <str name="facet.date.start">NOW-5YEARS</str>
847        <str name="facet.date.gap">+1HOUR</str>
848        <!-- :[NOW-1WEEK/DAY TO NOW] -->
849        <str name="facet.query">date:[NOW-1HOUR/DAY TO NOW]</str>
850        <str name="facet.query">date:[NOW-1DAY/DAY TO NOW-1HOUR/DAY]</str>
851        <str name="facet.query">date:[NOW-7DAYS/DAY TO NOW-1DAY/DAY]</str>
852        <str name="facet.query">date:[NOW-1MONTH/DAY TO NOW-7DAYS/DAY]</str>
853        <str name="facet.query">date:[NOW-1YEAR/DAY TO NOW-1MONTH/DAY]</str>
854        <str name="facet.query">date:[* TO NOW-1YEAR/DAY]</str>
855
856
857        <!-- Highlighting defaults -->
858        <str name="hl">true</str>
859        <str name="hl.fl">text)general FullLog ApplicationName text class method Action Level</str>
860        <str name="hl.snippet">5</str>
861        <!--str name="f.name.hl.fragsize">0</str-->
862        <str name="f.name.hl.alternateField">FullLog</str>
863
864
865        <!-- Spell checking defaults -->
866        <str name="spellcheck">on</str>
867        <str name="spellcheck.collate">true</str>
868        <str name="spellcheck.onlyMorePopular">false</str>
869        <str name="spellcheck.extendedResults">false</str>
870        <str name="spellcheck.count">3</str>
871      </lst>
872    <arr name="last-components">
873      <str>spellcheck</str>
874    </arr>
```

spellings.txt

This file provides a file-based spell check and can be enabled by specifying the following code in `solrconfig.xml`:

```
<searchComponent name="spellcheck" class="solr.SpellCheckComponent">
  <lst name="spellchecker">
    <str name="classname">solr.FileBasedSpellChecker</str>
    <str name="name">file</str>
    <str name="sourceLocation">spellings.txt</str>
    <str name="characterEncoding">UTF-8</str>
    <str name="spellcheckIndexDir">./spellcheckerFile</str>
  </lst>
</searchComponent>
```

In this file, you can write a list of correct words. This file is used to define a dictionary for users. You need to enter each word on a new line as follows:

```
solr
solar
```

Once the dictionary is created, it needs to be built by calling `spellcheck.build` using the following URL:

```
http://<solr-url>/select?q=*:*&spellcheck=true&spellcheck.build=true
```

Then you can simply check `spellchecker` by calling the following code:

```
http://<solr-url>/select?q=solar&spellcheck=true
```

synonyms.txt

This file is used by synonym filter to replace the tokens with their synonyms. For example, a search for "DVD" may expand to "DVD", "DVDs", "Digital Versatile Disk" depending on your mapping in this file. The following is how you can specify the synonyms:

- GB, gib, gigabyte, gigabytes
- MB, mib, megabyte, megabytes
- Television, Televisions, TV, TVs
- Incident_error, error

In this file, you can also make spelling corrections, for example, assasination can be changed to assassination.

protwords.txt

You can protect the words that you do not want to be stemmed. For example, a stemming would cut the word manager to manage. If you do not wish to protect them, you can specify those words in this file line-by-line as follows:

```
manager
Exception
Accounting
......
```

stopwords.txt

Using this file, you can avoid the common words of your language that do not add a significant value to your search. For example, a, an, the, you, I, and am. You can specify them in this file line-by-line as follows:

```
a
an
```

Index

Symbols

.NET
  interacting, with Solr 56

A

access pattern, enterprise data
  random access / direct access 59
  streaming data / sequential access 59
ACL (Access Control List) 134
Acquia
  Drupal-Solr SaaS 233
  URL 233
administration 17
AJAX-Solr
  components 121
  URL 121
  using, for Apache Solr integration 121
Amazon CloudSearch
  working with 231, 232
Amazon Elastic Compute Cloud
  (Amazon EC2) 219
Amazon Machine Images (AMIs) 219
Amazon Web Services. *See* **AWS**
Apache Hadoop
  about 236
  installation verification, URL 238
  URL 236
Apache Lucene 152
Apache Solr. *See* **also Solr**
  about 7, 12, 31, 107, 152
  architecture 19, 20
  Cassandra, working with 247-249
  configuring, for enterprise 45
  deduplication 76

Drupal, working with 123-126
embedding, as module in enterprise
    application 108-110
examples, running 39
features 12-18
HDFS, working with 236
horizontal scaling 207
images searching, LIRE used 78
information, extracting from scanned
    documents 77
integrating, with JavaScript 119
integrating, with PHP 114-116
integrating, with R language 252-254
issues 40-42
performance, monitoring 180
running, as IaaS on Cloud 219
running, as PaaS on Cloud 219
running, on Windows Azure 226
running, with AWS 219-225
running, with OpenSolr Cloud 227, 228
scaling, with dedicated application 211
setting up 31
solutions, for issues 42, 43
URL, for JDK 32
used, for partitioning index 138
using 132
vertical scaling 207
working, in web application 111-114
Apache Solr 1045 patch
  using 243, 244
Apache Solr 1301 patch
  using 245-247
Apache Solr attachment module 126
Apache_Solr_Document class 116
Apache Solr Facets 153
Apache Solr indexing time 182

W

warming up cache 201
web application
  Apache Solr, working 111-114
Weblogic 191
WhiteHouse.gov 25
Windows Azure
  Apache Solr, running on 226
  URL 226
WordPress CMS 126

X

XML data
  working with 65
XML style sheets (XSLT)
  about 122
  used, for Solr XML parsing 122

Y

yum install command 34

Z

zkCLI command 147
zkHost=<host>:<port> parameter 139
zk-host parameter 246
zkRun parameter 139
znode 134
Zookeeper 161
  URL, for downloading 175

Thank you for buying
Scaling Apache Solr

About Packt Publishing

Packt, pronounced 'packed', published its first book "*Mastering phpMyAdmin for Effective MySQL Management*" in April 2004 and subsequently continued to specialize in publishing highly focused books on specific technologies and solutions.

Our books and publications share the experiences of your fellow IT professionals in adapting and customizing today's systems, applications, and frameworks. Our solution based books give you the knowledge and power to customize the software and technologies you're using to get the job done. Packt books are more specific and less general than the IT books you have seen in the past. Our unique business model allows us to bring you more focused information, giving you more of what you need to know, and less of what you don't.

Packt is a modern, yet unique publishing company, which focuses on producing quality, cutting-edge books for communities of developers, administrators, and newbies alike. For more information, please visit our website: www.packtpub.com.

About Packt Open Source

In 2010, Packt launched two new brands, Packt Open Source and Packt Enterprise, in order to continue its focus on specialization. This book is part of the Packt Open Source brand, home to books published on software built around Open Source licenses, and offering information to anybody from advanced developers to budding web designers. The Open Source brand also runs Packt's Open Source Royalty Scheme, by which Packt gives a royalty to each Open Source project about whose software a book is sold.

Writing for Packt

We welcome all inquiries from people who are interested in authoring. Book proposals should be sent to author@packtpub.com. If your book idea is still at an early stage and you would like to discuss it first before writing a formal book proposal, contact us; one of our commissioning editors will get in touch with you.

We're not just looking for published authors; if you have strong technical skills but no writing experience, our experienced editors can help you develop a writing career, or simply get some additional reward for your expertise.

[PACKT] open source
PUBLISHING
community experience distilled

Apache Solr 4 Cookbook

ISBN: 978-1-78216-132-5   Paperback: 328 pages

Over 100 recipes to make Apache Solr faster, more reliable, and return better results

1. Learn how to make Apache Solr search faster, more complete, and comprehensively scalable.

2. Solve performance, setup, configuration, analysis, and query problems in no time.

3. Get to grips with, and master, the new exciting features of Apache Solr 4.

Apache Solr High Performance

ISBN: 978-1-78216-482-1   Paperback: 124 pages

Boost the performance of Solr instances and troubleshoot real-time problems

1. Achieve high scores by boosting query time and index time, implementing boost queries and functions using the Dismax query parser and formulae.

2. Set up and use SolrCloud for distributed indexing and searching, and implement distributed search using Shards.

3. Use GeoSpatial search, handling homophones, and ignoring listed words from being indexed and searched.

Please check **www.PacktPub.com** for information on our titles

Scaling Big Data with Hadoop and Solr

ISBN: 978-1-78328-137-4   Paperback: 144 pages

Learn exciting new ways to build efficient, high performance enterprise search repositories for Big Data using Hadoop and Solr

1. Understand the different approaches of making Solr work on Big Data as well as the benefits and drawbacks.

2. Learn from interesting, real-life use cases for Big Data search along with sample code.

3. Work with the Distributed Enterprise Search without prior knowledge of Hadoop and Solr.

Administrating Solr

ISBN: 978-1-78328-325-5   Paperback: 120 pages

Master the use of Drupal and associated scripts to administrate, monitor, and optimize Solr

1. Learn how to work with monitoring tools like OpsView, New Relic, and SPM.

2. Utilize Solr scripts and Collection Distribution scripts to manage Solr.

3. Employ search features like querying, categorizing, search based on location, and distributed search.

Please check **www.PacktPub.com** for information on our titles